Inside Society, Culture and Public Health

Inside Society, Culture and Public Health:

Readings in Anthropology

Edited by

Milonjyoti Borgohain

Dr. Dhritiman Sharma

KALPAZ

First Published, 2020

Published by

Kalpaz Publications
C-30, Satyawati Nagar,
Delhi – 110052
Ph.: 011-47034999, 9811692060
www.kalpazpublications.com
E-mail: kalpaz@hotmail.com

Printed at: Gyan Press, Delhi

Cataloging in Publication Data—DK
Courtesy: D.K. Agencies (P) Ltd. <docinfo@dkagencies.com>

Inside society, culture and public health : readings in anthropology / edited by Milonjyoti Borgohain, Dhritiman Sarma.
pages cm
Contributed articles.
ISBN 9789353242749

1. Ethnology—India. 2. Tribes—India—Social conditions. 3. Tribes—India—Economic conditions. 4. India—Civilization. 5. Tribes—Health and hygiene—India. 6. Public health—India. I. Borgohain, Milonjyoti, editor. II. Sarma, Dhritiman, editor.

LCC GN635.I4I57 2020 | DDC 305.800954 23

Contents

Foreword 9
Preface 11
Acknowledgement 13
List of Contributors 15

Introduction **17**
— *Milonjyoti Borgohain and Dr. Dhritiman Sharma*

Society

1. **Livelihood Security in Flood Prone Areas of Assam: An Agrarian Perspective** **25**
   — *Bruhid Rabha*
2. **Cultural Resource Management in North East India** **43**
   — *Dhritiman Sharma*
3. **Rural Poverty is Multidimensional Phenomena in Nepal: An Anthropological Review** **53**
   — *Dilli R. Prasai*
4. **Access to Non Timber Forest Products and Its Impact on the Irula Tribes of Nilgris** **61**
   E. Tamil Selvan
5. **Impact of Education on the Social Status of Bodo Women in Assam** **69**
   — *Franky Boro*
6. **Changing Livelihood Resources and Coping Strategies among the Tai Khamti of Namsai District, Arunachal Pradesh** **77**
   — *Heerock Jyoti Baruah*
7. **PVTG: An Ethnographic Profile of Jenu Kuruba of Basavanagiri, Mysuru, Karnataka** **101**
   — *Karuna Gogoi*

8. **A Study on Consumers Response to Online Market and its Impact on Local Market with Particular Reference to Guwahati City 115**
— Panna Garg

9. **Symbiotic Relationship between Tribe and Their Ecology: A Case Study of the Nyishi Tribe of Rilloh Village, Pakke Kessang District, Arunachal Pradesh 121**
— Ranjit Pachani

10. **Changes in Socio-Economic life of the Garo in Meghalaya 131**
— Shyam Babu Choudhury

CULTURE

11. **Traditional Religious Beliefs and Practices of the Sonowal Kacharis of Tinsukia District of Assam 147**
— Biswajit Kumar Singh

12. **Sacred Place and Its Rituals: Beliefs and Practices of the Deoris of Dhemaji District, Assam 151**
— Humen Chutia

13. **Ke-che-cham or Lord Shani Puja among the Hill Karbis of East Karbi Anglong District, Assam 161**
— Leena Laskar

14. **Role of Ethno-Medicine in the Provision of Primary Health Care among the Ahoms of Chiring Chuk Village of Lakhimpur District, Assam 173**
— Pallabi Gogoi

15. **Ancestor Worship among Ahom Community 181**
— Prasanna Bharali

16. **Social Folk Customs Associated with Birth, Puberty and Death Rites of the Sonowal Kacharis of Assam 199**
— Suravi Gohain Duwarah

17. **Transformation in Nyishi Festival, Nyokum: An Overview 207**
— Yora Bathey

PUBLIC HEALTH

18. **Prevalence of Hypertension and Its Associated Risk Factors among the Tengaponia Deoris of Dibrugarh District, Assam 227**
— Anand Sharma, Nitul Kumar Gogoi & Prasanta Kumar Borah

19. **Psychology in the Shade of Global Pandemics: A Brief Note** 235
— *Barnali Sarma*

20. **Antenatal Care Practices among the Mog Women of Upper Assam** 241
— *Falguni Roy Barua & Deepanjana Dutta Das*

21. **Relationship between BMI and Percent Body Fat among the Adult Mishings of Dhemaji District** 249
— *Mayurtrishna Hazarika & Sarthak Sengupta*

22. **Hygiene and Sanitation Practices among the Mising Tribe of Dhemaji District, Assam** 259
— *Milonjyoti Borgohain*

23. **Childhood Mortality among the Santals and Tantis of Upper Assam** 267
— *Parishmita Gogoi- & Deepanjana Dutta Das*

24. **Impact of Reproductive Aging on Women's Health** 277
— *Rita Taid*

25. **Physical Activity Level of Young-Adult Males of Bakarapara Area of Guwahati** 289
— *Sanjeeb Mallick & Dr. Chandana Sarmah*

Index 297

Foreword

I am delighted to write the foreword of "Inside Society, Culture and Public Health: Readings in Anthropology" as such kind of books are necessary to highlight the expanding scope of anthropological enquiries pertaining to various social and heath issues of human society.

This book is the result of many years of researching and it is important for students to reflect and develop skills that are based research from different fields within the discipline and even other related disciplines. This book places a clear emphasis on sheding light on ethnographic skills and analysis and ensures that those skills and unserstanding are based on current research. I am glad to learn that Mr. Milonjyoti Borgohain and Dr. Dhritiman Sharma has made an incessant effort to compile research articles addressing multiples cases and issues of the rural societies from across the country. Therefore, I welcome such a noble venture and I hope other engaged in the field of empirical research would follow this example and engage themselves in producing literature of this type, which would help not only to enrich their knowledge and experience but will add to the literature on rural Indian culture published so far.

The text speaks of reasearcher's experiences of information about a wide variety of groups, including family and the society at large. This literature has been updated drawing upon the recent theory and issues. It is my hope and expectation that this book will provide an effective learning experience and referenced resource for all students, scholars and researchers caring for enthographic work for better cause of human society.

I wish both of them success and luck.

D. Dutta Das

(Dr. Deepanjana Dutta Das)

Professor (Retd)

Department of Anthropology

Dibrugarh University, Assam

Preface

This book emerged out of a series of conversations and debates about the nature of contemporary anthropological enquiry and knowledge production with some of the discipline's leading scholars and emerging researchers of India. What the volume offers are twenty five structured accounts of anthropologists from both physical and social spheres, their key enquiries, and how they analyse the current human issues within the line of anthropological thought. The result is a series of candid, first hand narratives that reveal something quite close and thoughtful about the nature of the anthropological accomplishments. In the pages that follow our contributors examine a range of key issues including the issues of hypertension among rural dwellers, psychology during pandemics, how anthropological knowledge can be used to evaluate the beliefs and practices in indigenous communities; what distinguishes anthropology as a way of seeing and engaging in cultural resource management; how anthropology's self-understanding identify factors associated with changing livelihood and understand adaptation; the nature of childhood mortality and how reproductive aging affects women health; and how the rural cultures transform and structures itself and the role of ecology and modernisation in such processes. While each of the twenty five research articles in this book offers a uniquely rich and emic account of what concerns anthropologists among rural societies, taken as a whole these accounts highlights the wider issues and challenges that define, and continue to delineate, the past, present and future research within anthropology. Keeping in perspective the processes, the accounts offered up by the authors in this book provide a view of the life and times in which societies live and their history, particularly from the viewpoint of the respondents themselves. In bringing this book together, we have attempted to confine a sense of the familiarity that characterised our primary debates. Our aim is to offer the readers an ethnographic perspective on the work of anthropology than can hardly be found in textbook or academic volumes. We have attempted to portray our author's more personal and informal reflection to shed light on the major themes in the discipline. Whether they have lived up to that challenge is for the reader to judge.

Milonjyoti Borgohain
Dr. Dhritiman Sharma
Assam, 2020

Acknowledgement

The production of this book was made possible by the contribution of quality time, ideas, designs, and intellectual creativities of many, students, colleagues, friends and well-wishers. We will be failing in our duty if we do not acknowledge the help and advice from them.

We convey our heartful appreciation and gratefulness to the contributors for this unique initiative and for the continuous support. The authors of the units made their best attempt to provide the material according to our requirements in a short time and obliging to our request to take this work on priority basis. They showed the patience to review more than two or three times. We are deeply indebted to each one of them.

Milonjyoti Borgohain
Dr. Dhritiman Sharma
Assam, 2020

List of Contributors

Anand Sharma is a PhD scholar in the Department of Anthropology, Dibrugarh University. He is also serving as the district epidemiologist, DSU, IDSP, Bongaigaon, Assam.

Barnali Sarma is a PhD scholar in the Department of Psychology, Cotton University, Assam.

Biswajit Kumar Singh is an Assistant Professor, Margherita College, Assam. He is pursuing his PhD from Dibrugarh University, Assam.

Bruhid Rabha is a PhD scholar in the School of Economics, University of Hyderabad.

Dr. Dhritiman Sharma is an Assistant Professor of Anthropology, Rajiv Gandhi University, Arunachal Pradesh.

Dilli R. Prasai is an Associate Professor in the Department of Anthropology, Tribhuvan University, Nepal.

E Tamil Selvan is a PhD scholar in the Department of Anthropology, University of Madras, Tamil Nadu.

Falguni Roy Barua is a PhD scholar, Department of Anthropology, Dibrugarh University, Assam.

Dr. Chandana Sarmah is an Associate Professor, Department of Anthropology, Gauhati University, Assam.

Dr. Deepanjana Dutta Das has retired as an Associate Professor from the Department of Anthropology, Dibrugarh University, Assam.

Dr. Humen Chutia is an Assistant Professor, Department of Anthropology, Subansiri College, Assam.

Franky Boro is an M.Phil scholar in the Department of Anthropology, Assam University.

Heerock Jyoti Baruah is a PhD scholar in the Department of Anthropology, University of Hyderabad, Telangana.

Karuna Gogoi is a PhD scholar in the Department of Anthropology, Gauhati University, Assam.

Leena Laskar has completed her Post Graduation from the Department of Anthropology, Cotton University. She is a life member of the Indian National Trust for Art and Cultural Heritage, New Delhi (Kamrup Chapter).

Mayurtrishna Hazarika is a PhD scholar in the Department of Anthropology, Dibrugarh University, Assam.

Milonjyoti Borgohain is an Assistant Professor, Department of Anthropology, Moridhal College, Assam.

Nitul Kumar Gogoi is a Professor in the Department of Anthropology, Dibrugarh University, Assam.

Pallabi Gogoi is an M.Phil scholar in the Department of Anthropology, Rajiv Gandhi University, Arunachal Pradesh.

Panna Garg is a PhD scholar in the Department of Anthropology, Cotton University, Assam.

Parishmita Gogoi is an Assistant Professor in the Department of Anthropology, North Bank College, Assam.

Prasanna Bharali is an M.Phil scholar in the Department of Anthropology, Rajiv Gandhi University, Arunachal Pradesh.

Prasanta Kumar Borah is serving as Scientist E at ICMR-RMRC, Dibrugarh, Assam.

Ranjit Pachani Department of Anthropology, Rajib Gandhi University, Arunachal Pradesh.

Rita Taid is a PhD scholar in the Department of Anthropology, North Eastern Hill University, Shillong, Meghalaya

Sanjeeb Mallick is a PhD scholar in the Department of Anthropology, Gauhati University, Assam.

Sarthak Sengupta is a Professor, Department of Anthropology, Dibrugarh University, Assam.

Shyam Babu Choudhury is a PhD scholar in the Department of Anthropology, Gauhati University, Assam.

Suravi Gohain Duwarah is a PhD scholar in the Department of Folklore, Gauhati University, Assam.

Yora Bathey is a PhD scholar in the Department of Anthropology, Rajiv Gandhi University, Arunachal Pradesh.

Introduction

— Milonjyoti Borgohain and
Dr. Dhritiman Sharma

Anthropologists have long been engaged in studying human society and the continuous venture have elucidated various emic aspects of different cultures. This approach of bridging facts through first hand observation has been the core of a fruitful ethnographic writing. This book stresses such subjective encounters across various societies and explores the correlation between the personal experiences and knowledge generation. The aim behind production of this book is to set forth the professional practices and direction of ideas that shapes anthropology today. This book sets out to highlight how anthropologists involve in contemporary issues and challenges facing societies across India. In addressing these questions, it is expected to illuminate broader issues and reproduction of knowledge within the discipline. The practice of anthropology has been diverse with each of its sub-fields exploring and deconstructing personal experiences and self-reflexive accounts in their own way. Many of these have focussed exclusively on their fieldwork experiences; some stressed on more objective research on human anatomy, and while others provided narratives of more case based societal issues.

This book corresponds to anthropological approach in three important ways. First, the effort is to examine the practice of anthropology in addressing contemporary issues challenging both urban and rural societies. Anthropology as a discipline does not restrict to writing ethnography, but set forward major theoretical paradigm to address contemporary challenges. Second, there is effort to create narratives of personal experiences gathered through structured questions that sought to bridge relationship between transforming social structures and the human induced factors. Third, the book strives to highlight major concept associated to public health that have influenced modern human populations. This collaborative approach has enabled to look across various themes and concepts while drawing out generalized patterns related to national contexts and academic options.

The twenty five essays featured in this book have all devoted towards highlighting the relationship between the major concerns that occupy anthropologists and policy making at different level and would further inspire subsequent and aspiring students nationally. By exploring their individual works, the book aim to grasp some of the wider social and contextual subjects that are occurring within human race, as well as within the discipline as a whole. Ensuring livelihood security among the rural communities has been a major goal among policy planners in order to attain sustaibale development objectives.

From the narrative accounts in this book we can deduce distinct trajectories into anthropology. This book begins with an essay that analyses the factors affecting livelihoods in agrarian economies and sets forth community based approaches undertaken by the poor houiseholds to secure their livelihood avenues. Reconstructing peronal experiences and knowledge generation within the discipline is well sought in the second article that highlights the author's encounter with the training and association in Cultural Resource Management, which has emerged as a new direction in applied archaeology. Management and vulnerability shares a close relationship in contemporary policy planning. Vulnerability originating from poverty has been a major hindrance of social development that requires continuous management efforts for its regulation. The third article discusses the nature of poverty in Nepal and the agents that contribute to it. Vulnerability also stems from the scarcity of resources harnessed by any community. In the case of tribals access to non timber forest produce bears significance towards securing their livelihood. The fourth article analyses the situation of the Irula tribes, regarding their traditional depence on forest produces and highlights the functioning of the Forest Right Act 2006 in securing their livelihoods. Apart from attaining a sustainable livelihood, members within a society strives for a higher social status that enhances their wellbeing. The fifth article sheds lights on the importance of women education among the *Bodo* for the enhancement of social status as well as economic upliftment.

Changing livelihood resources bears significant impact on the social structure of any society. Resources remain crucial towards satisfying societal needs and thus every society undertakes measures to ensure their uninterrupted flow. Locating the livelihood capitals available within the Tai Khamti society, the sixth article attempts to highlight the strategies adopted by the forest dependent tribe to adapt to the changing livelihood resources. Ethnographic writings shed light on underlying complexities of rural societies. The seventh article follows the anthropological tradition of ethnography to highlight the profile of the Jenu Kuruba tribe of Basavanagiri, Mysuru, Karnataka. They are Particularly Vulnerable Tribal Group and were rehabilitated from their original place. Their ethnic identity has been endangered due to assimilation and very low rate of population growth. Social identity and social functioning cannot be understood without considering the influence of the ecology. Since its emergence anthropological writings have stressed the impact of environment on human society. The ninth article attempts to understand the underlying relationship manifested in the dependence of the Nyishi tribe with their ecology and highlights the changes in the relation with modernization of the society. The socio-cultural life entangles with the economic activities and thus forms the compound structure of any society. Different ethnic group of Meghalaya and their colorful lifestyles have significantly enriched the entire culture of Meghalaya. Economy is an important constituent of the community life. It plays a vital role in the formation of cultural and social structure of the society. As the activities associated with the fulfillment of material wants of the people are the parts of economic life, the study of socio-economic life of the tribal people helps us to understand the important aspects of the culture. The tenth paper tries to examine the changes in the socio-economic sphere of the Garos life and inter-relationship between the economy and culture by providing examples from the Garos society. The eleventh article portrays the use anthropological field investigation as a tool for understanding the traditional religious beliefs and practices of Sonowal Kacharis of Tinsukia District of Assam. The study reveals that the elderly population is more attached to various religious beliefs and practices as compared to the younger generation. Follwing a similar approach the twelfth article explores the traditional religious belief and practices associated with the village sacred place among the Deoris of Dhemaji district of Assam. The Deori is one of the plain tribe of Assam who are mostly distributed in Upper Assam. The village sacred place and the traditional priest of Deoris play a significant role in their society. Beliefs and practices forms a major subject matter of social anthropology and ancestors worship remains crucial within the discipline. Ritual is a religious ceremony and social behaviour. In Anthropology, it is an action with intentional symbolic meaning undertaken for a specific cultural purpose, such as a rite of passages from childhood to adulthood. The thirteenth study attempts to study the existing culture and associated socio-cultural practice of Ke-che-cham or Lord Shani Puja among the Hill Karbis of Thero Bey Village of East Karbi Anglong District, Assam. Ke-che-cham is performed only for those who receive death unnaturally. Ke-che-cham is performed to purify the evil soul of unnatural deaths. The Ke-che-cham ritual is an inevitable part of Karbi society.

First-hand accounts in anthropology have been highlighted in the preceding paragraphs. People with different cultural orientations and experiences have different notion with regard to the concepts of disease, cure and treatment and have different expectations from the physician. The fourteenth paper offers first-hand information about the indigenous health care practices and beliefs among the Ahoms of Chiring Chuk Village of Lakhimpur, Assam. Ancestors worship has been widely practiced since ages among most human societies and bear significant importance towards maintaining the social fabrics. The fifteenth article highlights the indigenous practices associated with the ancestor worship ceremonies of the Ahom community. Socio-cultural structure beholds a well organized life cycle mechanism that regulates activities of individual members through sanctions and taboos. The sixteenth article highlights the different social folk customs and the beliefs associated with the birth, puberty and death rites of the Sonowal Kacharis of Assam. Folk customs and practices reflect the social order and shed light on the indigenous knowledge and inherited capabilities of members. The seventeenth article speaks about changes that are occurring in the *Nyokum* festival of the Nyishi and analyses how every aspect and parts of the *Nyokum* can be seen affected by the agents like globalization, assimilation, acculturation, etc.

With its crtical and reflexive perspective, medical anthropology bears a lot to contribute towards the development of policies associated to public health. It can bee seen that despite anthropology's potential for informing health policy, its contribution has been limited. An ethnographic inquiry has the potential to generate a great deal of rich information which can influence public health planning. This book attempts to strengthen this approach of studying health and health care practices by allowing authors to critically address the health needs of various societies across the country. The eighteenth article attempts to estimate the prevalence of hypertension and its associated risk factors of hypertension among the Tengaponia Deoris of Dibrugarh district, Assam. A community-based cross-sectional study was conducted among 100 individuals in the age group of 18 years and above which reveals that the prevalence of hypertension was 24% which was higher among females in comparison with males. There was an increase in the prevalence of hypertension with an increase in age. Implementation of health promotional measures aiming to reduce alcohol & tobacco consumption, detection and treatment of hypertension, a dietary modification will help in decreasing the future risk of hypertension and its complications. The ninteenth essay discusses the psychological effects of pandemics. Of the late the spread of Covid 19, one of the biggest global challenges in our lifetime has changed the experience and behavior of the people and exert an overriding influence over the humanity across the gobe. These kinds of pandemics bring awful situation, growing public health crisis, economic challenges etc. Therefore to fight against these pandemic diseases having plethora of varied options can help people become better equipped to tackle the stress. The twentieth study aims to understand about the antenatal health care practices among the Mog women of Upper Assam. Mogs are the Aracan tribes who came to Assam through Chittagong Hill Tract. It is found in the present study that the areas where the study had been conducted have modern health institutions within their vicinity. Most of the Mog women taken under consideration for the study seemed aware of the importance of antenatal health care and hence they availed modern health care facilities. In the twenty-one article, the author aims to assess the age-related changes in anthropometric characteristics and indices thereof among the adult Mishing based on body mass index and percent body fat. The Mishing are the second-largest group of the plains scheduled tribe of Assam. In article twenty-two readers can generate knowledge on the hygiene and sanitation practices in rural areas of North East India. The study focuses on the Mishing tribe and highlights their health culture. In article twenty-three the authors examines the determinant of childhood mortality and differential mortality. The first hand study was conducted among the Santal and Tantis of Upper Assam and findings revealed that the childhood mortality (0-5 years death) among the Santal was higher (5.49) than the Tanti (2.96). The difference in childhood mortality among the Santal and Tanti was in regards of certain bio-social factors e.g. birth interval, age at marriage, age at menopause, family type, maternal education are non-significant. Significant differences were observed in regards of religion and age at menarche among these populations. Aging is an inevitable and a universal process, but the female reproductive organ ages first among humans. Today, with better medical facilities and improving life style most women live long enough to become postmenopausal. The twenty-four article presents a literature review on the impact of reproductive aging on women's health. The last paper attempts to highlight the Physical Activity Level (PAL) and Total Daily Energy Expenditure (TDEE) of Young Adult males of Bakarapara area of Guwahati, Assam.

The aim among our contributors was to highlight a few key areas where anthropologists can contribute to understanding the dynamics that are reshaping society, culture and health system in the contemporary rural and urban societies. In bringing together the twenty five articles, the aim was to elicit deeper insights into the general processes in anthropological knowledge formation.

Society

Chapter - 1

Livelihood Security in Flood Prone Areas of Assam: An Agrarian Perspective

— ***Bruhid Rabha***

Livelihood consists of capabilities, material and social resources, and requisite activities for a means of living (ILO, 2006). Dynamic interfaces among the components like natural, human, physical, financial and social capital constitute livelihood (Ashraf et al, 2013). In the 70s, the Brundtland commission familiarised the concept of sustainable livelihood in terms of ownership and access to basic needs and livelihood security. In simple terms, livelihood is concerned with people's capabilities to means of living in order to enhance their well-being and that of their future generations[1]. Modern welfare states undertake several policies, programs, acts, and schemes to ensure economic security, health, and livelihood security. However, in agrarian and rural economies, ensuing livelihood security is a great challenge as most of these economies operate under the conditions of the vicious cycle of poverty. The natural calamities like floods, drought, cyclones, windstorms, epidemics, etc. also pose challenges for livelihood in agrarian economies.

The concept of livelihood security

Livelihood security entails having access to means of living. It simply refers to ways and means of securing the necessities of life. We may say that livelihood security is having access to adequate earnings and resources to meet our day to day needs like food, clothing, safe drinking water, housing, health facilities, time for social integration, etc. Each household can have various sources of entitlement which together comprises its livelihood. The risk of failure to secure livelihood points to the level of vulnerability to income, nutritional and health security. Therefore, livelihoods are secure when we have secure access to resources or income-generating activities to offset shocks and to ease our risks (Chambers, 1989). A sustainable livelihood can withstand and recover from the shocks and stress, maintain its assets and capability and provide livelihood opportunities for the future generation (Chambers and Conway, 1992). In fact, livelihood is a multidimensional concept. The SOIL report defined livelihoods as "a set of activities a household engages in on a regular basis in order to generate adequate cash and non-cash income to maintain a minimum desired standard of living, both on a day to day basis and over a longer period of time. Oxford English dictionary defines livelihood as a means of earning money in order to live. Deriving from the above definitions, we can say that livelihood security covers economic, nutritional, health, educational, habitat, environmental security and community participation, etc. The definition put forward by Chambers and Conway may be considered as a standard working definition and can regard livelihood security as the assets and capabilities of human beings for securing means of living. This chapter considers these aspects and makes an attempt to examine the question of livelihood security in the agrarian economy of Assam in the context of the recurring nature of floods and consequent damage to property, life and other valuable resources.

Assam and flood scenario

Assam, located in the tropical latitudes (24.3° N and 28° N) and eastern longitudes (89.5° E and 96.1°E), occupies an area of 78438 km^2 representing 2.39 percent of the Indian landmass and is the gateway of the north-eastern region of India. The rivers Brahmaputra and Barak, in the north and south respectively carve out deep valleys that represent the major part of the state (Bhagabati et al., 2012). Arunachal Pradesh, Nagaland, Manipur, Mizoram, Tripura, and Meghalaya surround Assam and along with Sikkim constitute the north-eastern region. Geographically, Assam and other north-eastern states are connected to the rest of India via a strip of land in West Bengal called the Siliguri Corridor. Assam shares an international border with Bhutan and Bangladesh. The state supports 2.58 percent of the country's total population as per the 2011 census and occupied 15th rank in the country in terms of population. As against the decadal growth rate of 17.64 percent in the country, the population of the state grew at a rate of 16.9 percent in the period 2001-2011. The literacy rate increased to 73.18 percent in 2011 from 63.25 percent in 2001. Nearly 85.92 percent of the population in the state lives in rural areas.

The economy of the state is rural-based where more than 85 percent of the total population lives in rural areas. Although agriculture is the backbone of Assam's economy, production technology is dominated by traditional technology and has been a predominantly rain-fed system. Nearly 80 percent of the total cropped area is rain-fed in Assam indicating the dependency of the farmers on the uncertainty of nature (Bhowmick et al., 2005). The state is endowed with abundant water resources. The state can be termed as a land of rivers as by virtue of its unique geographical location, innumerable rivers, and their tributaries have covered most parts of the state. However, irrigation development in the state is very low. While existing irrigation facilities are not enough for the agriculture sector, a large portion of irrigation potential already created remains unutilized. The irrigation potential utilised in Assam has not been able to keep pace with that of potential created (Goyari, 2008). The annual rainfall in the state varies from 1800 mm to 3000 mm. However, in recent years, except for 2007 and 2008, *rabi* or summer season have been experiencing deficient rainfall for crop cultivation. Kharif season also experienced deficient rain during the years 2009, 2011 and 2012.[2]

Agricultural growth is essential to support the ever-growing population and to pave the way for achieving a higher growth rate of the economy by an agrarian state like Assam. Since land is a limited natural resource, future strategies for higher production of agricultural output will have to rely on increasing the level of productivity. The productivity of agriculture can be raised through the adoption of modern agricultural techniques, an increase in input use efficiencies or intensified cultivation. The agricultural productivity has been improving in Assam too along with other agriculturally developed states of India. However, the recurrent nature of flood in Assam raises a serious concern over the sustainability of agricultural production and productivity in Assam.

Extent of flood damage in Assam

Flood in Assam is a recurring feature. Flood and erosion are the two main natural disasters challenging agricultural sustainability in Assam. The Brahmaputra and Barak valleys of Assam experiences four to five major flood problems every year which cause significant loss of life, livestock and damages existing infrastructures and properties thus retarding agricultural growth in particular and growth of the economy in general. The flood of a particular season also has long term impact as severe flood scatters our livelihood. Apart from damaging and submerging crops and houses, water-logging also delays and affect crop in the next season (Bordoloi et al, 2013). It is said that the flood problem of Assam became severe after the great earthquake of the 1950s as it is believed that the river bed of the Brahmaputra River rose due to the great earthquake. Various man-made factors are causing frequent floods in Assam today. The Brahmaputra and the Barak River which generally carry a huge volume of water and sediment load witness a heavy concentration of rainwater during the monsoon period and thus cause an enormous flood in both banks of the river. The flood-prone area in Assam is estimated to be about 31.5 thousand sq km which is about 39.5 percent of the total land area of Assam. Significantly, Assam shares about 10 percent of the total flood-prone area of India. The data reported in the Economic Survey of Assam, 2018 shows that on an average of about 9.3 lakh hectares of area experiences flood in Assam. The Brahmaputra valley had witnessed severe floods in 1954, 1962, 1966, 1974, 1986, 1996, 2000 and 2004.[3] Assam suffers an average annual loss of about Rs. 200 crore due to severe floods and particularly in 2004, the loss suffered was to the tune of Rs 770 crores.

Assam experiences a sub-tropical monsoon climate with an average rainfall of about 1500 mm per year. Due to its unique geographical position, Assam experiences a wide array of climatic conditions. In comparison to many Indian states like West Bengal, Uttar Pradesh, Haryana, Punjab, Madhya Pradesh, etc. the north-eastern states including Assam receive higher average annual rainfall. However, the distribution of rainfall in the state is not uniform in a single year. The normal rainfall in Assam is very high during the monsoon (June to September). The normal rainfall is about 1700 mm during the monsoon, 648.90 mm in Pre-monsoon months, and 167.4 mm in post-monsoon (Basumatary, 2005). The *rabi* season receives very low or no rainfall in Assam. In recent years since 2007, except in the years 2007, 2008 and 2016, all the years received deficient or scanty rainfall during the *rabi* season. On the contrary, most of the years received normal rainfall during the Kharif season in Assam with some exceptional years which experienced deficient rainfall. The deficient pattern of rainwater experienced in some years sends a grievous message for the whole agricultural community of Assam. Since rainfall is not uniform in the state throughout the year, many farmers cannot cultivate paddy during the summer season due to a lack of proper irrigation facilities.

The flood problem of Assam is the result of the heavy monsoonal downpour. Every year during May-October, Assam receives heavy south-west monsoon rainfall resulting in floods. It causes instability in agricultural productivity and production in Assam every year. As a consequence of a regular flood, the cultivation of paddy is severely hit in Assam. The main crop season is Kharif in the state during which '*sali* rice' is grown after the harvest of *'ahu'* paddy during May-October. Unfortunately, the huge and devastating floods also occur during this crucial period. Further, floods in early parts of the Kharif season may cause huge damage to standing *'ahu'* crops as well. This also hampers the adoption of modern agricultural techniques and eventually results in low productivity. Flood also brings about significant change in the occupational pattern of people in Assam. Since agricultural lands and crops are damaged, people engaged in agriculture have to earn a livelihood as a fisherman, rickshaw puller, wage workers, salesman, drivers, small business, etc. The change from traditional occupation to new occupation seriously affects their socio-economic life (Hazarika, 2018).

The extent of flood damage to the total cropped area and value of crops damaged is still significantly high in Assam. Besides, many people lose their lives during the floods. During 1970-80, the flood-affected about 12 percent of Assam's geographical area and 7.4 percent of Gross Cropped

Table 1.1: Flood damaged crop area in Assam.

Year	*Crop Area Affected (Percent to GCA)*	*Area Affected (percent to state's total area)*	*Value of Crop damaged (Rs Cr)*	*Human Lives Lost (No.)*
1970-80	**7.40**	**12.40**	**13.50**	**37.00**
1981	4.00	5.80	7.00	21.00
1982	2.40	8.80	8.90	16.00
1986	6.40	5.50	98.00	15.00
1988	31.90	48.70	334.00	232.00
1980-90	**10.40**	**14.50**	**65.20**	**67.00**
1991	0.90	12.70	115.00	108.00
1992	0.10	2.90	17.80	12.00
1996	12.80	6.50	NA	NA
1990-98	**4.70**	**10.00**	**NA**	**NA**
2005	2.53	2.84	23.47	29.00
2006	0.26	0.74	1.11	7.00
2007	17.93	19.18	NA	134.00
2008	8.18	5.30	3.29	40.00
2010	3.58	NA	36.78	17.00
2013	1.75	NA	NA	0.00
2014	9.08	NA	NA	90.00
2015	8.06	NA	NA	64.00
2005-15	**6.42**	**7.01**	**16.16**	**47.63**

Source: Statistical handbook of Assam.

Area. In aggregate, about 37 people lost their precious life and the damage caused to the crops was to the tune of Rs.13.5 crore. The intensity of damage further increased during the decade 1980-90. More than 10 percent of GCA was severely affected by the flood and the value of damaged crops reached the level of Rs. 65 crores. The GCA affected by flood reduced significantly to 4.7 in 1990-98 and then to 6.4 during 2005-15. On average, about 47 people lost their lives and the value of damaged crops stood at around Rs. 16 crores during 2005-15 (Table 1.1). If we consider the individual year figures, it becomes clear that the crop area affected as a percent of GCA, the area affected as a percent to Assam's total land area, the value of crop damaged and human lives lost was the highest in 1988 during which the flood-affected almost half of the state. The flood and associated riverbank erosion have already emerged as one of the serious challenges in the way of securing our livelihood in many districts of Assam.

Table 1.2: Crop-season wise average rainfall in Assam.

Year	*Actual*	*Normal*	*Deviation*	*Pattern*	*Actual*	*Normal*	*Deviation*	*Pattern*
2007	1816.6	2118.2	-14.2%	Normal	259.7	313.6	-1.7%	Normal
2008	1773	2038.1	-13.0%	Normal	275.1	314.8	-12.6%	Normal
2009	1512.4	1953.6	-22.6%	Deficient	187.8	302.2	-37.9%	Deficient
2010	2066.3	1976	4.6%	Normal	189	306.2	-38.3%	Deficient
2011	1411.1	2001	-29.5%	Deficient	155.5	295.3	47.3%	Deficient
2012	1953.2	2001	-2.0%	Deficient	198.6	294.8	32.7%	Deficient
2013	1529.5	2016.3	-24.0%	Deficient	177.3	294.8	-40.0%	Deficient
2014	1774.6	2001	-11.0%	Normal	79	294.8	-73.0%	Scanty
2015	1936.5	2001	-3.2%	Normal	196	294.8	-33.3%	Deficient
2016	1789.7	2001	-11.0%	Normal	289	294.8	-2.0%	Normal

Source: Directorate of Agriculture Assam.

Cropping pattern of Assam

Cropping pattern is the proportion of area under various crops at a point of time as it keeps changing with the passage of time. Various factors like climatic, socio-economic, historical, political, etc. can affect the cropping pattern of a region. Table 1.3 represents the crop-wise shares in the gross cropped area in Assam. It is seen that the cropping pattern has been more or less stable with only marginal changes in the importance of a few crops. Among the various crops grown, rice is the most important crop with a share of more than 60 percent in the Gross Cropped Area (GCA). The other important crops cultivated in Assam are wheat, maize, pulses, tea, jute and mesta, sesamum, tobacco, banana, sugarcane, tapioca, potatoes, etc. The GCA in the state has been growing at a very slow pace from 3489 thousand hectares in 1980-90 to 3793 thousand hectares in 1990-00 and

Table 1.3: Cropping pattern across Assam *(NER data bank)*

Crops	*Area in 000 hectares*				*Percentage share of GCA*			
	1980-90	*1990-00*	*2000-10*	*2010-18*	*1980-90*	*1990-00*	*2000-10*	*2010-18*
A. Cereals								
1. Rice	2329.61	2507.36	2470.40	2474.52	66.76	66.09	66.11	64.41
2. Maize	19.24	19.22	19.13	28.75	0.55	0.51	0.51	0.75
3. Small millets	9.69	10.19	7.63	5.43	0.28	0.27	0.20	0.14
4. Wheat	106.92	81.78	61.99	22.17	3.06	2.16	1.66	0.58
Total Cereals	2465.46	2621.53	2543.04	2530.88	70.65	69.10	68.06	65.88
B. Pulses								
5. Gram	3.82	2.92	2.05	2.16	0.11	0.08	0.05	0.06
6. Arhar(Tur)	8.67	6.80	6.61	5.95	0.25	0.18	0.18	0.15
7. Other Pulses	115.24	104.75	102.49	137.60	3.30	2.76	2.74	3.58
Total Pulses	127.73	114.45	111.14	145.72	3.66	3.02	2.97	3.79
Total Foodgrains	2593.19	2735.99	2654.18	2676.60	74.31	72.12	71.03	69.67
C. Oilseeds								
8. Sesamum	14.06	15.29	13.61	11.87	0.40	0.40	0.36	0.31
9. Rapeseed &	287.59	285.82	247.32	284.63	8.24	7.53	6.62	7.41
10. Linseed	7.70	9.36	8.88	5.34	0.22	0.25	0.24	0.14
Total Oilseeds*	311.49	315.88	280.17	307.04	8.93	8.33	7.50	7.99
D. Condiments & Spices								
11. Dry Chillies	11.07	13.62	15.27	19.99	0.32	0.36	0.41	0.52
12. Turmeric	8.46	9.41	12.40	16.43	0.24	0.25	0.33	0.43
13. Onions	4.56	7.04	7.17	8.15	0.13	0.19	0.19	0.21
14. Ginger	NA	17.25	17.08	17.63	NA	0.45	0.46	0.46
15. Garlic	NA	7.87	6.95	10.26	NA	0.21	0.19	0.27
16. Coriander	NA	20.73	20.42	28.49	NA	0.55	0.55	0.74
17. Areca nuts	53.86	71.48	71.78	66.63	1.54	1.88	1.92	1.73
E. Fruits & Vegetables								
18. Coconut	7.95	17.23	19.95	20.29	0.23	0.45	0.53	0.53
19. Banana	29.58	40.67	43.53	50.63	0.85	1.07	1.16	1.32
20. Pineapples	10.70	13.50	13.16	15.94	0.31	0.36	0.35	0.42
21. Potato	49.44	69.70	77.21	102.11	1.42	1.84	2.07	2.66
22. Sweet Potatoes	9.14	9.11	7.99	5.50	0.26	0.24	0.21	0.14
23. Tapioca	1.88	2.38	2.93	3.25	0.05	0.06	0.08	0.08
Spices, fruits, vegetables (11-23)**	190.88	371.39	398.97	385.13	5.47	9.79	10.68	10.02
F. Fibres								
24. Cotton (Lint)	3.40	1.81	1.41	0.95	0.10	0.05	0.04	0.02
25. Jute	106.32	88.60	62.85	71.11	3.05	2.34	1.68	1.85
26. Mesta	10.91	5.96	5.01	3.95	0.31	0.16	0.13	0.10
G. Plantation								
27. Tea	217.02	231.02	292.63	314.29	6.22	6.09	7.83	8.18
28. Natural Rubber	5.22	10.26	14.60	52.45	0.15	0.27	0.39	1.37
H. Others								
29. Tobacco	4.46	1.81	0.87	0.23	0.13	0.05	0,02	0.01
30. Sugarcane (Cane)	46.71	34.77	25.87	30.11	1.34	0.92	0.69	0.78
Others (24 to 30)	394.04	374.23	403.25	473.08	11.29	9.86	10.79	12.31
Gross Cropped Area	3489.60	3793.90	3736.62	3841.85	100.00	100.00	100.00	100.00

then to 3841 thousand hectares in 2010-18. Rice dominates the cropping pattern of Assam. In the present scenario, rice occupies about 65 percent of the GCA in the state. Rice area increased from 2329 thousand hectares during the decade 1980-90 to 2507 thousand hectares in the decade

1990-00. In 2010-18, the rice area in Assam stood at 2474 thousand hectares with a slight increase from the decade 2000-10. But this dominant crop has registered a slight decline in its relative share in the GCA. The acreage share of rice in GCA has declined by about 3.5 percentage points during the whole period considered here. It is evident that Agriculture in Assam is cereal-based. Total food-grains account for about 70 percent of GCA and within the food grains, rice is the dominant crop with the acreage share of about 60 percent. However, due to a declining share of rice, small millets, wheat, gram, and other crops, the share of total food grains also has witnessed a gradual decline. The oilseeds like sesamum and linseed are also experiencing a slight decline in the area share in Assam. On average, more than 300 thousand ha of the area is under oilseeds in Assam. It shares about 8 percent of the GCA.

Over the years, plantation crops like tea, coffee, natural rubber, etc. have been gaining importance in Assam. Assam occupies a key position in the production of tea in India. It produces more than 50 percent of the total Indian tea. There are about 86 thousand small tea growers and 767 big tea growers in Assam. The absolute area under tea plantation increased by 97 thousand hectares during the period from 1980-90 to 2010-18. Its relative share in GCA also has shown an increasing trend from below 6.22 percent in 1980-90 to 8.18 percent in 2010-18. The acreage share of coffee and natural rubber is smaller in comparison to tea. As of 2017, the area under coffee and natural rubber plantation is 1.2 and 57.9 thousand hectares respectively.

India is one of the main wheat-producing and consuming countries in the world. After the introduction of the Green revolution during the 1970s and 1980s, there has been growing production of wheat in the country. However, Assam's share in all India wheat production is almost insignificant at around 0.07 percent only (2011-13). The area allocation under wheat cultivation also has decreased sharply from 106.92 thousand hectares in 1980-90 to 61 thousand hectares in 2000-10 and then to 22 thousand hectares.

It is evident that many crops in the state have shown a gradual decline in their shares in GCA. Pulses like arharand gram; oilseeds like sesamum and linseed; fibers like cotton, jute, mesta; and others like tobacco, sugarcane all have shown declining trends in their shares in GCA. However, most of the condiments and spices have shown a positive trend in their shares in GCA. Likewise, in the fruits and vegetable category, crops like coconut, pineapples, banana, sweet potato, tapioca, etc. have registered positive trends.

Therefore, it can be inferred that, although food grains occupy the highest share in GCA in Assam, in recent years, there has been a gradual shift in the cropping patterns towards high valued crops like fruits, vegetables, spices, and plantations crops.

Sustainability of seasonal crops

Livelihood security in an agrarian economy must ensure the sustainability of seasonal crops particularly the staple food crops like rice or wheat. Rice is the staple food of Assam. Rice production is one of the important segments of the state's economy. Growth and development of rice cultivation are still very important in Assam as in addition to generating income and employment it provides staple food to more than 25 million people (Talukdar and Beka, 2005).

Cropping pattern of seasonal rice

Rice cultivation occupies more than 60 percent of the gross cropped area in Assam. Likewise the rice area, as a percentage of the total food grain area amounts to about 90 percent. Based on harvesting time, three kinds of rice i.e. autumn, winter and *boro* are grown in Assam. The state basically depends on winter rice crop which is sown in the month of June-August and harvested in November-December. Autumn is another important crop season that is grown from February to August. In recent years, due to the frequent occurrence of floods in Assam during monsoons, farmers have adopted a risk-averse strategy during winter rice. Instead, many farmers in flood-prone areas have started their crop cultivation in *boro* or summer season, which is free from flood risks. Several studies also suggest that Assam's agriculture is diversifying towards high valued horticultural crops and cash crops (Deka et al., 2013). *Boro* rice cultivation starts in November-December and is harvested in May-June. *Boro* rice is generally an irrigated rice crop with a high productivity potential (5-6 tonne/ha) popularly cultivated in deepwater areas, where yield has traditionally been very poor during the Kharif season (Lal et al., 2013).

In the agro-climatic condition of Assam, winter rice occupies the largest share in total area under seasonal rice cultivation (Table 1.4).On average; winter rice has a share of 70 percent in total area under seasonal rice. Autumn rice with 9 percent and *boro* rice with 16 percent of the total area

Table 1.4: Area, production and yield of seasonal rice in Assam

(Economic Survey of Assam and NER data bank)

Year	Area				Production				Yield		
	Autumn	*Winter*	*Boro*	*Total*	*Autumn*	*Winter*	*Boro*	*Total*	*Autumn*	*Winter*	*Boro*
	In percent			*In '000 ha*	*In percent*			*In '000 tonnes*	*In Kg/ha*		
1980-85	26.19	72.14	1.66	2294.60	18.40	79.83	1.77	2458.20	752.70	1185.40	1135.20
1985-90	25.34	72.31	2.35	2364.70	16.15	81.05	2.81	2636.40	707.40	1248.70	1304.50
1980-90	**25.76**	**72.23**	**2.01**	**2329.65**	**17.23**	**80.46**	**2.31**	**2547.30**	**730.05**	**1217.05**	**1219.85**
1990-95	25.07	69.83	5.10	2503.10	17.25	76.21	6.53	3287.50	903.60	1433.80	1678.40
1995-00	23.80	68.24	7.96	2511.70	15.50	73.13	11.37	3443.30	893.40	1468.40	1900.40
1990-00	**24.44**	**69.03**	**6.53**	**2507.40**	**16.36**	**74.63**	**9.01**	**3365.40**	**898.50**	**1451.10**	**1789.40**
2000-05	18.85	68.37	12.78	2522.00	11.47	70.66	17.87	3848.20	921.50	1577.30	2128.90
2005-10	15.54	70.35	14.11	2418.80	9.81	70.94	19.26	3757.90	980.90	1554.60	2119.60
2000-10	**17.23**	**69.34**	**13.43**	**2470.40**	**10.65**	**70.80**	**18.56**	**3803.05**	**951.20**	**1565.95**	**2124.25**
2010-17	**8.94**	**74.98**	**16.08**	**2504.59**	**4.97**	**72.91**	**22.12**	**5118.97**	**1349.00**	**1969.00**	**2870.00**

under seasonal rice are less significant as compared to winter rice. However, in the pre-reform period, the share of autumn rice was considerably high at 25 percent and the corresponding share of the *boro* rice was only about 2 percent. A substantial change occurred in the cropping pattern of seasonal rice in Assam in the post-reform period. In this period, the share of winter rice had slightly declined to 69 percent particularly in the decades 1990-00 and 2000-10. However, recently the share of winter rice has shown an increase to some extent. Further, the share of autumn rice has been continuously declining and the share of *boro* rice has been continuously increasing in the post-reform period.

The major change has taken place in the context of area allocation under *boro* rice. The acreage share of *boro* rice was only 2.01 percent in the pre-reform period; however, its share has gone up to almost 16 percent in the recent period. It is interesting to note that the shrinkage of the area under autumn and winter rice in recent years due to the regular occurrence of floods in many flood-prone areas is compensated by a significant increase in area under *boro* rice cultivation. The substantial increment of area under *boro* rice can be attributable to some extent to the fact that the state of Assam has launched a massive crop diversification program in the post-reform period to support multiple cropping, facilitate shift in cropping pattern towards cash crop and horticulture crops and support development of non-farm allied services (Deka et al., 2013). On the other hand, according to Goyari (2008), many farmers in the state have adopted risk-averse strategy to cope with crop losses from the frequent occurrence of floods as a result of which there have been gradual decline in the area share of Kharif food grains and an increase in the area share of Rabi food grains and vegetables.

As in area under seasonal rice, in production also the percentage shares of autumn rice and winter rice have been declining over the years. On the contrary, the percentage share of *boro* rice in total rice production has experienced an increasing trend over the years. At present, the winter rice shares about 72 percent and *boro* rice shares about 22 percent in total rice production in Assam. From the preceding analysis, it is clear that in terms of area allocation and production, winter rice dominates both autumn and *boro* rice in Assam. However, in terms of yield, *boro* rice dominates both autumn and winter rice. *Boro* rice contributed about 1200 kg/ha during the pre-reform period; however, the yield attained was about 1300 kg/ha during the late 1980s. The level of the yield of *boro* rice started to increase from the early 90s and recently it contributes about 2800 kg/ha, which is the highest yield of *boro* rice achieved so far in Assam. This higher yield of *boro* rice explains the increasing share of boro rice in the share of total rice production. As pointed out by Gogoi and Bordoloi (2011), one of the reasons behind the higher productivity of *boro* rice is the use of other modern farm inputs. This *boro* season or summer season has emerged as an important crop season in Assam for paddy and other Rabi crop cultivation. Unlike autumn and winter seasons, which are affected by devastating floods every year, *boro* season is comparatively risk-free in terms of large scale damage caused by recurring floods. This season can be promoted for growing various high yielding varieties of paddy and other horticultural crops in flood-prone areas to generate sufficient income for securing our livelihood. As the Kharif season is subject to various natural risks and most farmers adopt a risk-averse strategy of not using costly HYV seeds, chemical fertilizers, etc., *boro* season can really come out as the engine for agricultural growth in Assam.

Boro season and crop sustainability

Although, crop cultivation during *boro* season has gained momentum in eastern Indian states in recent years, however, this season also poses many challenges. During this season, the crops are grown from November to about May. Unfortunately, Assam experiences significantly low rainfall for sustaining paddy and other long-duration food and other horticultural crops during this period. Therefore, for sustaining crops, the first priority should be accorded on the assured irrigational facility. This raises questions over the availability of irrigational infrastructure for seasonal crops in Assam.

Assam is endowed with abundant water resources. Interestingly, Assam is rich in both surface and groundwater resources. The Brahmaputra and the Barak river basins constitute about 32 percent of India's total surface water potential (Dutta, 2011). Assam also shares about 6.6 % of the annual replenishable groundwater resources of India. However, irrigation development in the state is progressing at a very slow pace. It is clear from Table 1.5 that Assam has witnessed a declining net irrigated area. It has reduced from 21.1 percent in the mid-1980s to 5.2 percent in 2000-10 and then to 7 percent in 2010-15. Currently, many Indian states like Andhra Pradesh, Haryana, Punjab, Uttar Pradesh, West Bengal, etc. have maintained a higher net irrigated area than Assam. Another concern in Assam is the low utilization of irrigation potential created. Irrigation potential utilized refers to the gross area actually irrigated during a year

Table 1.5: Net irrigated area as percentage to net sown area.

States	*1985-90*	*1990-00*	*2000-10*	*2010-15*
Assam	21.14	15.02	5.26	7.69
Andhra Pradesh	35.75	39.48	40.70	40.70
Haryana	70.30	76.62	83.73	83.73
Karnataka	18.09	22.22	27.88	27.88
Maharashtra	11.19	15.91	18.52	18.70
Odisha	28.17	28.55	33.26	28.07
Punjab	90.05	91.46	96.31	99.17
Tamil Nadu	43.11	49.46	54.18	57.97
Uttar Pradesh	58.72	67.47	78.56	83.86
West Bengal	35.80	43.08	57.68	59.23
India	31.43	37.32	42.58	47.15

Source: Ministry of Agriculture, Govt. Of India.

Table 1.6: Utilization of created irrigation potential

Year	*Irrigation potential utilized (in 000 ha)*			*% utilization*	
	Kharif	*Rabi*	*GIA*	*Kharif*	*Rabi*
1980-90	163.06	23.87	186.93	87.2	12.8
1990-00	131.20	22.50	153.70	85.4	14.6
2000-10	83.96	14.52	98.48	85.3	14.7
2010-18	160.20	36.00	196.00	81.5	18.4

Source: Irrigation Department, Govt. Of Assam.

under consideration. Defective distribution systems, inappropriate operation, crop diversification, conversion of irrigable land for other purposes, etc. have widened the gap between irrigation potential created and utilized in Assam over the years. The utilization of irrigation potential created has declined from 186 thousand hectares in 1980-90 to 153 thousand hectares in 1990-00 and further to 98 thousand hectares in 2000-10. The situation has improved significantly in recent years (Table 1.6). It is evident that irrigation potential utilized has been more during the Kharif season in Assam in all the years. Even after 30 years of economic reforms, Rabi or *boro* season crops share only about 18 percent of irrigated area in Assam. The interesting fact is that the utilization rate has been gradually increasing for the *boro* season. The sustainability of crops during the *boro* season depends on the availability of assured irrigation. However, the declining utilization rate of irrigation potential could prove to be detrimental towards overall food security in the north-eastern region.

Strategies for livelihood security in flood-prone areas

From the foregoing discussion it is clear that in the agrarian economy of Assam, one of the ways of securing livelihood is through modernization of the traditional method of agriculture. However, due to its unique geographical location of Assam, the adoption of modern agriculture is more feasible during the *boro* season in comparison to the winter season. This is due to the fact that the winter rice *(sali)* season is severely hit by flash floods in many districts. The diversification of cropping patterns towards the *boro* season further brings newer challenges. The first and foremost challenge is the availability of irrigational facilities. This necessitates water management during the *boro* season. In Assam, more emphasis could be laid on the development of shallow or deep tube well or dug well based minor irrigation. Various water saving methods of crop cultivation can be successfully implemented during the *boro* season for mitigating the water scarcity problem. In many south Asian economies, SRI (system of rice intensification) and AWD (Alternate Wetting and Drying) method is used as a strategy to save scarce irrigation water in many regions. Likewise, dry direct seeding of rice also helps in reducing the requirement of irrigation water. Likewise, by integrating fish cultivation into *boro* rice cultivation, farmers can attain higher returns from the *boro* season. The rice-fish-horticulture model significantly improves the economic condition of small and marginal farmers. It also results in economic utilization of land, saving of cost for manuring nearby pond, and additional income generation (Bordoloi et al., 2013). Therefore, while undertaking irrigation development policies of the state, these water-saving modern technologies should be popularized in the flood-prone areas of the state.

Assam possesses a huge potentiality for developing irrigation infrastructure. The Kharif season usually experiences more than sufficient rainfall. Instead of the requirement of newer irrigational infrastructure for the Kharif season, the need for the time is to protect and strengthen already existing irrigational infrastructure. However, for the *boro* season, there is a need for more irrigational infrastructure like surface flow or lift irrigation. In areas with the high water table, the use of bamboo bore wells can be popularized to reduce the cost of irrigation infrastructure for the poor and marginal farmers.

Guidance and training are vital inputs in scientific crop production. Many small, marginal and poor farmers in the state are not aware of various government schemes for the upliftment of poor farmers. While formulating agricultural policies, care should be taken of the dire need of training for the illiterate and poor farmers. Through audio-visual and publication medium, awareness has to be generated about the arrival of flood-resistant varieties and other new high yielding varieties of seeds, their benefits, cultivation practices, and various farm management methods.

Financial capital is one of the components of sustainable livelihood. It is not feasible to achieve sustainable livelihood depending on agriculture alone. Particularly, in flood-prone areas of Assam, economic security must be ensured through other economic activities apart from modernizing our traditional agriculture. The authorities can provide more livelihood opportunities through income-generating projects like MGNREGA. The funds of such schemes also can be successfully utilised for constructing infrastructures for controlling floodwater. The government also should properly study the unemployment scenario of the state and take corrective measures by creating other employment opportunities for unemployed youths. The withdrawal of excess labour from the agricultural sector would release surplus labour supply to the manufacturing and service sector of the state. Besides, rigorous efforts should be made to popularize handicraft products of Assam at national and international markets. The authorities can take initiative for marketing the handicraft products made in Assam through various online marketing platforms. Such steps would certainly relieve many flood-displaced farmers of Assam. In addition, the promotion of the tourism industry, particularly the promotion of rural tourism would provide lots of income-generating opportunities for the rural masses.

Assam's agro-climatic condition is suitable for growing various plantation crops like tea, coffee, sugarcane, natural rubber, oil palms, fruit plantations like banana, mango, etc. The concerned authorities must take initiative in this regard by providing sufficient aid and information for growing plantation crops in severely flood-prone areas. Mere dependence on growing rice and staple food crops cannot generate sufficient revenue and income opportunities for sustainable livelihood.

Conclusion

In the agrarian economy of Assam, flood and erosion are some of the biggest challenges for sustainable agricultural growth and productivity. Except for the hill districts, all the districts of Assam more or less experience few major floods each year. In Assam, the *sali* or winter season is the main crop season. Unfortunately, the flood also occurs mainly in this season. From the agrarian perspective, with limited land supply for extensive crop cultivation, the only possibility is raising the productivity of crops. However, due to large scale damage of crops during the monsoonal flood, many farmers adopt a risk-averse strategy for crop cultivation during *sali* season. Therefore, the *boro* season provides us enormous scope for growing rice and other horticultural crops. However, this season also confronts challenges. The prominent challenge for the *boro* season is the lack of sufficient natural rainwater and underdeveloped irrigation infrastructure. Therefore, while designing policies for agricultural development in flood-prone areas, the focus should be laid on making available assured irrigation along with the supply of improved high yielding varieties of various crops for the *boro* season. Various water saving methods of crop cultivation also should be popularized through active participation of authorities at ground level. Dissemination of information on various flood-tolerant varieties of paddy and other crop varieties to be grown during the *sali* season is of utmost importance. The next line of intervention could be directed towards providing assistance for growing plantation crops in flood-affected areas. Besides these, it is also important to provide employment opportunities and skill development training for unemployed youths for securing financial stability. Most importantly, both central and state government has to design long term policies for mitigating flood problem in Assam. Controlling flood problems in the state permanently would pave the way for agricultural development in particular and the economic prosperity of Assam as a whole.

References

Ashraf, S., Iftikhar, M., Shahba, B., Khan, G.A. and Luqman. (2013). Impacts of flood on livelihoods and food security of rural communities: A case study of southern Punjan, Pakistan. Pakistan Journal of Agricultural Science, 50(4), 751-758.

Basumatari, D. (2005). Rice cultivation in Assam: An analysis on productivity (Unpublished M. Phil dissertation).University of Hyderabad, Hyderabad, India.

Bhagabati, A.K., A.K. Bora & B.K. Kar (2012).Geography of Assam (5thed.). New Delhi, India: Rajesh Publications

Bhowmick, B.C., B.C Barah., S. Pandey & N. Barthakur (2005). Changing pattern of rice production systems and technology in Assam: A spatio-temporal analysis of performanceand prospects. Retrieved November 07, 2015, from System of Promoting Appropriate National Dynamism for Agriculture and Nutrition: www.spandan-india.org

Bora, P. (2013). Manifesting livelihood: The role of MGNREGA in Assam. International Journal of Innovative Research and Studies, 2(5), 462-473. Retrieved from www.ijirs.com

Bordoloi, R., Tamuli, K., Baishya, S. and Hussain, I. (2013). Rice-fish-horticulture model-An approach to improve the livelihood security in the flood affected areas of Dhemaji District, Assam. Environment and Ecology, 31(3A), 1429-1432. Retrieved from www.environmentandecology.com

Buragohain, R., Hazarika, J., and Deka, N. (2014). Agricultural sustainability in Assam-An economic analysis. International Journal of Research in Economics and Social Sciences, 4(8), 31-41.

Chambers, R. (1989) Editorial Introduction: Vulnerability, Coping and Policy. IDS Bulletin 20(2): 1-7

Chambers, R. & Conway, G. 1992. Sustainable rural livelihoods: practical concepts for the 21st century. IDS Discussion Paper No. 296. Brighton, UK, Institute of Development Studies.

Datta, S. and Sharma, V. (2008). State of India's Livelihoods: The 4 P Report. New Delhi: ACCESS Development Services. Retrieved January 2020, from www.livelihoods-india.org

Deka, P., C. Hazarika & P. Das (2013), Agricultural Diverfication in Assam under Trade Liberalizaiton, Journal of Academia and Industrial Research, 2 (5): 301-307.

Dutta, M. K. (2011). Irrigation potential in agriculture of Assam. Concept Publishing Company.

Goyari, P. (2005). Flood damages and sustainability of agriculture in Assam. Economic and Political Weekly, 40(26), 2723-2729.

Hazarika, A. (2018). Impact of flood on traditional occupational pattern: A case study in Dhemaji development block, Assam. Indian Journal of Applied Research, 8(7), 29-30.

International Labour Organization

Kumar, K., Singh, M. and Bandooni, S. (2018). Sustainable livelihoods through rural tourism: A case study of Majuli island, Assam. Journal of Water and Land use Management, 16(1).

Lal, B., P. Gautam & B. Panda (2013,April). Boro rice: A way to crop intensification in Eastern India. Retrieved December 21, 2015, from Academia: www.academia.edu

Mandal, R. (2010), Cropping patterns and risk management in the flood plains of Assam. Economic and Political Weekly, 45 (33):78-81.

Talukdar, K.C. &B.C. Beka (2005), Cultivation of summer rice in the flood plains of Assam-An assessment of economic potential on marginal and small farms, Agricultural Economics research Review, 18 (1).21-38.

Notes

1. Drawn from International Institute for Sustainable Development
2. Economic Survey of Assam, 2013-14.
3. Data drawn from Assam State Disaster Management Authority

Chapter - 2

Cultural Resource Management in North East India

— Dhritiman Sharma

In 2003, while choosing for archeology as special paper, I dreamt of going for some archeological fieldworks based on stone tools, may be belonging to Paleolithic or Neolithic sites, if available. Most of the works of archeology specialization was usually conducted in Garo Hills traditionally in terms of stone tools, or Karbi Anglong for megaliths. However, the trend changing approach that came in 2003 was the decision of conducting the fieldwork of archeology in Majuli by our late Professor Abdullah Ali Ashraf, from the perspectives of Majuli pottery makers. In fact, this was my first attempt or training in the field of CRM, as Majuli is considered as the cultural capital of Assam (although Guwahati is the capital city). CRM is a very recent field of archeology, as it is coming under the applied direction of archeology. Cultural Resource Management is the vocation and the practice of managing cultural resources, usually the arts and the heritage. It includes the physical aspects of culture like artefacts and also the intangible cultural items including folklore, storytelling, ethnomusicology and various other aspects. CRM encompasses the innovative and progressive urban culture too, rather than simply preserving the traditional aspects of culture

Origin and history

1990 may be considered as the beginning of CRM. It started with the protest and some legal measurements by the US Government in 1990, when they implemented a law named Native American Grave Protection and Repartiation Act, 1990. Prior to this, none of the countries implemented any such law to respect and preservation of gtaves, burials of other communities from their perspectives. However, India always practiced such acts, though no formal law, but respecting several communities' culture and artefacts have been deep rooted in Indian culture. The US Government's works initiated the academic pursuit of CRM and the archeologists and anthropologists started looking into the culture in different perspectives. As a result, the concept of archeology has changed and has become an issue from applied perspectives (Sarma, 6: 2012).

Cultural Resources Management (CRM) is the vocation and practice of managing cultural resources, such as the arts and heritage. It incorporates Cultural Heritage Management which is concerned with traditional and historic culture. It is also related to the material culture of archeology. Cultural resources management encompasses current culture, including progressive and innovative culture, such as urban culture, rather than simply preserving and presenting traditional forms of culture.

However, the broad usage of the term is relatively recent and as a result it is most often used as synonymous with heritage management. In the United States, cultural resources management is not usually divorced from the heritage context. The term is, "used mostly by archeologists and much more occasionally by architectural historians and historical architects, to refer to managing historic places of archeological, architectural, and historical interests and considering such places in compliance with environmental and historic preservation laws."

Cultural resources include both physical assets such as archeology, architecture, paintings and sculptures and also intangible culture such as folklore and interpretative arts, such as storytelling and drama. Cultural resource managers are typically in charge of museums, galleries or theatres, especially those that emphasize culture specific to the local region or ethnic group. Cultural tourism is a significant sector of the tourism industry.

At a national and international level, cultural resource management may be concerned with larger themes, such as languages in danger of extinction, public education, the ethos or operation of multiculturalism, and promoting access to cultural resources. The Masterpieces of the Oral and Intangible Heritage of Humanity is an attempt by the United Nations to identify exemplars of intangible culture.

Worldwide phenomenon

Cultural resource management in the heritage context is mainly concerned with the investigation of sites with archaeological potential, the preservation and interpretation of historic sites and artifacts, and the culture of indigenous people. The subject developed from initiatives in rescue archaeology, sensitivities to the treatment of indigenous people, and subsequent legislation to protect cultural heritage.

In the 1970s, archaeologists created the term "cultural resource management" as a parallel to natural resource management to address the following resources:

1. Historic properties
2. Older properties that may have cultural value, but may or may not be eligible for the National Register
3. Historic properties that have cultural value beyond their historicity
4. Archeological graves and cultural items
5. Shipwrecks
6. Museum collections
7. Historical documents
8. Religious sites
9. Religious practices
10. Cultural use of natural resources
11. Folklife, tradition, and other social institutions
12. Theater groups, orchestras, and other community cultural amenities (www.culturalpolicies.net)

A significant proportion of the archaeological investigation in countries that have heritage management legislation including the United States and United Kingdom is conducted on sites under threat of development. In the US, such investigations are now done by private companies on a consulting basis, and a national organization exists to support the practice of CRM. Museums, besides being popular tourist attractions, often play roles in conservation of, and research on, threatened sites, including as repositories for collections from sites slated for destruction.

Debates

It is commonly debated in cultural resource management how to determine whether cultural or archaeological sites should be considered significant or not. The criteria that is stated by the National Register of Historic Places is said to be able to be "interpreted in different ways so that the significance, may be subjectively argued for many cultural resources." Another issue that arises among scholars is that "protection does not necessarily mean preservation." Any public projects occurring near the cultural resource can have adverse effects. Development plans for a proposed project may not be able to be changed to limit impact and to avoid damage to the resource (Crowell, 2012: Fairfax County Park Authority Cultural Resource Management Plan).

Management of cultural organization

The vocation of management in cultural and creative sectors is the subject of research and improvement initiatives, by organizations such as Arts and Business which take a partnership approach to involving professional business people in running and mentoring arts organizations. Some universities now offer vocational degrees (Crowell, 3: 2012).

The management of cultural heritage is underpinned by academic research in archaeology, ethnography and history. The broader subject is also underpinned by research in sociology and culture studies.

Anthropology and cultural resource management

Understanding the traditional cultures of all people is essential in mitigating the adverse impact of development and ensuring that intervention by more developed nations is not prejudicial to the interests of local people or results in the extinction of cultural resources.

Policies

Cultural resources policies have developed over time with the recognition of the economic and social importance of heritage and other cultural assets.

The exploitation of cultural resources can be controversial, particularly where the finite cultural heritage resources of developing countries are exported to satisfy the demand for antiquities market in the developed world. The exploitation of the potential intellectual property of traditional remedies in identifying candidates for new drugs has also been controversial. On the other hand, traditional crafts can be important elements of income from tourism, performance of traditional dances, and music that is popular with tourists and traditional designs can be exploited in the fashion industry. Popular culture can also be an important economic asset.

India

India has always been very tolerant to other cultures since historic times. In 1904, the Protection of Monuments Act was implemented and since then, the protection of monuments is taken care by the Government irrespective of any place or community. Prior to that in 1861, Archeological survey of India was established. Such establishment of archeological offices or implementation of law is one of the parts of cultural resource management from Government perspectives. The Archaeological Survey of India is an Indian government agency attached to the Ministry of Culture that is responsible for archaeological research and the conservation and preservation of cultural monuments in the country. It was founded in 1861 by Alexander Cunningham who also became its first Director-General.

ASI was founded in 1861 by Alexander Cunningham who also became its first Director-General. The first systematic research into the subcontinent's history was conducted by the Asiatic Society, which was founded by the British Indologist William Jones on 15 January 1784. Based in Calcutta, the society promoted the study of ancient Sanskrit and Persian texts and published an annual journal titled Asiatic Researches. Notable among its early members was Charles Wilkins who published the first English translation of the Bhagavad Gita in 1785 with the patronage of the then Governor-General of India, Warren Hastings. However, the most important of the society's achievements was the decipherment of the Brahmi script by James Prinsep in 1837. This successful decipherment inaugurated the study of Indian palaeography.

The Archaeological Survey of India is an attached office of the Ministry of Culture. Under the provisions of the AMASR Act of 1958, the ASI administers more than 3650 ancient monuments, archaeological sites and remains of national importance. These can include everything from temples, mosques, churches, tombs, and cemeteries to palaces, forts, step-wells, and rock-cut caves. The Survey also maintains ancient mounds and other similar sites which represent the remains of ancient habitation.

The ASI is headed by a Director General who is assisted by an Additional Director General, two Joint Directors General, and 17 Directors (Sarma, 2012: 4-6).

Careers in CRM in North East India

North East India, being the home to hundreds of tribes and their undocumented material culture provides an ample opportunity in the field of Cultural Resource Management. Cultural resource management features people from a wide array of disciplines. The general education of most involved in CRM includes sociology, archaeology, architectural history, cultural anthropology, social and cultural geography, and other fields in the social sciences.

In the field of cultural resource management there are many career choices. One could obtain a career with an action agency that works directly with the Ministry of Culture or anything related to it, like Museum, and other Centers for Local Folklore and Traditions. There are also careers that can be found in research organizations like the Indian Council of Historical Research, or the state research offices. Beyond these choices, one could also obtain a career as part of the local government and work with planning agencies, housing agencies, social service agencies, local museums, libraries, or educational institutions. Jobs at private cultural resource management companies can range from field technicians to principal investigators, project archaeologists, historic preservationists, and laboratory work. One could also become a part of an advocacy organization, such as the National Trust for Historic Preservation. (FEMA, Integrating Historical Property).

Analysis

Whatever has been created in the past are the historic properties. However, all historic properties have not yet been listed by the Archeological Survery of India due to problems in relation to the remote localities. As a result, researches are leading to the discovery of new items everyday by the researchers, and these are subject to scrutiny for inclusion into the list of heritage. Several older properties have their cultural value, but so far, they may not have been registered. Such registration is usually not taken place in the heterogeneous countries like India, USA or Brazil, as culture is viewed in the official portrait from the National manners, and several ethnic minorities' cultural views and items are usually gone unnoticed due to the ignorance from the majority perspectives. For example, in the USA, when White Historians go for the archeological sites, there is no doubt that he might miss several cultural items of the Native Americans, Blacks or the Asian migrants due to his expertise in his own race, or from the family which he is hailing. Similarly, in India too, whenever the people from majority community search for historical items, several cultural items of the tribes or even religious minorities may be gone unnoticed depending on the state of origin. In National level, historical monuments are recorded mostly from the view of Taj Mahal or those Mughal architecture from the historical perspectives or the temples. In this point, we can cite the example of the discovery of tombstone by my research team comprising of Shyamalee Gogoi and Chandan Boruah, in West Kameng district of Arunachal Pradesh. Tombs are used in burial purposes in different parts of the world. It is generally made up with stone rubbles or large stone slabs with one or more chamber for the preservation of the dead and the shape and sizes of the tombs are found differently in different human societies. Tomb is the most common type of megalith in Europe and it is found in many European countries like France, Portugal, Netherlands, Germany and Denmark and on the basis of its construction the megalithic tomb of Europe is divided into three categories: portal tomb, pasasge grave and gallery graves. The radio carbon dating of the Europen tomb date back to 4800 BC. And hence it belongs from Neolithic period in Europe. Normally in Europe, three divisions of tomb stones are common. These are:

1. Portal tomb: Consisting of two or more vertical megaliths or menhir, supporting with a flatstone, and supporting with a flat slab stone over it.
2. Passage grave: It has a narrow passage made of large or sometime medium flat stones. It has one or more burial chambers consisting with stone rubbles. This has found in the Jamiri tomb stone, where the fieldwork has been conducted by the researcher.
3. Gallery grave: This kind of tomb is rectangular in shape and consisting with stone slabs, but sometime found narrow at one end. It was a form of community burial site. Those placed in a gallery graves were most likely themembers of the same family or hamlet, and probably were intended to reinforce the sense of community (Price, 2013:185).

In India so far, the megalithic tombs are only found in South India and they are known as Kudaikal and Topikal in Karnatka and Kerala. The Kudaikal consist with four vertical stone slabs and the burial urn is placed under these stones. A hemispherical stone slab is placed over the stones. In Topikal, the burial urn is placed under ground and it is covered by a convex type circular stone slabs. These chambered tombs were containing human burials and grave goods like black and red ware pottery and some pieces of iron which indicate that the megalithic tombs were appearing in South India during the Iron Age of India.

The discovery of tomb in Jamiri among the Hrusso of West Kameng district opens a new chapter of megalithic culture. These tombs are square in size and made up with stone chips or rubbles with a narrow passage. Structurally it is completely different from the South Indian tombs. These tombs have no written history or even oral history related with it and hence, it is difficult to trace out the origin and choronology of the tombs in Jamiri. As per the historical evidence, the Hrusso of Jamiri settled in this place under the rule of their chief Thage Raja i.e. first half of 19th century and they have no relation with those tombs. Thus it may be concluded that before the settlement of the Hrusso in Jamiri, this place was occupied by some unknown society and they had the tradition as tomb burials.

Morphologically, so far, the North East Indian megaliths are divided into only three divisions: menhir, dolmen and cist. Thus the finding of tombs in the hilly area of Arunachal Prdeash is opening a new way to anthropological as well as archeological research in Arunachal megaliths leading to new four divisions. In fact, the tombstone in West Kameng is a matter of cultural items, which are present here beyond their historiocity.

Another important aspect in applied archeology is the study and analysis of museum collections. In this case, while talking about the stone tools present in the museums of North East India, credit goes to the stone tool experts like TC Sharma, HC Sharma, MC Goswami and Abdullah Ali Ashraf. Because of their tireless efforts, today, most of the stone tools in the museums of Gauhati and Dibrugarh University and even in the museums of all the 8 states of North East India are also exhibited. Now, if someone is willing to do research on the stone tools of North East, then under the aspect of applied archeology, it can be conducted by collecting the samples from the Museum of Gauhati University, in the Department of Anthropology. In museum, such collections are authentically documented. Hence, from the study of museum items, the researchers can organize the research in a new direction and that without much pain from the field, which is a matter of sacrifice from the previous scholars.

In case of Religious sites, religious practices and cultural use of natural resources, anthropological training and knowledge help us to identify such sites. This is the reason, why we can't ignore anthropology while doing research in archeology, be it theoretical or applied aspect ever.

Conclusion

Archeology is not only the study of stone tools and fossilized bones, nor is it solely the study of extinct culture alone. To understand archeology deeply, the applied aspect is mandatory. In fact, several aspects of human society and culture developed during the Prehistoric times, but those predecessors who started all these traditions are no more, either through extinction and evolution, and the new evolution of Homo Sapiens occurred, who are ruling the world at present. In such case, we can cite the examples of agriculture, religion, pottery tradition, burial practices, house type and material culture, which had the prehistoric root in the human history. As a result, to conduct the full fledged archeological study of any of the topics of these, one must see the comparison in terms of pas present continuum, and as a result, the concept of ethnoarcheology has emerged, which studies the current traditions as well. Hence, today we are seeing the ASI or the Research Offices and Academicians of Archeology to get involved in the fields of Cultural Resource Management, where, the making of archival and digitalization of the processes of such archeological works have helped the future generation to learn and preserve the indigenous culture of their own, which in turn shall be saved and the cultural perspectives of human culture will continue. This is the ultimate goal of applied archeology or Cultural Resource Management at present.

References

Crowell, Elizabeth. 2018. Cultural Resource Management Plan. Retrieved from google books, page 3.

Price, P Douglas. 2013. Europe before Rome: A Site by Site Tour of the Stone, Bronze, and Iron Ages: 185.

Sebastian, Lynne. Archeology and Cultural resource Management. Retrieved from www.sarpress.sarweb.org.

Sharma, Dhritiman. 2012. Glimpses of North East India Archeology. Eastern Book House, Guwahati. 4-6.

State and Local Mitigation Planning. 2005. Integrating Historic Propertyand Cultural Resource, retrieved from google books. www.culturalpolicies.net

Chapter - 3

Rural Poverty is Multidimensional Phenomena in Nepal: An Anthropological Review

— Dilli R. Prasai

Rural poverty in Nepal is a widespread, complex and multidimensional phenomenon. Poverty is deeper, more intense, and more severe in rural (as compared to urban) areas; and even more so in the hills and mountains and in the western, Mid-western and Far Western regions. Even within rural areas, the poorer segments of the population have less access to fertile land, irrigation, modern inputs credit and marketing facilities and road infrastructure. The rural areas are badly under-served in terms of quality and coverage of basic education, health care, drinking water, roads and access to other infrastructure and markets. Poverty is also closely related to the degree of social, political and economic inclusion/exclusion. Women and ethnic groups are left out of the mainstream of development, because they lack voice, empowerment, representation and access to economic opportunities and resources. Thus, they are serious included in vicious circle of rural poverty (15th plan NPC, 2019: 5).

The concept of poverty

Poverty has different meanings in different stages of development. It doesn't exist only in developing countries but also in developed countries. In the context of poverty, there are various definitions which conclude that hunger, insufficiency of basic needs for minimum requirements, malnutrition, frequently ill health, illiteracy; poor clothing, weak health, low purchasing power, low life expectancy and landlessness are the criteria by which to judge poverty. In developed countries, poverty can be defined as the failure to maintain the desired level of living, where as in developing countries, it reflects the picture of hunger, malnourishment, illiteracy, high infant mortality, inadequate shelter, rapid growth rate of population and unemployment (Todaro: 1981: 33).

The World Bank defines poverty as the inability of people to attain a minimum standard of living. The measure of living standard for an individual is (or household's) real income of expenditure. The magnitude and extent of poverty in any country depends upon the average level of income and the degree of inequality in its distribution.

Poverty can also be defined in absolute and relative terms. Absolute poverty refers to a situation where people receive an income below the minimum level required for survival and physical efficiency whereas income level higher than the minimum subsistence requirement but below national average per capita income is considered to be relative poverty. So far as the process of the measurement of relative poverty is concerned, it is measured in terms of general standard of living and accepted quality of life in society. In fact the people, who have a less amount of goods compared to others in the society, are called relative poor. Relative poverty is also expressed inequality of income.

Glimpse of poverty in Nepal

Nepal is one of the poorest countries in the world with a per capita income 210 $ in 1997 (WBR: 1998/99) and a corresponding low level of consumption i.e. 51 percent of the total income of household is spent on food. In the context of Asia, Nepal lies at the second poorest position. Most of the poor live in the rural areas of Nepal. During the fiscal year, 1995/96, 44 percent of the rural people and 23 percent of urban people were under the poverty line. (CBS, NLS Survey: 2016:67)

The rural poverty is one of the burning problems of an underdeveloped country like Nepal. Around 38 percent of the total population of Nepal was below the poverty line at the end of the ninth plan (NPC 2016). The majority of the people in study area are below the poverty line due to a high dependency on limited resources. To some extent rural poverty spills over into the urban sector. For example; the rural poor eventually migrate to the urban areas in search of food and work.

Poverty in Nepal can be viewed from two levels micro level and macro level. At micro level, it focuses primarily on an individual's experience of extreme poverty in terms of low caloric intake per day, lack of access to basic health facilities, inadequate shelter and clothing, low purchasing power, high infant mortality, high rural to urban migration and illiteracy. At macro level, it can be expressed in terms of high rate of population growth, unemployment, technological and administrative inefficiencies, low income level and lack of marketing facilities.

Poverty in Nepal is unevenly distributed with regards to various regions. There is particular pattern of poverty, which is found in the mountainous and rural hill, parts of the mid western and far western regions. It also depends upon socio cultural conditions. Most Nepalese spend large amount of money on ritual feasts and festivals like Dashain, Tihar, Marriage ceremonies and cultural programs. If they have no money, they put their land on mortgage or pawn their property for these occasions without hesitation. Poverty further deepens with the excessive use of alcohol, laziness, unproductive expenditure, debt, land disputes, sickness, superstitious and untimely death of the family head. The villagers are compelled to leave the village abandoning the traditional occupation and go to India or overseas for wage labor.

The rural and urban areas are not out of circumference of poverty. It is well known that an underdeveloped country like Nepal is affected by rural poverty. Nepal is an agriculture country where more than 81 percent of the total population is engaged in the agriculture sector (Joshi: 1998). The majority of the population lives in the rural areas of Nepal and is poor owing to low productivity of agriculture, the limited resource base and inadequate growth rate of agricultural activities in the economy. In addition, lack of rate of exploitable mineral resources, the low work force productivity, high rate of population growth, traditional technology, or and topological disadvantages are also responsible for its economic backwardness and poverty. The low rate of income results in a low rate of saving, investment and capital formation.

The extent and situation of the rural poverty is different according to the ethnicity of people. Low level of income or' the disadvantage groups in the Dhampus village is also responsible for the incidence of poverty. The social disadvantaged groups like Damai and Kami people are seriously suffering from poverty in comparison to socially advantaged groups like Brahmins, Chhetries and Giris in the sample study area. During the nine months rule of Nepal.Poverty in Nepal is a widespread and complex problem. So the different government in different time tried to lunch diverse programme in Nepal against poverty. Especially, National Planning Commission have been designing and implementing dissimilar programme for the poverty reduction. There are so many organizations are working against poverty in Nepal.

The research relevancy

The problem of poverty is found/exists everywhere in the world, both in developed and developing countries, it is particularly serious in developing country like Nepal. Nepal's poverty is mostly concentrated in the rural areas where 74 percent of its total population lives (NPC: 2011). Although, Nepal's economy is basically based on agriculture, its productivity has been declining continuously. The reasons for poor performance in the agricultural sector are due to the lack of irrigation, implementations of traditional methods, small and fragmented land holding, and lack of improved and credit facilities. Since the development like manufacturing and industrial sector has been perceived at unsatisfactory level in the rural areas of Nepal, the employment opportunities are lacking outside the agriculture sector. Thus, rural people have a low living standard and are affected by poverty. A large number of rural people are incapable of meeting basic requirements like food, cloths, shelter, health, education etc.

Anthropological research stresses that poverty leads to miserable problems in the society. Due to the deprivation of basic need i.e. food, clothes and shelter, the individual moves toward choosing further alternatives whether those are legal or illegal for his/her existence. An organized effort to alleviate poverty was initiated in 1975 by the Agriculture Development Bank of Nepal through its Small Farmer Development Programme. Likewise, Land Reforms Co-operative Movements, Go To Village Campaign, People's Participation Approach. Develop Your Village Yourselves and many similar programs which either implicitly or explicitly are related to alleviate poverty has been lunched throughout the country. But such poverty alleviation effort and programme have not fulfilled the expectations of the people. Likewise due to inability to identify the poor, a large share of the developmental benefits goes to the non poor. As a result, rural poverty in Nepal has reached at alarming state. The Government has repeatedly promised and committed to the people to abolish the massive poverty. So, poverty alleviation program has turned into a mere dream.

The 15th Plan (2019) tried to reduce poverty in Nepal from 38 percent to 30 percent. But it could not achieve the target of poverty reduction due to political instability, weak governance, violence, moist insurgency, corruption, lack of fund etc. By the end of 14th Plan, about 38 percent population was recorded below the poverty line.

The researcher has tried to find out some empirical answers to the following researchable issues related to the rural poverty of the rural area of Nepal. So, this study has been carried out to find out the answer of the following questions:

1. What are the main sources of income in rural areas of Nepal?
2. What are the different natures of poverty in rural area?
3. What is the employment status in rural area?
4. What is the occupational status among the poor population?
5. What is the prevailing polices and practices to reduce poverty?
6. Is there infrastructure development in the study area?

Objectives of the study

This study has set the following specific objectives:

1. To review the characteristic of poor households of Nepalese Society.
2. To highlight the situation of rural poverty and its causes.

Conceptual Framework

Poverty is a strong determinant factor of the others such as Human, physical, Economic and Social development. Poverty contributes to physical weakness through lack of food, malnutrition leading to low immune response to infections, and inability to reach or pay for health service; to isolation because of the inability to pay the cost of schooling, to afford to travel to look for work, or to live near the village centre or a main road; to vulnerability through lack of assets to pay large expenses or to meet contingencies; and to powerlessness because lack of wealth goes with low status; the poor have no voice. (Chamber 1983:86).

Vulnerability is part of many of the links. It relates to poverty through the sale of mortgage of productive assets; to physical weakness because to handle contingencies, time and energy have to be substituted for money; to isolation through withdrawal whether spatial (to a more distant marginal area) or social (to fewer reciprocal relationships) following shocks and contingencies; and to powerlessness through the dependence on patrons to which it gives rise.

Finally, powerlessness contributes to poverty in many ways, not least through exploitation by the powerful. It limits or prevents access to resources from the state, legal redress for abuses, and ability to dispute wage or interest rates; and it entails weakness in negotiating the terms of distress sales, and only feeble influence on government to provide services for the poorer people and places., Isolation is linked with powerlessness through the inability of those who are powerless to attack government aid, schools, good staff, or other resources. Powerlessness also makes the poor more vulnerable to sudden demands for the repayment of loans (Chambers 1983).This is variously described as the vicious circle of poverty, the syndrome of poverty and the poverty trap. This fame-work shows the actual causes of rural poverty in Nepal

Status of Rural Poverty

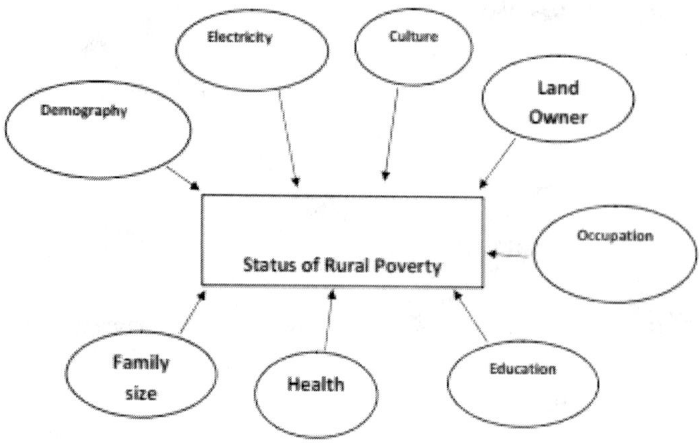

Conclusion and qualitative findings

An Anthropological view the rural poverty is one of the burning problems of an under developed country like Nepal. Around 38 percent of the total population of Nepal is below the poverty line at the end of 15ththree year interim plan (NPC 2019). The majority of the people in study area are below the poverty line due to a high dependency on limited resources like low level of income, small size of landholding. The extent and situation of the rural poverty is different according to the ethnicity of people.

Nepal has been founded that the productivity of agriculture sector is very low due to lack of irrigation facilities, unavailability of fertilizers to the required level, insufficient level of agriculture credit, traditional technology small and fragmented land holding etc. As a result, the living standard of the poor people is very low and there is poverty gap between rich and poor. On account of illiterate, low level of income, unemployed population, basic needs like food, clothing, shelter, and education, health care have remained unsatisfactory in rural areas of Nepal.

The main cause of poor socio economic condition of people in rural area is illiteracy or just literacy. Because of illiteracy, they are backward in every aspects of their life. They do not participate in many gainful programs carried out by the governmental and the non government sectors. So they are suffering from extreme poverty.

Poverty in the rural area has remained severe due to several reasons such as low literacy rate, unemployment, and small size of land holding low productivity of land, lack of market facilities, high dependency ratio, and high interest rate of loan, large family size and inequality income.

In the rural area, most of the poor households are either illiterate or just literate and so they are unemployed and they are forced to depend on wage labour for the means of livelihood.

In such a situation, it is necessary to reduce the extent of poverty in every rural area of the country. In order to reduce the extent and intensity of poverty problems effective programs and policies should be introduced in time. Further their socio economic problems should be addressed by the government as well as non governmental organization if they are really working for the betterment of the people in rural hills for poverty reduction

References

APPROSC 2010: Field Survey on Poverty, Situation of Nepal. Kathmandu, Agricultural Projects Service Centre

Bhattrai Andre. 1996: Caste, Class and Power. Changing Pattern of stratification in a Tanjore Village. Oxford University Press.

Bista, Dor Bahadur. 1991: Fatalism and Development. Nepal's Struggle for modernization. Calcutta: Lomiman

Blaikie, Piers. John Cameron and David Seddon. 1979: The Struggle for Basic Needs in Nepal, Paris. DECD

Bottomore. TB. 1905: Classesin .111odern Society, Allen and Unwin. London

Karl Marx : Selected writing in Sociology and social philosophy (Penguin Books, Harmondsworh, 1963)

Caplan Lionel, 2000: Land and Social Change in East Nepal. A Study of Hindu relations. Hirnals Books, Kathmandu

Chambers, R. 1983: Rural Development: Putting the last first, Harlow: Longman

NESAC, 2012: Review of Poverty Alleviation Indicatives in Nepal. Unpublished Report Submitted to UNOPS

NPC, 2019: Poverty Reduction Strategy Paper, Kathmandu: Nepal Planning Commission (NPC)

Saddon David. 1987: Nepal a State of 'Poverty, Vikash Publishing House Pvt. Ltd. New Delhi. India

The New Encyclopedia Britannica. 1978: Encyclopedia Britannia Inc. The University of Chicago. Chicago

Todaro, M.P., 1981: Economic Development in the Third World P. 33 Washington DC

UNDP. 2019: Human Development Report Washington DC

World Bank, 2020: Poverty in Nepal at the Turn of the Country, Vo. I. & II. Washington DC. World Bank

Chapter - 4

Access to Non Timber Forest Products and Its Impact on the Irula Tribes of Nilgris

E. Tamil Selvan

Tribes in India are forest or hill dwelling people and their livelihood directly or indirectly involved forest based economy. They enjoy major source of income through natural resources accessed from forest. There are 67.8 million Scheduled Tribe people, constituting 8.08 per cent of India's Population. There are 698 Scheduled Tribes spread all over the country barring States and Union Territories like Chandigarh, Orissa has the largest number – 68—of Scheduled Tribes. Tamilnadu is the southern part of India tribal population constitutes 1 percentage of overall population. Among 36 scheduled tribe six are considered as particularly vulnerable tribal groups one among them irula in Nilgris depend their economy through cultivation and natural resources from forest. They are hunter and gatherers in earlier period .In nilgri district they are relied on agricultural and allied activities and wage labour in tea and coffee plantations the other source income derived from collecting minor forest products.Tribal rights and recognition in forest is neglected due to non implementation of forest right act 2006 in TamilNadu.

Policies and its implications

About 10 million or more forest dwellers, mostly Adivasis (literally meaning "Original inhabitants" or "indigenous peoples"), will have much to celebrate. If the United Progressive Alliance (UPA) government in power in India takes the bold step to follow through on the recommendations of the report of the Joint Parliamentary Committee on Scheduled Tribes (Recognition of Forest Rights) Bill of 2005 (Bijoy). A wholesome feature of the revised National Forest Policy of 1988 is that, in Contrast to the 1894 and 1952 forest policies, it contains a specific provision for the integration of tribal interests with forest, inter alia, it states,

> *"Having regard to the symbiotic relationship between the tribal people and forests, a primary task of all agencies responsible for forest management, including the forest development corporations, should be to associate the tribal people closely in the protection, regeneration and development of forests as well as to provide gainful employment to people living in and around the forest. While safeguarding the customary rights and interests of such people, forestry programmes should pay special attention, among others, to protection, regeneration of minor forest produce along with institutional arrangements for the marketing of the produce".*

The Scheduled Tribes and other Traditional Forest Dwellers (Recognition of Forest Rights) Act 2006, (known as Forest Rights Act (FRA), 2006)consolidated the right of the community over MFP under section 3,1.c. It secures forest rights of individual or community tenure or both to the forest dwelling Scheduled Tribes and other forest dwellers on all forest lands for the "right of Ownership, access to collect, use and dispose of minor forest produce which has been traditionally collected within or outside village boundaries".

Forest Right Act 2006

This act has legal right to access land and forest resources for forest dwellers and tribal people. To ensure their rights in forest for their living was claimed by individual land right and communal rights

Minor forest produce

While PESA hasnot defined what constitute MFP, FRA defined MFP as "all non-timber forest produce of plant origin including bamboo, brush wood, stumps, cane, *tussar,* cocoons,honey, wax, *lac, or kendu* leaves, medicinal plants, and herbs, roots, tubers andthe like".

Area of study

The study was carried out, 19 tribal settlement, 5 different taluks which is located in Nilgiri District, Tamil Nadu. Those Tribal settlement are known as, Kollikarai, Melkoopu , Attadi, Kallampalayam, Alimayor, Annaipallam, Mooperkadu, Mavanalla, Atchangarai, Chokkanalli, Vazaithottom,

Koilpatti, Semmanathan, Thakkal, Kurumbarpallam, Thottulingi, Kengarai Annaikatti, and Sriyure. These tribal settlements come under the both forest and plantation based economy.Kothakiri taluk includes, Kollikarai, Melkoopu, Attadi, Kallampalayam, Alimayor. Coonur Taluk includes Mooperkadu, Annaipallam. Within Ootytaluk following the settlements are located such as Vazaithottam, Mavanalla, Kovilpatti, Kurumbarpallam, Anaikatty, Sriyure and Chokkanalli. In Annaipallam the houses are scattered along with cultivation land. Coffee is cultivated along with pepper. Coffee is the major source of income; it has two varieties harvest in the month of March. Pepper yield good amount of earning annually. Annaikatty, Chokkanali and Siriyure village situated inside the forest area. in these hamletstribal people mostly depend forest for their livelihood They do cultivation in forest land if monsoon favors. Ragi and maize, *thenai are* cultivated during the month of February. Every house in these hamlets has their own kitchen garden. Vazaithottum, Koilpatti, Kurumbarpallam, Thakkal, and Thottulingi these villages come under elephant corridor area. From these settlements these populations are facing lot of conflicts between forest officials and administration. Some of developmental programmes are restricted due to elephant corridor. Most of the population in these settlements is engaged in doing wage labour in resorts and guest house owned by non tribes. Alimayor and Kallampalam forest village which is located in the Thengumarda region. Most of them engaged in agriculture and animal husbandry. Atchangarai and Mavanalla are mostly exposed villages near the Mudumalai wild life sanctuary. They work as a fire watcher, government employee in different sectors.

Case study to understand the Forest Right Act 2006

The major outcome of this study to understand recognitionof forest rights over non timber produce extracted from forest. Most of irula villages located near forest and adjacent areas. The main form of occupation of irulas is agriculture, animal husbandry; wage labour and collection of minor forest products. They are symbiotic relationship with forest and have vast knowledge on flora and fauna. They have indigenous knowledge utilize the forest produce during availability. Earlier these people are allowed to collect non-timber produce from nearby forest. Nowadays Irulas are restricted to collect non timber products due to proper implementation of Forest Right Act in Nilgris, Tamil Nadu. Most of irula villages are converted in reserved forest and protected areas due to Wild life protection Act 1972. Some of the places are comes under Mudumalai Tiger Reserve. Occupation such as grazing, agriculture, minor forest produce collection, fire wood collection was regulated under Mudumalai Tiger Reserve was now banned. Forest department due wild life act they are trying to relocate people from forest to other places. Tribal people holding land half acre to one acre for cultivation without patta. Lacks of water during summer season tribal people are not able to do their agricultural activities. Unemployment cause major issues among them. Customary ritual and religious practices are restricted in the temples. Without permission from wild life warden they are banned to regular visits to their temple. During festival season only they are allowed to worship their deities. Due to restriction over forest resources and land accessibility adversely affects the livelihood of these tribals. Adi-Dravida and Tribal Welfare is a nodal agency to implement Forest Right Act. Forest right act are not implemented properly due to non- coordination with other departments and officials do not understand the legal rights as mentioned in the Forest right Act. Stay order was put in high court those who are claiming right to access land for cultivation and minor forest produce. Local administration consult with gram panchayat they collected information regarding land usage of homestead, cultivation, communal rights still they are not get individual claims or community titles over their land.

Food, housing, livelihoods is related with forest among these tribal people irulas grazing livestock in the forest areas. As observed during data collection most of agricultural lands have land ownership it creates more conflicts between forest officials. Since the settlers did not own land cultivated by them they could not procure loan for bank for the development of land and agriculture and animal husbandry etc. forest settlements decreases so far as the needs of forest department and wild life protection and reserved forest. Those Irula villages located in the periphery of the forest have received special attention. Minimum basic needs water; road educational facilities are not fulfilled. Some of villages in the irula settlement come under elephant corridor are so forest officials are restricted to do any developmental activities. Even though they are facing problem during harvest while the wild animals like wild boar, elephant enter in the agriculture field though the electric fencing is not allowed to protect the field. Interview with people reveled that they are exploited with officials. Literacy of both male and female in those settlements are low. Ration cards issued to these populations fall below poverty category. Inaccessibility in road causes to sell their products not in real value. So the outside people came and buy in very minimal price. They sell out these products in higher value. Mobile and TV has some better access in communication. Access to education, health, social backwardness, low level of literacy, simple technology, political marginalization need to address among them.

Statement of the problem

The impact of forest policy among irula tribe in nilgris andrecognition over non-timber forest produce.

Objective of the study

1. To understand the access and control over non – timber forest produce among irulas
2. To identify impact on nonimplementation of Forest Right Act in Tamil Nadu
3. To understand the problems faced through political and administrative agencies

Methodology

Data was collected through intensive field work through participant observation. Case study isadapted to addressing the challenges and issues facing relating to access and control over natural resources to conversation with those who engaged with collection of minor forest produce.

Results and discussion

Minor Forest Products collected from irula included Tamarind, Honey, Tubers, Sekakaai (Acacia sinuata), Resin, Mango, Mahuwa, Myrobalan, Hill Broom Grass, Tree moss, Turkey Berry.

Honey is important source of income for irula tribes during the seasonal times. It collected during the month of May to August of every year. Tamarind was collected in the month of May to June. Gooseberries are rich in vitamin C it has good valuein market price. It had two varieties it was collected during the month of January and March. Broom grass collected all over year. Tubers collected in the month of June. Turkey berry collected in the month of November. Hill broom grass is collected all over the annual year. Mango is mostly collected inthe month of May.

The scheduled tribes and other traditional forest dwellers act 2006. This gives rights to inhabit in forest, collect minor forest products, use the products of river and lakes and graze animals in the forest. It also guarantees and communal rights and right for clearance of land government funded facilities such as roads, schools, fair price shops and electric lines. This act ensures continue access to the forest and right to collect minor forest product but in Tamil Nadu non implementation of FRA rights denied to tribal those who depend forests for their livelihood.

Conclusion

The data reveals the forest right act implemented not completely sense. The implementation of forest right in Nilgris only individual claims are settled in very less number. According to tribal welfare department, data reveals so far totally 1333 titles are distributed in whole Nilgris. Community rights across nilgris so far 84 titles are distributed. It clearly indicates the ignorance of community rights over forest. In the forest act chapter iii (5) not fully filled. The panchayat is not able to regulate regular gram sabha meetings properly. Gram sabha is not functioning well in implementation of forest act. There is lack of awareness on communal rights among tribal as well as officials. This act provides 13 different type of right but it was rejected due to proper collaborations with forest officials and tribal welfare and people. The person claim individual rights have to struggle to get evidence. The actual tribal people suffer serious issues while claiming their rights. The nodal agency tribal welfare but land record details availed in forest and revenue department. So the individual and communal rights in implementation level have huge difference in nilgris. Due to Mudumalai Tiger Reserve irula tribes are facing problem in collection of non timber forest product. As a result this irula tribe switch on to their livelihood in cultivation, wage labour, and engaged on alternative jobs. Forest right act in Tamil nadu is very slow pace.So there is urgent need to implement policies very effectively.

References

Bijoy. C.A, et al. (2010), India and the rights of indigenous peoples Constitutional, Legislative and Administrative Provisions Concerning Indigenous and Tribal Peoples in India and their Relation to International Law on Indigenous Peoples. Asia Indigenous Peoples Pact (AIPP) Foundation. Thailand.

Forest Right Act, 2006 Act, rules, and Guidelines (2014). Ministry of Tribal Affairs, Government of India.

Table 4.1: Individual claims so far settled in Tribal settlements

S.No.	*Taluk*	*Panchayat and VillageName*	*No. of Claims*
1.	Gudalur	Cherancode Chembakakoli	67
2.	Ooty	Ebbanadu Anaikatty	15
3.	Ooty	Kookal Sriyure	59
4.	Ooty	EbbanaduAnaikatty	126
5.	Kotagri	Kengarai	88
6.	Coonoor	Barliyar	46
7.	Ooty	Denad Chokkanally	48
8.	Kotagri	Thengumarahada Kallampalayam	42
9.	Ooty	Denad Chokkanally	02
			Total = 493

Source: Data received from Tribal Welfare Department, Ooty.

Chapter - 5

Impact of Education on the Social Status of Bodo Women in Assam

— Franky Boro

Education is very essential for the development of a society and nation. It plays an important role in all sorts of human development such as social, political, economic perspective etc. There is close relationship between the woman education and their social status. A nation cannot move forward without the education of woman because the development of a society or nation depends on the progress of both male and female. There is close relationship between the women education and their social status. Napoleon Bonaparte said, "Give me good mothers, I shall give you a great nation." So a nation cannot move forward without the education of women.

It is known that the tribal societies are still lagging behind in terms of development process compared to other non tribal communities of the country. Assam is a land of rich cultural stock along with multiple ethnic groups. Bodo is an aboriginal tribal group of the region which is known for their rich cultural heritage and social identity. The social status of Bodo women is well-established because there is no social discrimination between man and woman in this particular community. But in some cases, due to the lack of education women face challenges whenever they come to contact with outsiders. However their social and economic status is equal to the man within the society and women contribute to the economic development of the family. This paper tries to analyse the impact of education on the social status of women among the Bodo society of Darrang district in Assam. The paper also attempts to focus on the overall status of Bodo women, i.e. their social, economic, and political position in socio-cultural life of the society. To collect primary data the intensive fieldwork was done and standard anthropological methods were applied to get detailed information regarding the studied issue.

Women education is very important to them for the upliftment of the entire community or society. The present paper is an attempt to study and analyse about the impact of education on social status of women among the Bodo community of Assam.

Objectives of the study

The main objectives of the study are:

1. To study the educational status of women of the society.
2. To study the economic condition of the village and contribution of women.
3. To study the overall social status of women in their socio-cultural life.

Materials and methods

The area of my present study is Gelaidingi village of Darrang district, Assam which is situated about 5km away in north side from Mangaldai town and particularly inhabited by indigenous Bodo people.

The paper is based on both primary and secondary data. In order to get primary data I had conducted my fieldwork among the Bodo people in Gelaidingi village of Darrang district in Assam. I had applied appropriate anthropological research methods such as participant observation, survey schedule and interview method to get the detailed information regarding the studied issue. In some cases case study method was also applied. Secondary data were collected from various books, journal, scholarly articles etc.

Results and discussion

From the study conducted in this village I have found the total population of village was 312. The male population of village was 178 and female population was 134. I have collected some information regarding the educational and economic status of women through household survey and interview by conducting a fieldwork among them.

Educational status of women

The awareness regarding the importance of education among the women of this village was comparatively low. Regarding the educational status of women out of total women 134 the result has been found that,

From the Table 5.1 it can be observed that the educational status of women is very low among the population. However the number of illiterate woman is also less. Only 6% women were illiterate. Otherwise majority of women population was middle school passed i.e. 38.8%. Only 3.73% of women are Graduate. The women were not much ambitious for higher education and the main reason for this circumstance is poverty, early marriage and lack of awareness about higher education. The girl child usually dropped out from the school in their early age and they used to get married by their middle adolescent period.

Table 5.1: Educational Status of Bodo women.

Educational qualification	*No. of women*	*Percentage*
Middle school passed	52	38.8
High school passed	37	27.6
Matriculate	20	14.9
H.S. passed	12	9
Graduate	5	3.7
Illiterate	8	6
Total	**134**	**100%**

Table 5.2: Economic Status of Bodo Women

Occupation	*No. of women*	*Percentage*
Agriculture	35	26.1
Service	7	5.2
Wage earner	15	11.2
Poultry/ Business	45	33.5
Housewife	32	24
Total	**134**	**100%**

Economic status of women

The people of this village were basically poor and the women of this village get equal opportunity to handle the economic function of the family with the male members of the house. Though it was a patrilineal society and head of the family was basically the father or any male member of the house however the women also contribute their labour or economic service to their family. The Bodo women of concerned village were hard working and they were skilful in any household works. The economic status of women of this particular village is as given below.

Regarding the economic status of women from the above table we have found that the majority of women of this village are economically independent. The community was basically agriculturist and they practiced domestication of animals such as pig, fowl, duck, cow, goat etc. The women helped their husbands in paddy field they do equal hard work with the males for the good production of crops. 26.1% women of this village were agriculturist and it includes from the age group of 15 to 70 years old. Besides the agriculture the people of this village were depended on domestication of animal and beverage selling as well. Almost in every household the beverage selling was a good way to earn money if they practice the domestication of pig. Because they can use the remaining rotten rice of beverage is as the food of pig. The highest numbers of women of this village were depended on this business and they became economically independent. 33.5% women had been practiced this poultry and beverage business. On the other hand the numbers of service holder woman was very less. Only 5.2% women had done job in both private and govt. sector in urban area. The main reason for the less number of service holder women was the lack of education among the women of the community. Likewise the housewives or depended women were 32 in number and 24% of the total women population. Other 11.2% women were wage earner and they do agricultural and household work in others house and rearing animals of others as well.

In the tribal societies besides working in the household the concerned women also have to work in the field. In this society also after marriage the young wife took care of her husband, her child and shoulders all the household responsibility including agriculture, cattle, poultry and everything belonging to her husband. Women even incurred the lone and repay it to the money lenders, sell the forest products in the local market. The tribal women performed an important role in the concerned economic life. The women of this village were involved in the collection of roots, tubers and fruits which constitute their food at certain season which is essentially considered as the job of the women. Women played a major role in the making and marketing of different home made products as well. Husbands go to the market for collection while the wives stayed at their home. Besides household activities the wives also had to visit the adjacent market with their home made products.

Balanced social status in socio-cultural life

The tribal women enjoy more social freedom because of their heavy demand in the economic life. In the plain land tribes the women are engaged in the field of agriculture and they are indispensable. The property is owned both by male and female folk and the women spent their income without any advices from the men folk.

The Bodo women of this village enjoyed a balanced social status with the men in their socio-cultural life. They could enjoy the full priority to participate in any event or festival of the village. Due to the economic independence the women had been played a vital role in maintaining the all kinds of household matters. They had been enjoyed an equal status with men in terms of socio-economic, cultural and religious functions of the society. Women in the said tribe were equal partner with men in shifting cultivation. Women participated in major agricultural activities and trade. Today almost all of their women worked as an agricultural wage labourer. The women's participation in the economic activities is universal among the tribals. Traditionally Boo women are equal with the men both in rights and privilege. They are equally respected and are equally responsible for making the Bodo society as a whole.

Religion is a part of the nature. Tribals worship trees and animals and believe in ancestral worship. The entire family or the village as a whole go to the groove and offer prayer as well as make offerings. Bodo worship *Sijou tree* and their main deity was *Bwrai Bathou.* Among the concerned society in religious ceremonies the age and sex had no bar in the participation. Despite that the concerned women folk in this village were engaged in organizing the religious festivals and helped the male to culminate the required materials needed to perform the rituals. Here the worship was done for the entire familial welfare and for the welfare of the entire village. Especially the prayer was being done to increase the reproductive aspects and fertility status of the concerned women folk. In this studied village the women folk except the priest hood, enjoyed participation and played an important role in their religious festivals.

Though the social status of both the gender was equal among the people of this village however the educated women got more privilege to stand out in any public event. They get more preference to express their opinion in any kind of decision making or any political issues of the society. Therefore we can say that the higher educated women had enjoyed a higher social status and illiterate or less educated women have enjoyed a lower social status in the society.

Moreover, the illiterate and less educated women had also faced some challenges in their social life. Particularly whenever they come to contact with outsiders or other advanced group of people they feel hesitated due to the lack of education and therefore they had to stay backward in terms of modernization and advancement of the global world.

Besides the education, the age of the woman also matters in any decision making or public opinion. The elderly women enjoyed the power to give their judgement in any illegal or unwanted issues of the village. On the other hand the educated younger generation also take suggestion or advice from their illiterate older generation regarding the all kind of social, cultural, economic and political matters.

Major factors of poor education

Though the women of this village were enjoying the equal opportunity and social status within their society but still they were lagging behind in case of educational status. There is close interrelationship between education, social status and economic condition of the society. One important factor of their poor educational status was economic condition. The people of this village were basically depended on agriculture and they lived on simple economic system. Due to the poor economic condition the people could not move forward for the further development. The male people were also not much educated and they were not sincere about their girl child's education.

Another important factor of the poor education was early marriage. Due to the poverty and unemployment the younger generation was getting depressed and they had been suffered from psychological imbalance. They fall in love in early age and used to get married. Therefore the new brides or daughter in laws from other villages were also not much educated and it effects the entire educational environment of the society. Because they were not able to teach and encourage their own children and they cannot maintain a higher social status as well.

Thirdly, the lack of awareness among parents was also an important factor of low education of the society. After completing their lower primary or middle primary school the boys do not want to go for higher studies. They wanted to earn money and joined in different company or factories in urban areas. But without education they had failed to do those jobs also and finally they have to come back to the village. Likewise the girls also after completing their middle or high school level education started to do household work and some girls used to get married before the age of 18. Parents were not aware about this matter and the main reason of this problem is the lack of education among the parents. Therefore we can say that there is a close relationship among these three factors and if anyone of these is not fulfilled properly it effects badly to each other. Due to the lack of proper guidance and motivation for gaining knowledge the people of this village are still lagging behind of proper education. Though some rich families preferred their children to get education from private institution or prestigious institution, however, the poor families were not even able to send their children to nearby government school.

Conclusion

The Tribal population provides an almost equalitarian status to their women folk. Women in tribal society are treated as an economic asset and they treat the women as the symbol of fertility and nature.

Even in their daily familial affair the concerned women had a very crucial role to play. In the economic perspective the concerned Bodo women played a crucial role because they maintained their household activities and along with that they were involved in cottage based work with the help of forest based resources and other raw materials.

From the above discussion we have found that there is a great impact of education on social status of women among the Bodo community of this particular studied area. Because of the lack of education the women could not move forward to the outer world of the community and they feel uncomfortable whenever they had to face any challenging situation in the day to day life. Since time immemorial the tribal people are lesser educated and mostly illiterate and they are known for their simplicity and elegant nature. The social status of women in tribal societies is equal to the men and they enjoy all the opportunity and privilege of the socio-economic, cultural and political life of the society. However in today's context the education is very important for all human being and community for the entire development of the society. The progress of a particular society or nation depends on the educational background and quality and standard of living of the people. The economic condition is also an important factor for the development of a society. The particular society of this studied area is still underdeveloped in terms of women education and for this reason their social status is also remaining lower in the greater advanced society though they have been enjoyed equal status within the society.

In the concerned society both the men and women played an equalitarian role to maintain their familial integration and its source of economic pursuit as a whole. Thus among the studied village the women were recognised as a part of resource which treats them to achieve the honour and prestige in their domain of daily life. Here the women were treated as mother and nature which provides them prestige and status in the society.

However, the facility for women education among the studied community is very necessary to uplift their social status as well as the economic development of the society. After all, the education of women is very important in each and every society to make a society or nation wealthy, developed and prosperous.

References

Ahuja, R (2017), *Research Methods,* Rawat Publications, New Delhi

Chatterjee, P (2014), Social and Economic Status of Tribal Women in India- The Challenges and the Road Ahead, *International Journal of Interdisciplinary and Multidisciplinary Studies,* Vol 2, No 2 ISSN 2348-0343 p 55-60

Majumdar, D.N and T. Madan (2009), The Status of Women in Tribal Society, *An Introduction to Social Anthropology,* Mayoor Paperbacks, Noida, p 121-129

Narzary, S.R (2016), Identifying Bodo Women through Education Empowerment with Special Reference to BTAD in Assam, India, *The International Journal of Humanities & Social Studies,* Vol 4.Issue 7. ISSN 2321-9203, p 134-137

Shunmuga, M. M.Sekar and A. Subburaj, (2014), Women Empowerment: Role of Education, *International Journal of Management and Social Sciences,* Vol 2, Issue 12 ISSN 2321-1784 p 76-85

Singh, K and C. Rajyalakshmi, (1993), Status of Tribal Women in India, *Social Change,* December 1993, 23(4). P 3-18

Suguna, M (2011), Education and Women Empowerment in India, *International Journal of Multidisciplinary Research,* Vol 1, Issue 8, ISSN 2281-5780. p 198-204

Chapter - 6

Changing Livelihood Resources and Coping Strategies among the Tai Khamti of Namsai District, Arunachal Pradesh

— *Heerock Jyoti Baruah*

Research-oriented towards explaining events in terms of environmental influence on human behaviours is not new. Since the nineteenth century, with the development of geography and anthropology as scientific disciplines, human interaction with the environment became the subject matter. Anthropological studies have shifted from analysing the casual relationship between human and their environment to a more focused and profitable study of understanding the internal dynamics and functioning of socio-cultural systems in relation to its surrounding ecology. The very basis of the interaction between nature and society lies in the extraction and utilization of resources from the surrounding ecology. Hence, there exists a crucial relationship between the governance of natural resources and the economic activities among the low-income communities; as such population relies on the availability and access to these resources in order to secure their livelihoods (Ellis, 2000). Since 1975, anthropologists have been critical towards evaluating the impacts of the development process and highlighted how conventional top-down approaches aimed at achieving the national and international interests have contributed to the further impoverishment of rural populations and stimulated degradation of their local habitats. Anthropological research on developmental understandings has contributed to persuading specialists and resources managers to relook at the expertise of rural people, who are the target and supposedly the beneficiaries of development actions and have demonstrated the internal complexity and socio-economic differentiation of local communities that are typically assumed to be homogeneous by planners.

Contemporary livelihood studies focus on the active involvement of people in response to change and vulnerability. Rather than considering them as victims, people are seen as performing active roles in achieving their livelihoods by decision making and continuously exploiting alternative opportunities. It is therefore highlighted that vulnerable community plays an active role in ensuring their own sustenance despite their lack of access to services and to an adequate income. Livelihood is defined by Ahmed and Lipton (1988) as "a set of flows of income, from hired employment, self-employment, remittances (usually in developing rural areas) to a seasonal or annually variable combination of all the above". It is understood as a system of how people make a living and whether their livelihoods are secure or vulnerable over time. Chambers (1988) on the other hand defined livelihood security as "secured ownership of, access to, resources and income-generating activities, including reserves and assets to offset risk, ease shocks and meet contingencies". The importance of livelihood approach derives from the fact that it focuses on people's assets (physical, natural, financial, human, social and political capitals). It further evaluates how people utilize these assets and negotiate their problems, which collectively determine the living gained by the individual or household. Sustainable livelihoods approach helps to understand the underlying constraints and links micro-level understanding of poverty into policy and institutional change processes (Farrington et. al, 1999).

Overseas Development Institute (2000) applied the sustainable livelihood approach in Kenya and Namibia to evaluate how community-based resources management and various policies tend to affect the livelihoods of the rural population. This study focussed on the impact of tourism and wildlife conservation efforts on the livelihood scenario of the local population. They tried to highlight the difficulties among the partners and skills required to assess the impacts and further illustrated the difficulties in quantifying the impact of various projects that contribute to the livelihoods of the people. Sustainable livelihood approaches recognise the importance of the ability to access resources and entitlements, reduce risk and vulnerability, and exercise voice. The emphasis is rather on the fact that the poor do have assets, options, and strategies, and that they are decision takers. Its concern with 'getting below the surface' to informal institutions and processes is particularly important. It offers the prospect of identifying entry points for pro-poor change, and of sequencing activities in such a way as to minimise the danger of appropriation of benefits by local elites (ibid, 1999).

Keeping this in perspective, this study focuses on the Namsai district of Arunachal Pradesh to evaluate the factors that affect the livelihood opportunities of the local communities and identify the strategies adopted by them to mitigate such shocks and further highlight the outcome. Cross-sectional data were collected from different natural resource users like families relying on minor forest produce, farmers, timber traders and development workers through interviews and group discussion. The result reflects that natural, institutional and physical factors have significantly contributed to creating livelihood vulnerability situations in the district. Each group of resource users varied in their possession of physical assets, their socio-economic capabilities and their access to financial capital and this created variation in their nature of vulnerability to livelihood shocks and capacity to cope with the constraints. The most popular strategies to mitigate the economic hindrances included cash cropping, crop rotation, agricultural diversification, occupational shift, the establishment of self-help group (SHG), etc. The livelihood outcomes were characterized by measures adopted to avert the irregularities of income, to adapt to the changes in resource use policies, and to improve existing agro-based activities to supplement the income opportunities. This study concludes that the livelihood assets, activities, and accesses are the underlying determinants of the livelihood of natural resource users and this regulates its vulnerabilities to various shocks, coping strategies and outcomes in the Namsai district of Arunachal Pradesh.

Arunachal Pradesh relies significantly on its natural resources, which remains the most volatile sector considering that the majority of its population have long been deriving their livelihood from their surrounding ecology either in terms of commercial as well as non-commercial usages. Furthermore, the lack of agricultural modernisation and lack of infrastructural development owing to remote locality further impairs their practice of self-employment. The changing natural resource conservation measures have been a dominant cause of the declining income generation among the local populations. Empirical studies involving the stakeholders have been missing in the Namsai district and thus the sustainable livelihood approach was used as the analytical framework. The application of the livelihoods approach is pliable and adaptable to specific local settings. Specifically, livelihood assets, vulnerability to shocks, coping strategies, and outcomes were evaluated based on the viewpoints of the stakeholders, collected through discussions, interviews and complemented by field observations.

Framework of the study

As discussed above, a livelihood embraces the means, possessions, and actions that are required for a means of living. Livelihood is regarded as sustainable when it can "cope with and recover from stresses and shocks and maintain or enhance its capabilities, assets, and activities both now and in the future, while not undermining the natural resource base" (Serrat, 2017).

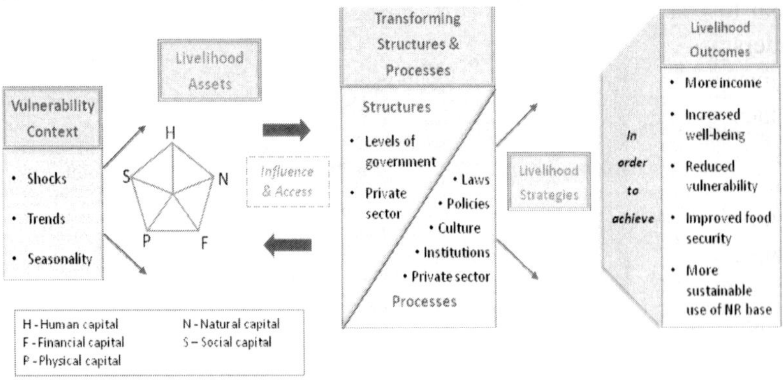

Source: https://www.soas.ac.uk/cedep-demos/000_P528_RF_K3736-Demo/unit1/page_22.htm

Fig 6.1: Sustainable Livelihood Framework.

The sustainable livelihoods framework (Fig 6.1) marks an attempt to conceptualise livelihoods in a comprehensive way, locating the multiple complications of livelihoods, and the limitations and prospects that they are subjected to. Such restraints and possibilities are regulated by numerous determinants, ranging from global or national level trends and structures over which individuals have no control, and may not even be aware of, to more local norms and institutions and, finally, the assets to which the households or individual has direct access (SOAS, 2020). The vulnerability context (Fig 6.1) signifies the external environment in which the population inhabits. Such setting further includes trends (such as national or international economic trends, changes in available technology, political systems), shocks (such as illness or death, conflict, weather), and seasonality (of prices, production cycles and so on) (ibid, 2020). The vulnerability context remains crucial within the framework as the three underlying factors impose a direct impact on the opportunities that the rural households have towards earning their living both in the present and in the near future. Serrat (2017) observed "wider economic conditions can create more or fewer opportunities; illness in the family can deprive a family of an important source of income and can force them to sell important assets that they have built up. Seasonal shifts in prices, production and employment opportunities are one of the most enduring sources of hardship for poor people all over the world".

Assets are another central component of livelihood analysis. The sustainable livelihood approach (SLA) conceptualise poverty by considering the availability of assets within the households that enables them to sustain their income to prosper rather than the traditional understanding of poverty that relates it to the lack of income. This framework further highlights that people's access to the five assets is influenced and regulated by policies, institutions, and processes, including social relations, markets and organisations (Ellis, 2000; Allison and Hormans, 2006). The 'transforming structures and processes' comprises of the 'institutions and policies that affect poor peoples' lives, and can change both the vulnerability context and the assets upon which the rural households rely upon. Based on the available assets and guided by the vulnerability context and depending on the changing policies and institutions, rural households formulate and undertake multiple livelihood strategies that tend to determine their livelihood outcome.

Strategies may vary between choices and activities that determine their consumption habits. Both short term and long term measures categorised as coping and adapting strategies respectively are adopted by the stakeholders and the final outcome would generally include more income, increased well-being, reduced vulnerability, and greater food security. The framework hypothesizes that with the increase of capacity to harness more assets, households are less vulnerable to the negative impact that emerges from the trends and shocks or the transforming structures, thus proving rural households with a better opportunity for securing their livelihood. Thus it is essential to evaluate underlying dynamics that determine whether rural households either succeed or fail in their efforts to sustain their livelihoods amidst adversities and such understanding would help in the design of policies and interventions to assist people's existing coping and adaptive strategies (Horemans, 2006).

Study area and the sample population

Namsai is the 18th district of Arunachal Pradesh carved out of the Lohit district in 2014 with a total area of 1587 square kilometre. According to the 2011 census, the district hubs a total of 19035 households among which

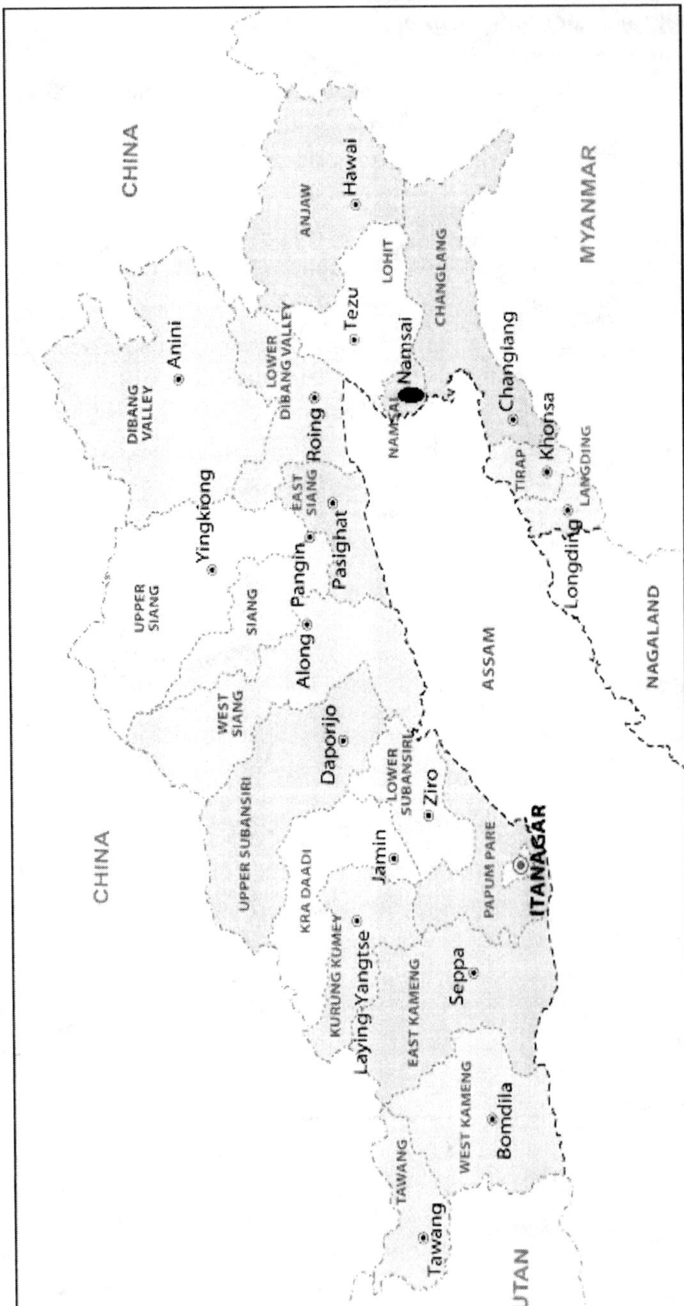

Map 6.1: District map of Arunachal Pradesh.

15890 (83.5%) reside in the rural areas adjacent to the forest landscape. The total population is 95950 and the region is dominated by the Tai Khamti tribe. Since their immigration into India in the 18th century, the Tai Khamti has been living in coherence with their ecology. Their economy is closely associated with the physical environment and can be easily visualised from their cultural traits. The Tai Khamti has a long history of involvement in the logging activities along with their dependence on settled agriculture. It was as early as 1948 when the first sawmill was established under the ownership of the Khamti elites. The locational advantage of the region led to a rapid expansion of timbering and a majority of the Khamti population gradually shifted towards the lucrative business. State initiatives equally triggered the growth of the timber industry and this flourishing economy led to the recognition of Chowkham (Khamti village of Namsai) as the richest village of Asia, back in 1990. Thus forest resource has customarily played a critical role in the livelihood of the tribe. Considering this economic dependency and the impact of forest resources in the socio-cultural life of the tribe, this region has been selected to highlight the impact of the policy changes and trends, and analyse the patterns of livelihood vulnerability witnessed by the tribe.

Objectives

The prime objectives of the present study are as follows:

1. Understand the livelihood system of the Tai Khamti in the context of natural resource use.
2. Evaluate the shocks that are particular to the livelihoods of the Tai Khamti.
3. Examine the decision-making capabilities with respect to coping vulnerability.

Methodology

The fieldwork was conducted between January and May 2017. Simultaneously secondary data was collected from sources like journal articles, census reports, newspapers, governmental annual reports, and local manuscripts were analysed. This study is largely descriptive in nature based on qualitative data collected through, semi-structured interviews, informal discussions, occasional group discussions, and case studies. Primary data collection was assisted by field observation and sample surveys consisting of 250 households from four Tai Khamti villages namely, Momong, Chowkham, Gunanagar, and Kherem. Informants were specifically chosen from individuals associated with diverse livelihood activities like farming, timber trading, cash cropping, with the purpose of evaluating the pattern of available livelihood capitals or assets harnessed by them. The focussed group discussion was categorically conducted among each of the above-mentioned stakeholders with eight informants within each category, aiming the total participants to twenty-four. The participants were chosen considering their comprehensive knowledge about the livelihood system and had better community acceptance and significantly involved in community activities. Pretested semi-structured interview questions were administered both at the individual and group levels. In the group discussion, participants were made comfortable to discuss their livelihood issues freely. Furthermore, the discussants were allowed to interact between themselves and respond to issues raised by each other. Such discussion helped to cross the data collected from personal interviews that increased the validity and reliability of the data. A questionnaire was administered consisting of open-ended question which helped the respondent to comprehensively discuss their issues simultaneously maintaining their anonymity. A series of field observations were carried out during planting, harvesting, timbering operations for the purpose of understanding variations in access to household resources and their daily livelihood activities and associated stress. The use of key informants has been specific to the study and three experts with comprehensive knowledge of the livelihood sectors like forest and land were selected through snowball sampling method and in-depth interviews were conducted for probing. This method provided ample opportunity to cross-check the information already gathered from various interviews and group discussions. Note-taking supplemented the whole study along with photographs and voice recordings when permitted. For data analysis, a comparison analysis was used to assess common themes and subthemes in reaching data saturation. Finally, every theme and subtheme was described using a narrative analysis or approach.

Results and discussion

Among the Tai Khamti, access to the five capitals has played a significant role in their livelihood system. Income generated through both forest resources and farming depended on the capabilities of individual households and their possession of the physical capital like machinery to enhance their productive endeavours and natural capital that stimulated their effort to secure alternate livelihood activities. The following paragraphs discuss the livelihood assets and their characteristics considering their relevance to income generated from both land and forest resource.

Local livelihood and assets

Human capital

The Tai Khamti has traditionally been considered as an advanced tribe in terms of their literary works and technological capabilities. Pemberton (1835) mentioned about the use of hydro-powered rice mills operating in the Chowkham village. Their small population provided them ample opportunity to exploit the land resources for settled cultivation. Borrowing the art from their ancestral territory of Bor Khamti in Burma, the tribe has long been involved in practicing *'hali'* cultivation. However, the practice was largely associated with their sustenance endeavours and less inclined to commercial usage. In the post-independence periods, the tribe secured stronghold in the state politics and such opportunities provided them to secure their livelihood avenues through political connections. Such advancement towards development gave way to better amenities like healthcare, education and enhanced their capacities to sustain traditional skills and knowledge like handicrafts and herbal medicine. The capacity to secure the livelihood possibilities did vary within the community, as the traditionally higher clans had better access to the resources and hence was well prepared to adapt.

Social capital

Tai Khamti society has practiced the clan-based division of their society, where the higher clans like *Lunkeing, Namchoom,* etc were regarded as rulers. Differentiation in the possession of livelihood assets did exist in the society and even an unequal distribution of income was reported. Such clan-based division has however improved the social relationship networks between remembers of the similar clans. It was found that members from the same clans were engaged in observing feast and share both financial and physical resources. In the course of agricultural activities, members shared tractors, harvesting machines among themselves. Further, timber traders were seen to borrow trucks, labourers, and elephants from clan members either in lieu of money or by promising help in the future. It was found that clan members shared information regarding market situations related to price change and also made each other aware of government schemes and programmes. It is necessary to note that, in the semi-urban households the cooperative ventures have diminished in course of time with the expansion of their business and entrepreneurs reported a desire for individual income. In contrast, rural households still maintain a strong cohesion with regard to socio-economic activities and engage themselves in sharing assets necessary for productive development. The desire of working together for the development of the community can be observed in the practice of organising annual community events like *Poi Pi Mou, Poong*. Such events are aimed at strengthening social cohesion and showcasing the rich heritage of the tribe. The two main community agencies performing towards the betterment of the tribe are the Tai Khamti Singpho Council and the Tai Khamti Development Society. Both these organisations are committed to the betterment of the tribe and take initiative to organize periodic meetings to discuss community issues and make key decisions for the community welfare which are later addressed at the State level through their political representatives.

Financial capital

Given the lack was infrastructural development; the Tai Khamti was less exposed to financial services. The availability of financial resources varied within society. The semi-urban residents had the earliest access to banking services which enabled them to accumulate a solid stock of financial resources during their involvement in timber trading. In the post timber ban period, such monetary savings supplemented their capacity to invest the capital as a means to diversify income avenues. In contrast, the rural residents lacked risk perception capacity and hence during their association with timbering, they neglected the banking services which maximized their vulnerability condition following the Supreme Court's ban. This has been a vital factor that restricted rural residents from immediately shifting their income sources. The lack of financial resources restricted the members from taking a risk by obtaining credit for their economic interests and minimized their effort to access funding that could have improved their economic stability by investing in enterprises for boosting resilience. Respondents indicated that in the post-ban period, most of the financial credit was acquired by the urban and semi-urban residents who were already wealthy and hence easily approved by the banks. Among the Tai Khamti, it is evidenced that the availability of financial stock and better access to credit enabled the semi-urban residents to achieve a rapid economic transition in the post-ban period than the rural dwellers.

Physical capital

Prior to its formation in 2014, the Namsai region was enclosed with the Lohit district. Like most other districts of Arunachal Pradesh, even this region experienced a lack of proper connectivity and transportation opportunities for a long time. Tai Khamti was known for their practice of elephant rearing which was used as a means of transportation across the region. The lack of communication further hindered the advancement of infrastructural development until the tribe gained access to the lucrative timber business. Traditionally the framing technology was rudimentary which mostly depended on the handmade implements used for both cultivation and harvesting. Mixed farming and crop rotation were non-existing and the use of fertilizer was restricted which significantly reduced the introduction of hybrid crop varieties. It was only with the emergence of the forest-based industries that gave way for the development of the physical capital in the territory.

Natural capital

Since their migration, the Tai Khamti society has largely been dependent on the surrounding natural resource that has defined their livelihood structure. Contemporary resource utilisation pattern still reflects the extensive collection of firewood as the primary energy source for cooking in the majority of households. Survey results indicated that lower-income groups constitute the major section of the firewood user and it comprises of the population entirely dependent on agricultural activities. Among 250 households surveyed, sixty families derive their livelihood through commercial extraction of firewood and procuring NTFP available in the vicinity. Indirect benefits of natural resources on livelihood are generated from the practice of grazing, wherein livestock are fed on the wild vegetation. Though the Tai Khamti rarely practices animal rearing in their household premises, they maintain a patron-client relationship with the Nepali community, who are entrusted to look after the domestic animals and share the dairy products. Among the surveyed households, 70% have leased out their animals to the serving community, while 15% of them were associated with self rearing the livestock. The natural vegetation across the territory has encouraged the maximum accumulation of livestock that guarantees income from milk and indirectly benefits agricultural production through the use of dung as manure.

The livelihood pattern reflects a close association with the ecological setting and family nourishment is extracted through fruit, roots, tubers, honey, fish and leafy greens, which form a major section of their diet. The respondents agreed that the traditional knowledge pertaining to wild plants and animals has helped them at times of crop failure. Though hunting was widely practiced by the tribe, yet in contemporary Tai Khamti society such activities are restricted and the forest is exploited largely for edibles and raw materials required for medicine making. The easy access to raw materials gave way to craftwork among the tribe which was largely adopted as a means of livelihood until the advent of urbanisation that minimised valuable tree species in the territory. Timber, thatch, and bamboo are used as different building materials components. These products were used for the floor, walls, poles, rafters, beams, roofs, and other parts of the houses. These forest resources were collected not only as a building material but also for cash generation.

Larger opportunities for income generation from forest resources emerged with commercial extraction of timber as early as 1948 when the first sawmill was started in Sunpura. Specific drivers stimulated the Tai Khamti population to adopt the new source of livelihood which included the low agricultural productivity of the sandy farmlands, cordial relation with the colonial empire throughout history, communal dominance in the region, political affiliations and the cultural expertise in elephant rearing, which was an essential requisite in the timber operations. Though initially the commercial extraction of timber was restricted to the elites, yet in due course, the lucrative income generation opportunity soon attracted individuals from different sections of the society. Between 1970 and 1996 significant number of wood-based industries came up in the Lohit district and 57.14 percent of such industries were located in the Tai-Khamti territory allowing them to extend their opportunities by trading timber products like plywood. The lowland occupied by the Tai-Khamti is characterised by river networks and dense evergreen forest and the industrial upspring escalated the locational advantage for the tribe. From a livelihood perspective, individuals turned reluctant towards owing salaried jobs and seem rather inclined towards timber trading or supplying elephants to the traders as a source of income. Indirect benefit from the timber-based economy was the rapid urbanisation in the Tai Khamti territory. Villagers received easy access to groceries, medicines, and enhancement in the possibilities of rural employment in various industrial workshops. The female members were not indifferent to this urbanisation and significantly increased their income through economic pursuits involving the selling of hand-woven dress material like *Sui* (shirt), *Fanoi* (dhoti), *Sin* (mekhela), *Langwat* (Riha) which are locally made in the weaving machine called *Houk*.

The spreading timber market and rapid urbanisation demanded frequent contacts with the neighbouring state of Assam as significant traders belonged to the Tinsukia district, which still remains as the commercial centre for the Namsai, Lohit, Changlang, Anjaw districts of Arunachal Pradesh. Such contacts induced a significant change in the social structure of the tribe. Respondents narrated incidents of emerging inter-community marriage which were largely driven by the intention of securing access to timber trading. As observed by the researcher, such instances are still prevalent in the Mishimi habitats who are the neighbouring tribe of the Tai Khamti. The introduction of the timber economy hindered the existing livelihood activities. With increasing individuals shifting to timber operations, agriculture was reduced to those who had limited access to assets necessary for timbering, like elephants, trucks, etc. Among other changes, increasing demand for material goods, the elaborate construction of houses, changing food habits, preferences for higher studies outside the state were noteworthy. A strict line of difference can be seen among the elites involved in the timber trade and sections of the community primarily dependent on agriculture. The elites hold a specific status within the community and their family members often reside outside the state either for academic or other economic pursuits. Respondents also revealed that the new economic avenues played an important role in challenging the traditional class hierarchy within the Tai Khamti society. With easy access to resources, individuals who were considered to be of lower status were then capable of harnessing significant monetary benefits and thus started maintaining a living standard to match the elites.

Vulnerability and coping mechanism

The term 'vulnerability' refers to any kind of trend, shocks or seasonality that affects people's livelihood and over which individuals have the least control. Trends may be understood as large movements or transitions of population, governance, and technology while shocks constitute the short intense burst like an epidemic, natural disaster, economic depression, and conflict, etc. Seasonality, on the other hand, is the cyclic events or seasonal shift in prices, employment and food availability. In any society, livelihood practices can be regarded as sustainable based on its ability to cope up and minimise the impact of shocks or stress. Sustainable livelihood must maintain or enhance the capabilities and assets now and in the future, while not undermining the natural resource base. Within human ecology, the process of sustainable adaptation to vulnerability situation is not only seen as a result of natural selection on the cultural or social system level but more specifically regarded as the outcome of thousands of individual decisions about how to best interact with the surrounding ecology for maximum benefit (Rambo, 1983). Within this perspective, individuals are assumed to be making choices constantly regarding the means of harnessing the available natural resources in a way to cope with the impending shocks or seasonality. Survival under such circumstances corresponds to the 'correct' choice-making while many who choose less wisely fails to survive the crisis (ibid). Thus the larger survival strategies within a society are associated with the decision making the ability of any individual and such an approach provides a valuable understanding of how different social systems function in response to environmental irregularities.

Forest conservation in India has seen a shift from production to conservation since the Colonial era. Forest has witnessed the pressure of unsustainable resource harnessing in the name of conservation which has collapsed the symbiotic relationship maintained by the forest dwellers with their ecology. Among many criticised forest regulations, the most enduring has been the Godavarman case or the Forest Case of 1996. Based on a petition filed by T.N Godavarman to protect Nilgiri forest land, the Supreme Court made a vital reformation of the existing forest policies. The order came with a suspension on tree felling across the country directly affecting the wood-based industrial economy. Following the judgment, the term 'forest' was interpreted by its dictionary meaning and as such, regardless of its ownership, the state government or other authority was restricted from allowing the use of any forest land for any non-forestry purpose without prior approval from the central government. It ordered a complete closure of sawmills in the forest-rich North-Eastern states and banned any transportation of timber out of the seven states. Curtailing the right of the State and Central government, the Supreme Court involved itself in national and local forest protection, timber pricing, timber transport, licensing of timber industries, management of forest revenue, and enforcement of its own orders concerning forest law. Such alienation soon created confusion among state and national level organisations leading to mismanagement of forestry and protection attempts came up at the cost of human rights with no considerations on the economic losses arising out of the ban. Due to non-representation in decision making, many State governments were reluctant to alter the local forest policies considering their political careers in future elections. Thus, by neglecting the state and local bodies, the Supreme Court failed to address the state-level needs, livelihood patterns, and possibilities in its order which created extreme difficulty in the desired implementation of the new forest regulations.

The Tai Khamti livelihood scenario experienced a drastic change with the timber ban. In the preceding section, it has been established that the emergence of the timber economy set forth new possibilities of employment in the region. The lack of infrastructure, efficient education, and alternative livelihood options compelled the tribe to extensively depend on the forest resource to earn their living. When the ban came into effect, the region was lacking the practice of cash cropping that might have substituted the crisis. Further, the new regulation made no attempt to understand the impact of the restriction on the livelihood of the forest-dependent population. It was a drastic step that shattered the economy of many Indian tribes like that of the Tai Khamti. As revealed by the respondents, the major economic loss of this regulation was the non-functional economic assets associated with the timber business. Trucks, machinery, elephants soon became non-valuable and had to be sold away at significantly lower prices. The lack of efficient economic surveys to access the loss of livelihood during the ban period compelled this study to solely depend on oral narratives to analysing the subsistence scenario. In search of alternative livelihood options, large sections of the tribe got engaged in illegally felling of trees which were left unattended due to the problem of transportation following the ban. Respondents held the view that since they were restricted from using the resource with which they had been associated with since ages, drove people to make unsustainable use of them which turned harmful for both the ecology and people's livelihood.

Following the ban, villagers started clearing tracts of forest land in the name of agricultural activities, however, due to the lack of modern technology they failed to cultivate a larger plot. This resulted in the misuse of land resource and the associated tree felling caused the extinction of valuable species of plants and trees that were essential for medicinal use and handicraft works. As far as livelihoods are concerned, the shift from agriculture and other occupation to timber business in the pre-ban period created a shock situation among the tribe. Amateur timber contractors found themselves devoid of savings following the lavish living standard maintained during the flourishing economy. This led a major section of the tribe towards opium consumption and this practice has still been affecting contemporary society. Anti-social activities sprung up following the economic crisis and a gradual decline in social capital was reported by the respondents. Though by 1998 the Honourable Court allowed few sawmills to be reopened by relocating them to a specific industrial area, yet only a handful could make it at the place called Gunanagar in Namsai district. By the time these industries were fully operational, most of the villagers either lost access to the trade or were hesitant to resume considering the lack of proper information about the court's order during those days. Moreover, the partial relaxation in the trade came with numerous trade regulations and a permit system was introduced soon. This had larger implications on the Tai-Khamti society as most of the economically superior traders belonged to the upper strata of the society and got hold of the permit through their political connections. In this process, the class hierarchy became prominent following the differences in income distribution across society.

There is a significant negative impact of the Supreme Court's regulation on the tribe at both its individual and community level. At the household level, families were forced to curtail expenses on education, material possessions, ritual and community feasts, etc, while from a societal viewpoint a significant lag in socio-economic development was experienced in comparison to its neighbouring tribes, who were relatively less developed than the Tai-Khamti. A close examination of the Tai Khamti society revealed that, though different initiatives have been undertaken to strengthen the socio-economic condition of the region, yet none of these efforts have been capable enough to generate a similar income for the tribe as derived from timber operations. Though the Tai-Khamti has been an agrarian society across history, yet the Court's judgement curtailed their rights and jeopardised their primary income source. Devoid of any other opportunities owing to their remote habitation and lack of training and skills to access alternative livelihood sources the tribe became the scapegoat of top-down forest policies that restricted them from utilising the forest resources to generate income.

The vulnerability context in the Tai Khamti livelihood system was subjected to ineffective forest management institutions and practices. Though the Tai Khamti traditionally practiced the *Tang-ton-mei* ritual, in which a new sampling has to be planted for every tree cut, yet with the rise in livelihood demand for timber such ritual soon lost significance and the spread of deforestation soon led to the complete removal of specific species of trees like *hollock* and *hollong*, which generated better revenue. Furthermore, stakeholders in general, and retired timber traders in particular, conversed that inadequate information about the proposed policy changes, lack of adequate measures to mitigate occupational crisis on the part of the government, inadequate commitment in arranging credit facilities or subsidies for alternate employment generation and inadequate awareness generation efforts were among the major factors which increased uncertainties of the Tai Khamti livelihoods. Timber traders also complained about the inequality of institutionally provided permits for timber extraction, which provided a better opportunity for the politically influenced traders and the biased attitude soon stipulated section of the tribe to involve in incessant exploitation of the resource.

The above-mentioned livelihood vulnerabilities and the shocks have been gradually managed by the tribe based on their capabilities. Such mitigation practice varies with households, depending on the wealth category, educational level, and experience. Among the Tai Khamti, household remains the primary decision-making agency. This study found that vulnerability reduction strategies were guided by individual choices based on the resources at their disposal and were subject to the economic status of the specific person. To minimise the effects of the resource crisis and maintain the stability of their livelihood, a gradual change in employment pattern and natural resource use was observed in the territory. Some of the major coping strategies have been listed in the subsequent section.

Alternate employment generation

In the post-ban period though timber industries continue to perform in the territory, yet villagers were engaged in creating livelihood opportunities for themselves rather than depending on the forest resource. Moreover, timber trade has become uncertain owing to the shortage of wood and the dominance of outsiders in the trade. In the contemporary Tai Khamti society, members are seen to engage in contact works like land supply in road construction, establishing stone queries, opening up grocery shops. Within the townships, rooms are leased out to outside traders and merchants, which has given new avenues for income generation and further helped the tribe to increase opportunities for trade of their indigenous commodities. Rural youths with specific skills like driving have taken up transport service as a profession. Within the Kherem village with fifty households, six of them owns auto-rickshaw, which is their primary source for livelihood. A growing preference for salaried jobs in both the private and government sector can be observed among the villagers. Reservations of seats have helped the tribe to secure a post in various service sectors. As an entrepreneurial effort, local youths have started shops which provide local delicacies and have been an attraction for tourist visiting the Parashuram Kund located in Wakro circle.

Agricultural intensification

Based on the economic condition, different households have adopted diverse measures to improve their agricultural income in the post-ban period. Tea cultivation was the choice among the elite Tai Khamti population given their easy access to industrial resources and manpower. This section of the tribe was capable of harnessing significant land which was easily accessible and this helped them to expand their cultivation without any difficulties as compared to those who had land at interior locations. Cash cropping is another significant innovation brought in by the tribe in recent times. Owing to the vast land resource in comparison to the scanty population, the cultivators have been engaged in clearing large plots of land for cultivating ginger, turmeric, mustard, etc. Apart from this, agroforestry has been a new inclusion where a handful of families have been cultivating betel nuts and pepper in the midst of tomato, tea, and vegetable cultivation. The Farmers Training Centre located at Kherem has been a major boon to the village farmers, which have been providing them easy access to a high yielding variety of seeds and frequent awareness programmes. Though illegal, this region has witnessed a significant increase in poppy cultivation. Respondents even compared this to the timber trade owing to the higher monetary gains. In the course of fieldwork, it was observed that local villagers were financed by outsiders to cultivate poppy for them for which they earn a handful. An adaptive adjustment was made to the crop production system, specifically in crop selection and their varieties based on the seasonal variability. As a result, adjusting planting time and selecting adaptive crop varieties are increasing in recent times. Farmers choose to grow early maturing crop species and varieties under the late onset of rain, with mid maturing or local late-maturing varieties under normal seasonal rainfall. Farmers increase seed rates to increase planting density and crop establishment; and reduce fertilizer rate to reduce its burning effect on germinating seeds, to promote seed germination, establishment, and to reduce the risk of investment in fertilizers following crop failure or yield reduction. New cropping approaches such as diversification has recently increased to spread farm risks. Such practices diversify income and nutrition and minimize crop losses that different crops, for instance, haricot bean and maize, are differently vulnerable to rainfall variability. Agricultural extensification, which increases farm size, used to be one of the farmers' strategies to ensure sustainable food security and livelihood. It is often practiced by bringing new lands into cultivation, with the perception that more land gives more food. Agricultural intensification, which raises farm yields on a given plot of land, is a practiced strategy to sustain livelihood pursuits.

Changing educational preference

The Tai Khamti has been known for their academic excellence among other North-Eastern tribes and is considered culturally advanced than its counterpart owing to their possession of original script called *Lik Tai.* Across generations, the tribe has successfully carried on its educational commitment. However, during the timber ban period, a significant increase in academic dropout has been reported by the respondents which were largely due to the failure of families to sustain educational expenses. In contemporary society, the scenario of accessing education has significantly changed. Parents were seen to opt for English medium school rather than government school considering the employment opportunities post studies. Preference for higher education for both genders has increased the movement of youths outside the state and has encouraged in the setting up of colleges in and around Namsai town. Educated youths have taken up initiatives to preserve and develop the Tai Khamti culture and have been organising awareness drive against social evils like consumption of opium and other kinds of intoxicants.

Financial resource management

During the flourishing timber trade, most of the households led a lavish living standard devoid of any monetary savings. Such practices created havoc in the post-ban period since families were devoid of financial resources to invest in other means of income. Lack of awareness and infrastructure like banking was the reason behind such anomalies. However, in present-day society, villagers are keen to make regular savings at the bank. Further, the self-help groups have emerged up allowing the females to better utilise their income. Subsidy loans are withdrawn for expanding agricultural activities. In every household, each of the earning members would secure a part of the income for personal expenses, irrespective of the gender. With the growing opium trade in the whole of Namsai and Lohit district, females have emerged out as efficient earners. Lending money on interest has become an important finance management strategy among households.

Livelihood outcomes

The agricultural intensification has seen an improved use of hybrid seeds, modern farming techniques and advanced agricultural practices like crop rotation and intercropping which have collectively contributed to increasing household livelihood conditions, generating income avenues and thus ensuring food security even in the lean seasons. Despite efforts to enhance cash cropping, the lack of well-established market and instability of prices still hinders the process of ensuring improved farm income and food security. Among the Tai Khamti, it was found that there has been a gradual change in the attitudes of the villagers towards the surrounding ecology. Respondents agreed upon the fact that depending too much on the forest ecology for their livelihood would mean hampering their environmental conditions. Though at the initial stages of agricultural intensification, deforestation became prominent as a means to extend land resources; yet in the present society, villagers reflected societal awareness of the role of natural resource management as a response to rainfall variability and further forest degradation. It was observed that there was an increase in households' skill, experience, and knowledge of realizing the impact of deforestation on rural livelihoods and ecosystem services.

With the change of educational preferences, the employability rate has significantly improved among the tribe. Likewise, increased awareness has improved efforts to acquiring jobs outside the state which have also influenced the standard of living among the tribe. Youths have taken up community-based activities under the various platform in order to bring out the issues of the tribe whether it is social or more specifically livelihood related. Community-based programmes have helped the tribe to strengthen their social ties which were significantly hampered by the unequal income distribution.

At the individual level, the capacity to take advantage of the information, related to technology, government schemes, financial assistance has created a favourable adaptive capacity among the members. Finally from a social viewpoint, the vital factor that enhanced community resilience relies on the degree to which values are shared, the willingness of community members to cooperate and mobilize resources and also to stabilise their relationship with other communities. However, it was seen that the entrepreneurial drive among the semi-urban dwellers was more pronounced due to their ownership of land in important centres and easily approachable locations. As a result, the semi-urban residents reported more engagements in infrastructure development like the establishment of shops, leasing out commercial spaces and providing accommodation on rent. Due to the better connectivity with the district headquarters, this section of the tribe appeared to be more informative about government schemes and technological innovations.

Conclusion

Forests and forest products have been accepted to contribute significantly to livelihood options of the world's people and its continuing existence. Though the Tai Khamti has been an agrarian society practicing settled agriculture, yet their dependence on the forest resources has been significant. The natural resource supplies basic day to day needs of the tribe including daily dietary requirements, construction materials. Their livelihood activities involve the extraction of resources for both commercial and household requirements. Firewood collection remains the main usage in every household. The Tai Khamti cultural pattern is associated with constructing multiple fire hearths which significantly increases the firewood requirement. The larger livelihood dependency on forest resources started with the emerging timber trade when the first sawmill was established in the year 1948. The densely forested landscape, river networks for timber transportation and knowledge of elephant rearing gave the tribe ample opportunity to spread the trade within a short time span. Though initially restricted among the elite section, the timber business soon attracted individuals from other sections of the society, which was seen as an opportunity to improve status across the class hierarchy through economic gains. The Supreme Court's judgement jeopardised the entire Tai Khamti economy since timber trade has become the largest employment generation sector in the territory. Devoid of infrastructural facilities, efficient education, lack of specific skills and training, the tribe to exploited the easily available resources of their vicinity. Occupational shifts from agricultural activities and other services during the timber trade created a shock among the community creating a vulnerability situation where villagers were unable to seek alternative livelihood sources. Economically stable section of the tribe was capable to limit the impact of the resource crisis by investing in tea plantation, while a large part of the population who lacked awareness regarding banking and savings soon found themselves in a pathetic situation which drove many of them towards consumption of opium leading to larger anti-social activities.

In contemporary Tai Khamti society, a gradual process of adaptation to the livelihood crisis could be noticed. In response to economic shock, households use different strategies, including choosing seasonally appropriate crop varieties to be cultivated, choosing appropriate cropping calendar and making decisions whether to use external inputs for every cropping season. Moreover, adaptive crop varieties, improved seeds, fertilizer application, intercropping, crop rotation, traditional rainwater harvesting are among the remaining strategies for adapting to the variable rainfall and for improving farm income, food security and the overall livelihoods. With the households being the primary decision-making agency, individual choices have resulted in the new entrepreneurial activities to strengthen their economic condition. The coping strategies are determined by the economic status of the particular household and by the nature of resources available at their disposal. In any human society, individuals' make choice as to how best utilise the resources and such collective decisions reflect the economic structure. Under the specific condition, not all decisions generate a positive outcome and less appropriate decision ceases to exist in the long run. Members within a society are aware of their capacities to exploit the ecology and hence the interrelationship between humans and their surrounding environment is largely dependent on the individual decision-making ability. In the post-ban period, different sections of the tribe have started exploiting the natural resources in a varied manner, but diversification of agriculture has turned out to be the most feasible in the territory which has given the tribe a new array of livelihood avenues. Since rural livelihood is primarily dependent on appropriate management of natural resources, it is recommended that policies, institutions, and communities should be integrated in order to reassure household capabilities and ensure effective governance of natural resources in order to minimise the stresses for sustainable rural livelihood.

References

Ahmed, I.I. and Lipton, M. (1988) *Impact of Structural Adjustment on Sustainable Rural Livelihoods: A Review of the Literature*, *IDS Working Paper*, Brighton: IDS.

Allison EH and B Horemans (2006) "Putting the principles of the Sustainable Livelihoods Approach into fisheries development policy and practice". *Marine Policy*, No 30, pp 757-766.

Bernstein, Henry, Ben Crow and Hazel Johnson (1992) *Rural Livelihoods: Crises and Responses*. Oxford University Press, Oxford.

Chambers R, Conway GR (1992) *Sustainable Rural Livelihoods: Practical Concepts for the 21st Century*. Institute of Development Studies: Discussion Paper 296.

Chambers, R. (1988) *Sustainable Livelihoods, environment and development: Putting Poor People first. IDS Discussion Paper No.20*, Brighton: Institute of Development Studies at the University of Sussex.

Ellis, F. (1998) Household Strategies and Rural Livelihood Diversification. *Journal of Development Studies,* no 35, vol 1, pp. 1-38.

Ellis, F (2000) *Rural livelihoods and diversity in developing countries*. Oxford University Press, Oxford.

Farrington, John, Diana Carney, Caroline Ashley and Cathryn Turton, (1999) "Sustainable Livelihoods in Practice: Early Applications of Concepts in Rural Areas". *Natural Perspectives*, No. 42, ODI and DFID.

ODI (2000) *Livelihood Diversification and the Rural Poor in Asia: Concepts and Methods* (Draft mimeo).

Serrat O. (2017) "The Sustainable Livelihoods Approach". In *Knowledge Solutions.* Springer, Singapore.

Pemperton, R.B (1835) "An outline history of Pong". In Lila Gogoi, *The Tai Khamtis*, Nabajiban Press, Calcutta, 1971.

Rambo, A. T. (1983) *Conceptual approaches to human ecology*. Honolulu, HI: East-West Environment and Policy Institute.

SOAS (2020). "What is Rural Finance, and How Does it Fit into 'Development'?". Accesses in January 22 https://www.soas.ac.uk/cedep-demos/000_P528_RF_K3736-Demo/unit1/page_22.htm

Chapter - 7

PVTG: An Ethnographic Profile of Jenu Kuruba of Basavanagiri, Mysuru, Karnataka

— *Karuna Gogoi*

The tribal population is identified as the aboriginal inhabitants of our country. They are the most vulnerable section of our society, living in natural and unpolluted surrounding far away from civilization with their traditional values, customs and beliefs. There has been a long and enduring debate among the social scientist to define a tribe. Tribe also called as scheduled tribe in Indian context is an administrative and legal term to refer to some ethnic groups based on their socio-economic status, religious and cultural customs in order to give special attention to them as mandated by the Indian Constitution.

According to the constitution of India, "any tribe or tribal community or part of or group within any tribe or tribal community as deemed under article 342 are scheduled tribes for the purpose of the constitution". On the basis of their anthropological characteristics tribal people of India are considered to be aboriginal. Risley (1891) defined the word 'tribe' as, "it is a collection of families or group of families, bearing a common name which as a rule does not denote any specific occupation, generally claiming common descent from a mythical or historical ancestry, occasionally the name is derived from an animal but in some parts of the country, the tribe is held together only by the obligation of kinship, member speaking the same language and occupy a tract of the country.

The tribal population according to the 1961 Census of India was 6.87 percent of the total population of India of 439.2 million. In 1971 census the percentage of scheduled tribes to total population of the State/ Union

Territory of India (548,159,652) was 6.94 percent. The tribal population of India in 1981 was 7.76 percent of the total population according to the Census of India 1991 the percentage of scheduled tribes to total population of India is 8.08 percent, excluding the population of the state of Jammu and Kashmir.

About 80% of the tribal population is to be found along the central belt starting from Gujrat, Maharashrta running through Rajasthan, Madhya Pradesh, Chattisgarh, Orissa, Jharkhand and West Bengal. The rest 20% populations are in North-Eastern states, Southern states and Islands.

The smaller tribal groups (earlier known as primitive tribal group) numbering 75 in our country have been categorized as Particularly Vulnerable Tribal Groups for special development assistance.

The Jenu Kuruba tribe of Basavanagiri settlement is a Particularly Vulnerable Tribal Group by the Government of India classification created with the purpose of enabling improvement in the conditions of certain communities with particularly low development indices. According to 2001 census, the total population of Jenu Kuruba tribe is 29,828.

PVTG (Particularly Vulnerable Tribal Group)

Dhebar commission (1960-1961) stated that within scheduled tribes existed inequality in the rate of development. During Fourth Five Year Plan a sub category was created within schedule tribes to identify the groups that considered being of lower level of development. This sub category was made as "Primitive Tribal Group". The features of Primitive Tribal Groups are:

1. Pre agricultural system of existence, i.e. practice of hunting and gathering.
2. Zero or negative population growth.
3. Extremely low level of literacy rate in comparison with other tribal groups.

In 2006, the Government of India proposed to rename, "Primitive Tribal Group" as "Particularly Vulnerable Tribal Group". The Constitution of India incorporates several special provisions for the promotion of educational and economic interest of Scheduled Tribe population and their protection from social injustice and all forms of exploitation. These objectives are sought to be achieved through a strategy known as the Tribal Sub-Plan strategy, which was adopted at the beginning of the Fifth Five

Year Plan. The strategy seeks to ensure adequate flow of funds for tribal development from the State Plan allocations, schemes/ programmes of Central Ministries/ Departments, other financial and developmental institutions.

The cornerstone of this strategy has been to ensure earmarking of funds for Tribal Sub-Plan by States/UTs. Besides the efforts of the States/ UTs and the Central Ministries/ Departments to formulate and implement Tribal Sub-Plan for achieving socio-economic development of STs, the Ministry of Tribal Affairs is implementing several schemes and programmes for the benefits of STs.

There are now 194 Integrated Tribal Development Projects (ITDPs) in the country, where the ST population is more than 50% of the total population of the blocks or groups of blocks. During the Sixth Plan, pockets outside ITDP areas, having a population of 10,000 with at least 5,000 scheduled tribes were covered under Tribal Sub-Plan called Modified Area Development Approach (MADA). So far 252 MADA pockets have been identified in the country. In addition, 79 clusters with a total population of 5,000 of which 50% are scheduled tribes have been identified.

The tribal group Jenu Kuruba lies under this PVTG category. The following are the factors that influence over all tribal populations in India. These are:

1. Poverty: Instead the resources keep decreasing, leading to making survival for a human being more and more competitive even for the basic necessities of life like food, clothing and shelter. But still there are some isolated areas that peoples of that place even using the pre industrial techniques for their livelihood.
2. The tribal peoples hold their religious beliefs, traditions and cultural Norms very tightly and it also effects the tribal population.
3. Mainly in isolated tribal regions hospital facility is not good so in many tribal groups have low birth rate and higher mortality rate.
4. Migration of outsiders to the tribal areas also affects the tribal population.
5. Unemployment and Illiteracy is the main factor that affecting the tribal population.
6. Food Resources: as the all forest lands that the tribes lived were captured by the government and other peoples their traditional food resources become limited.

These are the main factors that affecting tribal population. The Indian government has implemented many schemes for their development but it needs much more proper implementation in proper direction for a fruitful result.

The Jenu Kuruba of Basavanagiri, Mysuru, Karnataka

The ethnographic profile brings out the basic outline and the settings, both material and non-material that governs the research study. It comprises of ecological conditions, administrative setup, infrastructure and the type of the people among which the study was conducted. The tribe under study, Jenu Kuruba are situated in the Basavanagiri settlement Colony (A). Kasaba hobli, H.D. Kote taluk in Mysuru District, Karnataka. The Jenu Kuruba is the original inhabitants of the forests regions of the Western Ghats and also other places of South India. Jenu Kurubas are found mostly in the taluks of Heggadadevanakote and to some extent in Hunsur, Nanjangud, Periyapatna of Mysuru District.

Etymological origin of Mysuru

Mysuru district, like most of the district of Karnataka State, takes its name from its headquarters town. Mahisharastra, mentioned in the Buddhist text of ***Dipavamsha***, is identified with Mysore. Asoka is stated to have sent his Buddhist Missionaries to Mysore. Some identify it with ***Erumainad*** of the ancient Tamil texts. But such identifications are difficult to accept. The earliest reference to Mysore is in a copper plate inscription dated 862 AD from Kadalur, Mandya taluk, where the place is mentioned in inscriptions of the 11th and 12th centuries. By way of literary flourish, it is also spelt as Mahisurapura. The name of Mahisur or its anglicized form "Mysuru" is described as derived from Mahisasura or the buffalo-headed monster, who lived in this area and came to be killed by the Goddess Chamundi. The Chamundi Hills is associated with Mahishasura's execution by the Goddess. But, etymologically, the place can be associated with"May" (an antelope) than Mahisha (buffalo).

Administrative setup

Mysuru district consists of seven revenue taluks, namely, H.D. Kote, Hunsur, K.R. Nagar, Nanjangud, Periyapatna, T. Narasipura and Mysuru (Urban and Rural). For administrative purposes, Mysuru district is divided into two subdivisions, which are Hunsur and Mysuru and the district has 1,216 villages, 11 statutory towns, 235 gram panchayats and 226 wards.

The District Commissioner is responsible for managing the district administration and the Assistant Commissioners are responsible for managing the sub-divisions of the district. There are 7 revenue administrative blocks and 9 educational blocks. Mysuru block is divided into two educational blocks, namely, Mysuru Urban and Mysuru Rural. Mysore Urban is further bifurcated into sub- educational blocks, namely, Mysuru North and Mysuru South, for administrative purposes. H.D. Kote and Nanjangud blocks have vast geographical areas because of the forests. Nanjangud block has a large number of Gram Panchayats in the district and this is due to larger populations of the block compared to the remaining blocks of the district. Apart from the above, the district has 9 municipalities, 1 City Corporation (Mysuru), 7 taluk panchayats, 46 Zilla Panchayat Constituencies, 1 Parliamentary Constituency and 11 assembly constituencies.

Climatic conditions

The climate of the district is tropical and is greatly influenced by the two seasons, namely, the southwest monsoon and northeast monsoon. In regard to temperatures, there are mild temperatures during the months of December-March, but starting in April, the temperatures increase gradually to reach a peak in May and begin to decrease only after the end of the southwest monsoon, in September. The climate is salubrious for nearly 5 months because of the elevations, but is generally hot the rest of the year.

Topography

The River Cauvery is the lifeline of the district. It springs up on the Western Ghats at Talacauvery in Kodagu district, entering the district near Abbur in the northwest of K.R. Nagar taluk. It meanders through the district for about 250 km. The other rivers of the district are the Hemavathi and the Kabini. All these are the tributaries of the Cauvery. The Cauvery flows through the taluks of K.R. Nagar and T. Narasipura. The Kabini River flows through the taluks of H.D. Kote, Nanjangud and T Narasipura.

Soil types of the district can be broadly classified as the laterite, red loam, sandy loam, red clay and black cotton soils. Laterite soil occurs mostly in the western parts of the district while the red loam is found in the northwest. The two account for nearly half the area of the district. Black cotton soil is mostly found in the northeastern parts of the district. Red sandy loam soils are derived from granites and gneisses. The western taluks of Periyapatna, H.D. Kote and Hunsur are covered with hilly terrain and contain red, shallow gravelly soils. In the taluks of T. Narasipura and Nanjangud, there is deep red loam, occasionally interspersed with the black soils.

Forests and forestry

Mysuru District has 10 percent of the total geographical area of the State. Even this is also deteriorating. Hence, the Zilla Panchayat is interested in developing social forestry in the Government and private lands with the cooperation of people instead of just improving the reserved forests. Much importance has been given to involvement of rural people at the Grama Panchayat level. According to a Census report, the total geographical area covered by the forests is 62,851 hectares. However, due to imbalances in the environment of Mysore District, the State has initiated various other programmes through Zila Parishad.

Irrigation

A total of 159,230 hectares is the net area irrigated in Mysuru district. The main rivers of Kabini, Cauvery and Harangi supply water for agriculture in the district. Among them, the Cauvery flows through K.R. Nagar and T. Narasipura taluks, Kabini flows through H.D. Kote, Nanjanagud and T. Narasipura taluks and join the Cauvery. The minor irrigation systems such as the tanks, wells and bore wells have played a crucial role in the development of irrigation facilities to promote and enhance agricultural production in the district.

Cropping patterns

Diversity in cropping pattern is an index of agricultural development. The most common crops of the district are paddy, ragi, ginger, sugarcane and cotton.

Horticulture

Mysuru district is renowned for special horticultural crops like Nanjangud Rasabale, Mysuru betel leaves, Mysore Mallige (Jasmine) and Erengere brinjal. A total of 3,030 hectares of land are utilized for growing varieties of fruits and 1985 hectares of land utilized for growing varieties of vegetables in the district. However, it is most unfortunate that the varieties like the Nanjangud Rasabale (a variety of banana, tastier and nutritious) and Mysuru betel leaves are fast disappearing due to continuous indifference by the Government.

Heggadadevankote where the area of study is located forms the chief town of the Taluk which bears its name and a municipality. It is situated in a wild forest tract, 36 miles south-west of Mysuru, on the Sargur- Hunsur road. The place can boast of considerable antiquity. Its puranic name was Brihad-bhanu-pura. Pandus ruled this area and they may be regarded as the founders of this city. The Heggada Deva after whom it is now named, appears to have rebuilt the fort and restored in his own person the ancient line of rulers about the tenth century.

H.D. Kote taluk has the highest number of tribals (23880) which accounted for 51.67 per cent followed by Hunsur taluk with 14580 (31.55), Periyapatna taluk with 6005 (12.99), Nanjangud taluk with 1235 (2.67 %). Mysore had the lowest tribal population with 518 which accounted for 1.12 per cent. K.R. Nagara and T. Narasipura taluks have no tribal population. (as per annual report 2009-2010, DSO, Mysore)

As per annual report 2009-10, Mysuru District has the highest number of Jenu Kuruba population (35,068), followed by Soliga tribe (5013), Betta Kuruba tribe (2430), Yerava tribe (1640), Hakki Pikki tribe (1625) and lowest number of 442 Dongri Gerasia tribes.

History of the Jenu Kuruba

Jenu Kuruba's are descendent of ancient Kurubas. They thought that the world was submerged in water and there is an instrument that was floating on the water and from that instrument one brother and sister produced and they created kids with mud and from their children Jenu Kurubas were born.

Jenu Kuruba Tribe of Karnataka are the original residents of the forest regions of the Western Ghats and also other places of South India. In the Kannada language, the term 'Jenu' signifies honey and 'kuruba' stands for caste. Therefore their name suggests that Jenu Kuruba tribe has adapted the profession of honey gathering.

Physical appearance

Jenu Kuruba's were Dravidian origin.their structure is lean. Head form is dolichocephalic to mesocephalic (71.0-80.9). Their skin colour is dark brown. Jenu Kurubas stature is short to medium. Their hair form is narrow weavy.

Dress pattern

The male dress is, they used to wrap a cloth around their waist with upper part naked. But now they wear Trousers, Shirts and Dhotis. The female wear Saree wrapping it around having the shoulders under the armpit. They put a piece of cloth around their shoulder. They also wear bangles. They don't have traditional tattoos on their body but some of them done on their own interest. Formerly they used to wear thread with turmeric on it during the marriage ceremony. But now they used to wear saree and blouse.

Language

The Jenu Kuruba dialect is *Jenu Nudi* and their script is Kannada. Their dialect is mixture of a mixture of Tamil, Malayalam and Kannada. Their second language is Kannada. Now, as the young generation goes to school they are accustomed with English, Tamil, Malayalam and can understand.

Food habits

Their traditional foods are Honey, Small Game Meat, Fruits, Tubers, Raggi, Rice. They are non-vegetarian. Raggi is their staple food. But now due to eviction from their original habitat and also having connection with the non tribals, they eat Raagi, Rice, Eggs, Meats (but not beef), Samber and Vegetables.

Settlement pattern

The study was conducted in the Basavanagiri settlement, Colony(A) of H.D. Kote taluk, Mysore district, Karnataka. They were originally inhabitants of the forest regions of Western Ghats and also other forest areas of Karnataka. They were relocated in this place by Indian Government in the year 2003. The settlement of the tribe is linear. The houses are brick wall with cement plaster. The ground of the houses is cemented and the roof is tiled. An extension of the houses is also seen to support the family size wise. The extended parts are having mud wall and thatched roof. Every household has separate toilet.

At the entry of the settlement there is a bus stop near the main road. The settlement is in the right side of the road. There is a Kuccha road to enter to the settlement. In the settlement two main lanes and the houses are situated side by side of the lanes. At first the Ashram school left side of the lane and there is a big water tank just beside the school. The Anganwadi school is in the middle of the settlement. There are four small shops in the settlement and three small water reservoir and community tapes are there. There is one *Basappa* god temple of the tribe in north-west side of the settlement. There is one Jenu Kuruba community hall in the middle of the settlement. There are total 31 Jenu Kuruba house hold found in that settlement. The total population is 197 and out of which 99 are males and 98 are females.

Economic activities

The Jenu Kuruba traditional economy is Honey collection, Food gathering and Small Game Hunting. But now they are engaged in daily wages labour, coffee estate labour and agriculture.

Festivals

The Jenu Kuruba people celebrate three main festivals in a year in the present days. These festivals are – Ugadi, Ganesh chaturthi, Dipawali. Ugadi is the festivalthat celebrates as their New Year celebration. In the Ganesh Chaturthi, they prey the Hindu god Ganesha. Dipawali is also the same Hindu festival they adopted and celebrated as the festival of lights and happiness.

Life cycle rituals

Birth ceremony

In Jenu Kuruba tribe, the first delivery takes place in the parental house of the woman. They observe pollution for 12 days. On the 12th day chey clean their houses. The mother is not allowed to enter the kitchen or to the temple. During the post delivery pollution the woman must remain away from her husband. The naming ceremony is performed on the 12th day. Elderly person select the name but the name is announced by the father of the child.after the announcement a ceremony is performed by mixture of dry coconut and juggery for the baby on his lap and symbolically cut the hair.

Puberty

When a girl attends puberty, she tells her mother, then father and after that to *Yajman*. The *Yajman* then goes to the forest and brings bamboos to construct the hut and gives it to the father. The maternal uncle constructs the temporary hut for the girl to stay there. The duration is approx 1 month. She takes bath each alternative day. First day she eats on leaf and from the next day food is given in separate utensils. For three days black gram, juggery and dry coconut pieces are given to eat. After completion of one month she takes bath with hot water. This bath is to pure her from the pollution. New cloths are given to her, all relatives and neighbors are invited for the celebration. The girl gets gifts from them. But traditionally, there was no festival in this occasion. Now due to contact with the non tribal peoples they also celebrate it like them.

Marriage

Jenu Kuruba seems to have exogamous clan like structure. They usually follow the territorial exogamy. The Jenu Kuruba peoples are free to marry out of their clan. They marry both arranged by their parents and marriage by choice. No bride-price and dowry is prevalent among them. But now, with the connection of outsiders they give some gifts with them. After divorce or separated the bride comes to the parental house and lives there with her children. The *Thali* and the toe rings are symbol of marriage for woman. The *Thali* is made of copper or silver.

Death ceremony

Immediately after death takes place among the Jenu Kuruba, information is sent to relative and neighbors. The dead body is bathed and laid out on the *chatta* (bier). The body is placed in north-south direction, the head facing to the south. After placing the body in a grave the eldest son puts a full hand mud in to the pit. He is followed by others. Woman also goes to the burial ground. Milk is poured on the grave. Funeral ceremony is performed on the 12th day as a mark of ending death pollution.

Healthcare facilities

In the Basavanagiri settlement, they have a Primary Rural Health Care Centre in Metticuppe, which is two kilometer away from the settlement. There is one tribal Hospital in Seregu, which is twenty kilometer away from the settlement and one government hospital named Swami Vivekananda Memorial Hospital in H.D. Kote, they send ambulance every week to the settlement to free health care check-up of the peoples.

Educational facilities

There is one Anganwadi school for the below five year children and one Ashram School, which have from class-I to class-VII in the Basavanagiri settlement. For the further study they have to go to Metikuppe, where there is a government high school and for the higher studies they go to H.D. Kote and Mysuru city.

Transport and communication

Basavanagiri settlement can be accessed by road, with Buses, private jeep and auto from H.D. Kote. The buses are very few, but private vehicles charge a nominal fee for transportation. Communication facilities are through mobile phones. Most of the people possess mobile phones. There is a sub centre of post-office in mettikuppe, which is 2 km from the settlement. The head post-office is in H.D. Kote.

Conclusion

It was found that the broad settings within which the study was conducted play an important role in shaping the behavior of the people. There have been seen changes in the external realities of their livelihood as they are rehabilitated from their original place. So, they are not being able to maintain their core cultural values for which it is very much difficult to brought out ethnographic information during the study.It is suggested to make more effective awareness of child and maternal health among them, implementation of effective programmes and schemes in their area, promote education and give them facilities and opportunities to study for higher levels of study, give employment in some work places to the members to make their econonmy level to a better position.

References

Aiyappan, A. (1948). *Report on the Socio Economic Conditions of the Aboriginal Tribes of the Province of Madras*. Government Press, Madras.

Buchanan, F. (1807). *A Journey from Madras through the countries of Mysore, Canara and Malabar*, Vol. 1, London.

Enthoven, R.E. 1922. *Tribes and Castes of Bombay*. New Delhi: Asian Educational Service, Vol. 1.

Kamath, Suryanath U. (1988). *Karnataka State Gazetteer, Mysore District*. Government Press, Bangalore.

Kundu, Manamatha (1990). *Cultural Anthropology and Tribal Education*. Amar Prakashan, New Delhi.

Nanjundayya, H. V, Ananthakrishna Iyer, L. K. (1931). *The Mysore Tribes and Castes*, Volume IV, Mysore Government Press.

Prasad, Ravi Shankar (2012). *Ethnography of Indian Tribes*. Anmol Publications Pvt. Ltd., New Delhi.

Rao, K. L. N. (1951). *Kurubas of Mysore*. Bharatiya Adimjati Sevak Sangh, Kingsway, Delhi.

Sashi, S. S. (1995). *Tribes of the Southern Highlands*. Anmol Publications, New Delhi.

Sharma, P. Dash, (2006). *Anthropology of Primitive Tribes in India*. Serials Publications, New Delhi.

Singh, K. S. (2003). *People of India- Karnataka*, Volume XXVI, Part Two. East-West Press Pvt. Ltd.

Sirajuddin et al, (1989). *All India Anthropometric Survey: Southern Zone, Karnataka State*. Anthropological Survey of India, Calcutta (Report).

Thurston, E. (1909) 1975. *Castes and Tribes of South India*, Volume IV: 155-177. Cosmo Publications, New Delhi Reprint.

Venkataiah, C. (2009). *Scheduled Tribes of India, A Statistical Report States and Districts*, Volume II. Arise Publications and Distributors, New Delhi.

Plate 7.1: Jenu Kuruba women.

Plate 7.2: A Jenu Kuruba man.

Chapter - 8

A Study on Consumers Response to Online Market and its Impact on Local Market with Particular Reference to Guwahati City

— *Panna Garg*

The concept of market seems to be as old as civilisation. People from time immemorial are been exchanging goods and services among themselves. When it comes about definition, a market can be viewed as that particular set up in which people go in search of their necessary goods, and fetch them in return of some standard amount of other goods, mostly money. In other words a market is a public gathering which is mainly held for buying and selling goods and services. Traditional concept of market holds the view that it is a physical location where things are exchanged through some sort of transactions.

With the passage of time, the forms of retail market evolved into some sections like departmental stores, discount stores, weekly markets, super markets and malls etc. This evolution is nothing but the effort to fulfil customer satisfaction.

However the advent of online market and its increased popularity among consumers is creating a major threat to the traditional local market system. Here, in this paper, an attempt is made to concentrate on this particular aspect of the challenges and helplessness faced by the local vendors due to the increased consumer inclination towards online purchasing.

Significance of the Study

The traditional market set up is been breaking down due to the introduction of e-commerce and its increased popularity among the consumers. The matter of profitability in local sector of market is now a tough job. This paper tries to highlight the aspect of changing mode of business. Again the threat faced by the retailers will surely make them aware about the outcome and may also help them to escape from the consequences. In the present scenario of changing market preference, this paper will help creating a major awareness among people and preparing adequate strategy to cope with it.

Objectives

The objectives of the paper are-

1. To see the factors contributing in the increased consumer tendency towards online market.
2. To find out the aspect of profitability and loss in the local retail market.
3. To find out the strategy if any adopted by the retail sellers to cope with the competition.

Methodology

The data collected through primary sources or direct fieldwork. The paper is based on empirical fieldwork carried out for a period of three months. As it is difficult for the part of the researcher to depend solely on one method while collecting the data, different methods such as - observation, interview (both structured and unstructured), case study, Focused group interview, etc., were simultaneously applied depending upon the nature of enquiry. A section of shopkeepers and a section of consumers were interviewed by direct interview method. Collected data is tabulated, analysed and presented through diagram. Samples were selected by Random sampling method based on convenience sampling. The sample covers 50 retail shops of Guwahati irrespective of any sector and 50 consumers irrespective of any age.

Study Area

The study was conducted in 50 random retail shops of Guwahati city which were irrespective of any sector, may it be wholesale market, showroom, departmental shop, malls and supermarket, etc. Consumers selected for interview were also from Guwahati city itself.

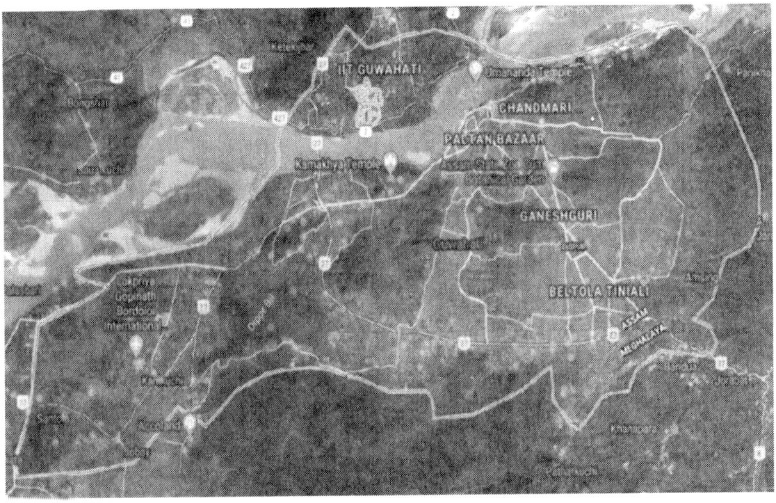

Period of Study

The study was conducted for a period of three months from November 2019 to January 2020. However it shows data for a period of three years.

Limitations of Study

1. Time is the major limiting factor of the study.
2. The study is confined to Guwahati city only.
3. The shops were selected depending on the convenience.

Findings and Analysis

While collecting the data some interview schedules were made for the retailers as well as the consumers. The responses are recorded for better understanding of the scenario.

The questions set for the retailers are depicted in the following table along with their responses-

Questions	*Yes*	*No*
Is there any decrease in the profit margin in the last three years	31	19
Do you update your stock for variety of products	42	8
Do you provide increased discount facility	29	21
Do you provide home delivery	11	39
Do you provide after sale serice	9	41

The responses are clearly depicted in the following bar diagram-

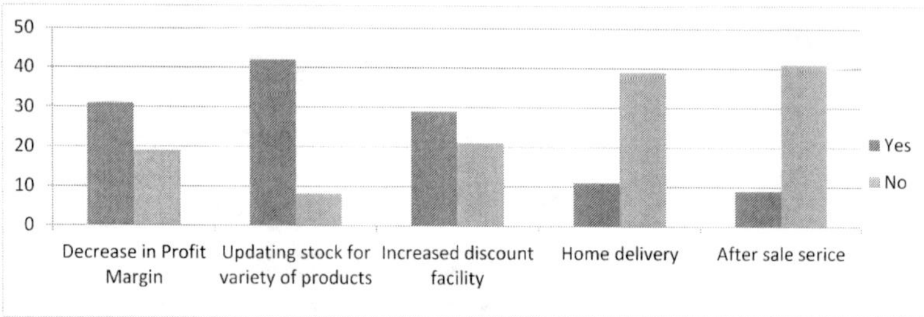

The questions set for the consumers are depicted in the following table along with their responses-

Questions	*Yes*	*No*
Do you have online shopping apps in your mobile	43	07
Have you ever experienced online shopping	40	10
Do you find it more easier to shop online	36	14
Do you find more variety and discount in online market	42	08
Do you want after sale service of the delivered products	46	04

The bar diagram of the responses will be as follows-

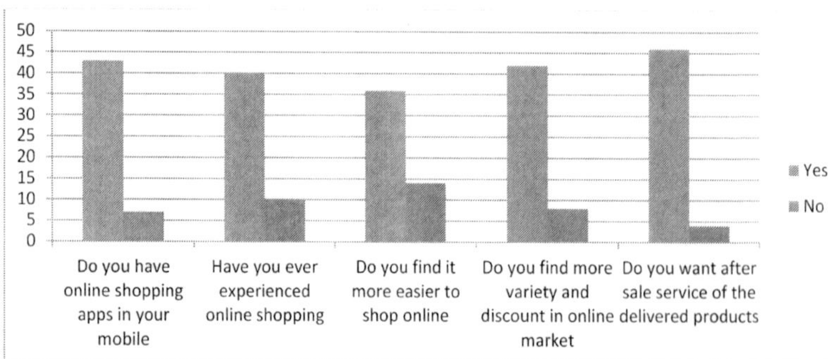

So it is inevitable that increased grasp of online market over consumer's inclination towards it is damaging the trend of traditional market system. The present work included shops of all categories like groceries, clothing, electronic gadgets, eyewear, footwear, pharmacies and so on. Differences were there. Some vendors said that they are undergoing a severe loss.

But one of the Titan clock shop in Chandmari, there was a reverse reaction. They said that when their stock gets empty then only new stocks are allowed to be sent. They don't have the warehouse to store things and keep it for future, that is why their stock remains always new. Customers appreciate it and as a result no loss is seen.

The situation is not the same in other shops. Some pharmacists said that as people go for online shopping many of their warehouse products don't get sold. As these products are to be used within definite expiry date, huge loss has been reported throughout the years.

The cosmetics and jewellery shopkeepers are also in the same stage. They are willing to know how some specific online sites manage to provide the goods in half price. How these sites manage to make profit by doing so. They also added that if that very question solves in clear light, they will also adopt the same strategy to keep their market alive.

Regarding the consumers response it is clear that they prefer click and order instead of bricks and mortar. Moving around from one shop to another in search of their daily things is a time consuming process. People want everything at their door in readymade form. Digitalization makes it possible for them. Marketing becomes easier and quicker now. The marketing time is now replaced by household and office activities. According to the consumers if such facilities can be fulfilled by local markets, they will definitely go for this market again.

Conclusion

Once getting habituated, it becomes difficult to move back to the old school market system. If the local shopkeepers comes out with some adaptive strategies like renewing their old stock, increasing their discount rate, providing door to door delivery, promoting after sale services and maintaining proper return policy, then only consumers attraction can be drawn back. It is the high time for the local sellers to refine their business policy. Otherwise one smart phone per hand will be enough to erase the whole market structure and to draw a new virtual set up called e-commerce.

References

Ember, Carol. R. Melvin Ember and Peter N. Peregrine, 2003 (reprint), *Anthropology (tenth edition),* Delhi, Pearson Education.

Kothari, C.R., 2009, *Research Methodology: Methods and Techniques* (second revised edition), New age *International* Pvt. Ltd., New Delhi.

Young, P.V. 2002, (reprint), *Scientific Social Study and Research,* Prentice-Hall of India, New Delhi.

A committee of Royal Anthropological Institute of Great Britain and Ireland, 1954 (reprint), *Notes and Quarries on Anthropology,* London, Routledge and Kegal Paul Limited.

Chapter - 9

Symbiotic Relationship between Tribe and Their Ecology: A Case Study of the Nyishi Tribe of Rilloh Village, Pakke Kessang District, Arunachal Pradesh

— *Ranjit Pachani*

Theoretical discourse on the human-environment interaction has been abundant within Ecological Anthropology since the twentieth century. Anthropological investigation on specific cultures revealed that man has been modifying the environment for long and there was a variety of responses possible to most environmental situations and this proved culture to be highly adaptive. The first major theory being the environmental determinism advocated that environment mechanically 'dictates' how a culture adapts (Sutton & Anderson, 2004). The next tradition followed categorisation of cultures based on their similarity of cultural aspects and the environment in which they existed. There was no illusion that the environment did not influence culture, but it became clear later that it was not the prime factor affecting cultural traits (Little, 2007). In possibilism, the environment was seen as limiting or enabling factor rather than a determining element. Following a similar approach, Steward came with his method of Cultural Ecology, where he stressed the fact that the environment influenced only certain elements of a culture, which he termed the 'culture core'; other elements of culture were subject to the autonomous processes of culture history (Moran, 2006). Rappaport's (1967) analysis of system ecology emerged as a new approach where the focus was diverted from culture to population. The approach advocated that the human population as a collective unit shapes their behaviour according to how they might best survive in a given ecosystem. Rambo (1983) in Conceptual

Approaches to Human Ecology discussed another approach in ecological anthropology namely, the 'actor-based model of human ecology'. The later approach highlighted that adaptation was a byproduct of the individual decision of how to interact with the environment. The 'correct' decisions thus made will survive and prosper against the odd ones and over time, the more successful adaptive decisions will become institutionalised as cultural norms.

From the time in memorial human beings have inhabited the forest landscape and maintained a close association with the environment. In the Indian context, the forest-dwelling population largely comprises of the tribals who have been surviving in harmony within the forest ecology mostly separated from the mainstream society. They are in a multiplex relationship among populations of organisms for sustaining their livelihood within their habitat. Forest has been a major determinant towards enhancing rural livelihood and further regulates the Forest has been an important source of renewable resources throughout the world. Around 1.6 million people worldwide depend on varying degrees of forests for their livelihoods (Banerjee & Chowdhury, 2013). In India, around 1.73 lakhs villages are located in and around forest areas (ibid). According to the World Bank report (2006), a population of 275 million inhabits the forest areas of India (MoEF, 2009). The livelihood of those people living close to the forest and within the forests is inextricably linked to the forest eco-system. People depend on the forest for a variety of products for food, fodder, agriculture, housing, and an array of marketable minor forest produces which can potentially degrade forest if harvested unsustainably (Nayak et al.).

The symbiotic relationship of tribals with their forest environment has often been highlighted in social science research as a feature which distinguishes the tribes from other communities. The symbiosis is reflected in the manner in which resources drawn from the environment are utilised by them and are crucial for their survival. Vadakumchery (2003) carried out his study among two geographically separated tribal groups known as the Bara and Chota Maria Gonds. The author stresses how the process of social fission and geographical displacement of a tribal community led to divergent attitudes towards nature and brought in vital changes in their social dynamics. Being separated from their original territory, the Chota Gonds lost access to nature's bounty and has to explore diverse ways of subsistence in an environment different from the one left behind. This struggle for survival brought in a variety of influences on their lives and eventually shapes a different social organization, cultural pattern, and value system. In the course of their adaptation, a virtually different paradigm of man-nature relationship emerged among the two groups. The Bada Marias have developed socially regulated uses of natural resources with a restrained consumption pattern and were, therefore, closer to nature. The Chota Marias started exploiting nature without such conservationist concerns and therefore lacked a harmony with their environment. This separateness further created a dichotomy in their respective social organizations where the Bada Marias retained community control over land and extraction and utilisation of natural resources, while the Chhota Maria markedly adopted individual ownership and use. In the process, the two groups of the community have shifted away from each other to such an extent that they have become two distinct communities.

Since human society is naturally connected to its surrounding environment, an alteration in the later often induces changes in the structure of the society dependent on it. In the introductory chapter of Introduction to Cultural Ecology, Sutton & Anderson (2004) argued that humans and their cultures are an integral part of the environment. Human activity affects the environment, which is then altered and in turn affects human activities. A similar reciprocal impact of the ongoing forest degradation in India has been documented by different scholars. Both forest dependent population and communities that are indirectly related to forest ecosystem has been facing such stress. The consequences of this loss in forest cover have resulted in climate change, habitat loss, resource crisis and further social and economic hindrances towards human society (Chakravarty et al., 2012).

Following the introduction, this study aims to contribute to the literature on the human-environment relationship and understand how the tribal population has been depending on the forest ecosystem to meet their basic need even in this age of scientific and technological development.

Materials and methods

The present research was aimed at collecting qualitative data. The major techniques used in the whole study included interviews (semi-structured), observation (participant observation when it was possible), use of key informant, group discussions, case studies, and household census schedules. As a pilot study, nearly 8 days were spent in the selected village. The main purpose of the stay was to secure permission for the research as well as to go through the available literature on the area. A brief content analysis was made on the official records (voter list, village map, demographic records, etc). This attempt had made the approach clearer.

Household census schedule was used at the initial stage of the study to develop a rapport with the villagers and to have a clear understanding of their economy and habitat, which will be helpful to proceed with the study. Being an outsider of the village, data collection was mainly through the observation method. Things that could not be explained by the informants could be better understood through direct observation. Observation also helped in analysing the reliability of the information generated from the informants. Regarding the purpose of the study, semi-structured interviews were conducted with the help of a checklist. Semi-structured interviews with open-ended questions provided my informants with greater scope to in-detail discuss their views. Both individual and group interviews were conducted. Most of the interviews were recorded in voice recorders. Group discussions became a major tool for the study which was much helpful in collecting data in the course of gossips and meetings. The use of key informant for the study was much helpful in data collection.

Objectives

The prime objective of the present study was to understand the nature of relationship shared by the Nyishi tribe with their environment.

Results and discussion

Arunachal Pradesh and the Pakke-Kessang district

Arunachal Pradesh is the 29th state of India. On 20th February in 1987, the state was granted statehood, before which it was a union territory. Formerly, it was part of Assam till 1972 and NEFA. NEFA was renamed as Arunachal Pradesh by then director of research Late Mr. Bibhabasu Das Shastri. By area, the state is largest in northeast India with an area of 83,743 sq km, making it the 15th largest state in India. The literacy rate of the state is 66.95% and the HDI is medium at 0.617. The state shares an international border with Tibet in the North, Burma to East and Assam and Nagaland to the south. The state has 26 major tribes with numerous sub-tribes. All the tribes have different languages and hence, the official language of the state is English, and all government schools from primary onwards run under the medium instruction as English. Along with English, Hindi and Assamese are two major languages of the state. Pakke Kessang is a newly created district carved out of the Ease Kameng district on 14th December 2018. Pakke Kessang district has five administrative units' Pakke Kessang, Sejosa, Pijiriang, Passa Valley and Dissing Passo. The district headquarter is Lemmi.

Demographic profile of Rilloh Village

Rilloh village is a small hamlet consisting of sixty households, situated at a distance of 78 km from Itanagar. The land area comprises beautiful scenic place and there was no electricity provided and as such solar energy from the government beneficiary was the only source of power. There was no network facility and communication was only through satellite phones that demanded high cost. Rilloh village was very rich and availed in natural resources like water, agriculture land, and forests. The government of Arunachal Pradesh has been started a good priority of development factor is imposed in the village. At the same time, water supply is 24 hours a day in the village, which is still a far cry in all over India or to be electoral promise even the capital of India. The Rilloh village was self-sufficient and the economic condition of the people was based on horticulture like cardamom, ginger, local potato, etc.

The people of Rilloh village belonged to the Nyishi community and their language was also Nyishi. Different sub-clans of Nyishi were settled in Rilloh village namely Teli, Techi, Nabam, Yanfo, and Tallang. Currently, very few educated persons were found to settle at the village because there was no availability of medical and network facilities. The people of Rilloh village were kind-hearted. They welcomed our team for the fieldwork in their village and they cooperated with us during the time of data collection. They have offered duck, firewood and some materials to our team.

Socio-economic life and man-nature relationship in Rilloh village

Arunachal Pradesh is the best place to explore the relationship between man and nature and this relationship is well established in the study village. The villagers were mainly dependent on nature. Nature abundantly provided them with the most necessary things, in their daily life. Most of their work was associated with nature. Some of their religious beliefs, socio-cultural works, etc. were almost dependent on nature. The villagers were still away from the modernised world of sophistication and therefore formed a strong relation with nature. Most of their daily needs such as firewood, food, wood, bamboo, water, medicines, timber, straw, etc. were collected from the nearest forest. Apart from collecting minor forest products the villagers mostly engaged in shifting cultivation and wet cultivation.

As the fire was the source of heat and light, most of the families in the village used firewood for cooking, water boiling and many other purposes on their daily needs. During the cold season, firewood was the primary source of energy for every household. For this reason, firewood forms the most frequently extracted products for household needs. Nowadays, a few households used gas stoves for day to day cooking. But still, they give preference in using firewood because of some reason like, the region remains the cold throughout the year, the availability of LPG cylinder was limited and expensive. Due to the lack of transport communication, the villager did not receive a regular gas cylinder in their native home; therefore they had to go to a place called Sepa to collect their gas cylinder, which was very far from their village.

According to the village headman, every village had a specific boundary and boundary name. They usually follow a rule to collect firewood from their nearest forest land. Every individual of this village gathered firewood at a particular place for their necessary use. They are allowed to cut trees or collect fallen branches and twigs from their boundaries; if they disobey this role then they had to pay penalty. Trees were also the main source to build their shelter. People of Rilloh villagers are used different species of trees available in the surrounding based on their requirements. Some of the commonly used trees include Taram tree, Kora tree, Kosu tree, Taku tree, Seri tree, Nealo tree, Sangria tree, Sanglo tree, Sansar tree. Sansar tree was regarded as the costliest among other species. The extracted timber was used for varied purposes like timber for construction, as fuel for cooking and heating, construction of fencing, storage containers, etc. Their houses were of unique style. Houses stood over four or more polls supporting from the corners of the house. These posts were usually made of wood or bamboo. Roofs were constructed from straws, bamboos and some leaves. The walls and floors were also made from woods and bamboos. The villagers believed that large size bamboo plant *Voluka bah*[1] was first introduced to the villagers by travelers from the neighbouring state Assam. This type of bamboo has a very good demand among them. They had been using the bamboo shoot as a healthy dietary supplement. Most of the household items like stools, utensils and some decorating things, etc were made out of bamboo, wood or from anything available in nature.

The most essential requirement for their subsistence is food. The main source of food is rice cultivation (plant-based source), animal husbandry

1. Voluka bah is the local name for Bambusa balcooa Roxb.

and hunting (animal-based source). Most of the time they depended on the natural product but at the same time, they also buy some necessary products from the market. Other than doing cultivation they also collected many wild products like fruits, shrubs, herbs, insects, etc from the forest. Each family of this village had its own agricultural field. They performed two types of cultivation, wet cultivation and shifting cultivation. Wet cultivation was now more common in their village. The villagers called wet cultivation and shifting cultivation as *halo rango* and *raksup* respectively. Wet cultivation was done in the plain areas or valley and shifting cultivation was restricted to the hilly terrains or small mountains. In wet cultivation, they generally grew rice and respondents narrated that the wet cultivation provided more amount of rice as compared to shifting cultivation.

Paddy fields covered a large part of the valley areas, which indicated that rice was the foremost dietary-product of the villagers. Rice was often consumed with boiled vegetables, meat, etc. The villagers made different types of delicacies like pancakes, rice beer, etc from the rice. The locally prepared rice beer was known as *Apong* which was much popular among them. This local wine was made up of rice or *Pona, monua,* and *poling oppo*. Most of the food items they eat were either boiled or smoked and the use of oil and fried foods was significantly limited.

Generally, the people of Rilloh village started wet cultivation in April and May. First of all, they clean the drains that surround the paddy field, for irrigation purposes. They construct a boundary of mud in their paddy field. These boundaries called *Ali.* Then the farmers start ploughing their field. This process of ploughing was known as *Hala*. They made their soil muddy and prepared it for the next step. Then the planters or *Am Dina* start planting single seedlings keeping space in between, in a proper sequence. After six months the paddy *(Ame)* was ready for harvest. Locally the process of harvesting was called *Ametilna.* The harvested grains were stored in their granaries located nearby the main house building.

In the study village, residents are also involved in shifting cultivation. In this type of cultivation, they first cleaned the land by cutting the trees and vegetations and thereafter burning them and as a result producing some amount of ashes which brings fertility to the field. The villagers were still devoid of any modern techniques of cultivation. In this type of cultivation, cattle were not used for ploughing. Therefore, the cultivators use some tools such as, spades, etc. to prepare their land for cultivation.

The vegetables they generally cultivated through shifting techniques included cucumber, chilly, potato, tomato, pumpkin, etc.

The villagers also domesticated cattle, buffalo, fowl, ducks, etc. Rearing these animals provided them with milk, meat, and fertilizer, etc. On the other hand cattle and buffalo were also used for ploughing in paddy fields. Hunting was another source for them to derived food. Hunting wild animals have been a traditional practice among the villagers. But nowadays the government had prohibited them from hunting, but they still engaged in hunting secretly. Some of the animals they usually hunt include- tiger, pig, Monkey, squirrel, etc. Among birds, species like *pio*, hornbill, maina, woodpecker, sparrow, etc were commonly hunted. Hunting mainly provided protein requirements to them and at the same time, they also use the remnants of these wild animals for medicinal and magico-religious uses. Remnants such as skin, feathers, horns, etc. are also used as decorative products, clothing, etc. Traditionally they used these remnants to decorate their dress which reflected their dependency and connectivity with nature and natural products. Fish is also an important natural product used by these people for survival. They generally caught fish from their paddy fields and nearby water sources. In the earliest days, the villagers generally used *Toun* gos for fishing that included two different varieties, one was a creeper and the other was a shrub. The creeper was locally called *Mupu gos* and the tree was called *Muta gos*. They used both the creeper and the bark of the tree as an intoxicating agent to catch fish. First of all, they grind the creeper or the bark as a poison and mixed into the water sources. Some of the people still follow this way to catch fish while most villagers were found to use baits.

There were many herbs, shrubs, and trees which provided them with medicines to cure diseases locally. Some of the important medicinal plants that were used by the villagers were, *Doi, Pas Iai, Loci loma, Tanda affa,* and *Nagin phul*. Water was another most necessary resource provided by nature. Every major activity such as drinking, cooking, washing, bathing, etc. needs water. Traditionally bamboo has been playing an important role in supplying water, which formed connectivity between spring water to their houses, for their daily use. Nowadays most of them used running water which was also connected with the springs by pipes.

From time immemorial, people follow the barter and exchange system as a means of market communication. In earlier, the villagers only used their homestead agricultural products for their daily life. But nowadays there had been a change in their economic and social lifestyles. The aged persons practiced handicrafts made from wood and bamboo and were sold either at the nearby markets or to visitors to the village. According to the village headman, the landslide has been a major constraint in the region. He narrated that landslide has been frequently and severely affected agriculture and communication facilities in the territory.

Conclusion

From the above discussion, it can be concluded that any tribal society, irrespective of their location of habitat are closely tied to their physical environment. The resource use pattern systematically structures their cultural traits over time and the material culture maintains an inseparable relationship with the forest environment. In the case of the Rilloh Village, despite their gradual advancement in socio-economic spheres, they were never alienated from their surroundings. Much of their livelihood needs were derived from the physical environment and the relationship further strengthened their knowledge about the judicial use of plant resources for subsistence. In any tribal society across India, similar nature of coherence dominates the social structure. Ecosystems and indigenous populations have evolved in symbiosis for thousands of years. They are highly dependent on the forest as the other sources of income from agriculture and daily wage labours are limited. The tribal people, the most disadvantaged section of society, subsist from the forest and both wood and non-wood products remain essential for their livelihood.

References

Sutton, M. Q., & Anderson, E. N. (2004). Introduction to cultural ecology. Walnut Creek, CA: AltaMira Press.

Little, M. A. (2007). Human Ecology in Anthropology: Past, Present, and Prospects. Anthropology Today: Trends, Scope and Applications, Anthropologist Special Volume 3, 25-38.

Moran, E. F. (2006). People and nature: An introduction to human ecological relations. Malden, MA: Blackwell Pub.

Rappaport, R. A. (1967). Pigs for the ancestors; ritual in the ecology of a New Guinea people. New Haven: Yale University Press.

Rambo, A. T. (1983). Conceptual approaches to human ecology. Honolulu, HI: East-West Environment and Policy Institute.

Banerjee, A., & Chowdhury, M. (2013). Forest degradation and livelihood of local communities in India: A Human Rights Approach. Journal of Horticulture and Forestry, 5(8), 122-129.

MoEF (2009). State of Environment Report. New Delhi: Ministry of Environment and Forest. Government of India.

Nayak, B. P., Kohli, P., & Sharma, Dr. J. V. Livelihood of local communities and forest degradation in India: issues for REDD+. Ministry of Environment and Forests, New Delhi, Retrived from www.moef.nic.in/assets/redd-bk3.pdf.

Vadakurnchery, J. (2003). Tribes and cultural ecology in central India - A study among the Chota and Bada Marias. New Delhi: Mittal Publications.

Chakravarty, S., Ghosh, S. K., Suresh, C. P., Dey, A. N., & Shukla, G. (2012). Deforestation: Causes, Effects and Control Strategies. Global Perspectives on Sustainable Forest Management, 3-28.

Chapter - 10

Changes in Socio-Economic life of the Garo in Meghalaya

— *Shyam Babu Choudhury*

Economy is an important constituent of the community life. It plays a vital role in the formation of cultural and social structure of a society. As the activities associated with the fulfilment of material wants of the people are the parts of economic life, the study of socio-economic life of the tribal people helps us to understand the important aspects of their culture. David Throsby opines as follows: Economic discourse and the operation of economic systems function within a cultural context; similarly cultural relationships and process can also be seen to exist within an economic environment and can themselves be interpreted in economic terms. If culture can be thought of as a system of beliefs, values, customs, etc. shared by a group, then cultural interactions among members of the group or between them and members of other groups can be modelled as transactions and exchanges of symbolic or material goods within an economizing framework. He argues that the interpretation of culture in functional terms, we can identify the notion of culture as economy and interpretation of culture as residing within an economic milieu. Both economy and culture of a community are inter-related. If economic condition of a society is developed or changed, the cultural life of the given society is also influenced accordingly. Similarly, the economic life and economic development of a particular society are always influenced by their cultural system. The study of economic system consists of many economic theories given by the eminent economists in different times. But this discussion focuses only on the changes in the socio-economic sphere of the Garo life and inter-relationship between the economy and culture by providing examples from Garo society. Economic organisation consists of the ordering and organisation of human relations and human effort in order to procure as many of the necessities of day to day life as possible with the expenditure of effort. It is the attempt to secure the maximum satisfaction possible through adopting limited means to unlimited ends in an organised manner. This is true of primitive and modern society (Madan and Majumdar, 1986). Economic life is the fundamental condition for the existence of human. Marx stated that the character of the society depends on the way in which the economic problems are solve by it. These ways develop into norms of trade, exchange and property. (Kuppuswamy, 1972). Economy can be divided into two broad categories, Viz. Productionconsumption type economy and production-consumption-distribution type economy. Tribal economy of Assam is mainly of subsistence type and they fall into the broad category of production-consumption economy. In production-consumption economy production is made according to the need. On the contrary, the production-consumption-distribution economy is based on the accumulation of economic surplus or surplus production. The following four stages have been mentioned by the economists as the main stages of economic development of the tribal people. Those are: (i) Hunting and food gathering, (ii) Pastoral, (iii) Agricultural and (iv) Technological. The economy of the tribes of North-East India is based on agriculture. Tribal agriculture is dependent on two types of cultivation, viz. shifting cultivation and settled cultivation. The hill tribes mainly depend on shifting cultivation that is known as Jhuming. Almost all the tribal people of the North East India are cultivators. Therefore, the economy of the people of these areas is dependent on agriculture. The basic principles of their economy are: production for consumption, no capital investment, investment of excess wealth for enhancement of prestige and kin oriented economic co-operation. The modem economy and the tribal economy are different from each other. Modem economy is related to production, distribution, exchange and consumption. S. L. Dosi and P. C. Jain state that, the tribal economy can be looked at from two different perspectives. One is from the point of view of production, distribution and consumption and another is actor oriented where the actors use available means to maximize value. The former is called system oriented or subsistence economy and the later is called actor oriented or formal economy. In system oriented or subsistence economy the actor or individual has no determining voice in production process. The actor oriented or fom1al economy is basically the economy of the present market, where individual maximize their value and base their behaviour on cost-benefit, and increase the value of economy. In other words tribal economy is the economy of household and generally their production is only for self-consumption. But they also exchange their surplus production in traditional markets like hat and *mela.* These traditional markets have important roles on their economy. On the contrary, modem economy is rational that wants to work on the cost benefit idiom.

Socio-economic life of the Garo

Agriculture is the basic economy of the Garo. In the hill areas they depend on shifting cultivation. But in the plains, permanent cultivation is practiced by them. Although there had been the legendary reference of hunting as the basic traditional profession of the Garo, in the present- social system it is neither popular nor practical. Now, almost 70 percent of the total populations of the Garo engage in cultivation. Agricultural works of the Garo started during the month of May-June. Both staple and cash crops are cultivated by the Garo. Wet cultivation is the major crop of the plains Garo and paddy are also grown. In November-December, the crops are ready for harvesting. Both men and women take part in harvesting, generally women reap the crop and men join only if the area of the field is large. For the completion of agricultural work there is the corporate activity like system among the Garo. Friends and relatives also help, but that would be on a personal basis and without compulsion. Besides the paddy cultivation, horticultural cash crops and seasonal vegetables like gourd, pumpkin, brinjal, orange, radish and chilli are also grown by plain Garo. The most common horticultural crop is areca nut, which covers a large area in the backyard. The produce is for home consumption as well as for sale. Bamboo is another important plant used for making baskets and fencing, construction and repairs of the houses, sheds for cattle and pigs or for granary. Mustard, jute and sugarcane are also grown in Garo families. In the plains the cultivation of land is done by ploughing. Surplus stocks of their products are sold in the markets for purchasing items of daily use. Besides the cultivation, spinning and weaving, fishery, piggery, poultry and basketry are also done by the Garo.

Study area

The study has been undertaken in the RI-Bhoi district, Meghalaya. Out of the total 2 Garo villages of RI-Bhoi district, Meghalaya, Pillangkatta was mostly inhabitant by Garo people. So I have been selected for the study.

Data base and methodology

A total sample size of 270 Garo households has been selected from RI-Bhoi district. Both primary and secondary data have been used for the study in order to get the present livelihood pattern, socio-economic conditions and changes in the occupation pattern of Garo tribe. General information of the study area and the Garo tribe has been collected from various secondary sources like Garo Association's census, Government records and article in books, journals and newspapers and from other reliable sources. Primary data have been collected from the selected Pillangkatta village of RI-Bhoi district through household questionnaires. For the field survey scheduled questionnaires were used to collect required data regarding the present occupational pattern and their trend of occupational shifting.

The predominant means of livelihood of the Garo is shifting cultivation that has helped them to survive over the years. Although agriculture was their principle occupation as an additional source of income, these farmers have also engaged in other part time activities.

Occupational structure of the Garo, RI-Bhoi District, Meghalaya

The data shows the present trend of occupational structure of the RI-Bhoi district, Meghalaya, in Pillangkatta.Out of the total working males 36.51% are in traditional agricultural work, followed by the business category with 17.43%. Only 8.71% Garo in RI-Bhoi district are engaged in low category government services. The rests are found in other tertiary sectors like garage works, machine repairing, tailoring etc. Most of the Garo females are housewives comprising about 69.4%, while 15.65 are unemployed. It can be concluded that most of them are trying to cope with adopting new means of livelihood through employment. But some enthusiastic Garo are still struggling to continue with their traditional agricultural work though their income is miserable. It has been found that even today some Garo are very ignorant about education and as a result most of them are found with high school level education, whereas an insignificant portion completes graduation. A small section educated in religious schools to get jobs in Church. On the other hand, while discussing about the female education they are much more backward in this regard. Most of them left school in high school level and get married. Unlike other ethnic tribes of Meghalaya, these Garo women rarely found contributing in family income. This educational backwardness and reluctance for any kind of income generating activities can be explained as the influence of their recently developed religious orthodoxy.

Traditional agricultural work is no more a sustainable livelihood system in today's changing economic scenario. Low income, poor entrepreneurship, problems of marketing, stagnant low wages of the agricultural work all these can be considered as the factors behind their occupational shifting.From the above study it can be stated that traditional work provides the least amount of the total per capita income, whereas the business and trade category and the government service holders have comparatively higher income. It can be concluded that this low income is the vital cause behind the extinction of this traditional occupation. It is quite obvious that people, in search of better livelihood will surely opt for other options which can support them with a better economic condition. Most of them do not have any savings except the government service holders and businessman and traders. Most of the enterprises are family owned. For agricultural work get low amount of daily wages comparing to other wage labourer.

Occupational trend through generations of Garo of RI-Bhoi District

Diversification of occupation exists in RI-Bhoi district throughout the generation: Here age group of 20-39 years contains about 19.4% agricultural work, whereas their parent's generation 47.2% agriculture and the number of agriculture workers enhance to 70.83% in the grandparents generation. New generation Garo are mostly found in various tertiary sectors like business, Government service and trade.

Changing trend of occupation among the Garo tribe in RI-Bhoi district, Meghalaya: It can be concluded that there is a gradual declination in the participation of agricultural work towards new generation.

The changing scenario of socio-economic life

The Garo are hard working people and start working hard early in their life. But most of them do not have sufficient land for cultivation. During the field visit it is found that most of them cultivate in the rented land of other people of neighbouring villages. It is locally known as Adhi loa system. In this system, the landless Garo get land and crops for cultivation from the original land owner. In return, they have to give half of their products to the land owner after harvesting it. Although some of the Garo have good agricultural lands, yet their agriculture is at subsistence level. The main cause of this state of affair is the age-old pattern of cultivation with indigenous tools and implements, use of traditional seeds and organic fertilizer. Though a small number of families have adopted improved agricultural practices like use of tractors, power tillers, high yielding varieties of seeds, chemical fertilizers and pesticides, yet these new practices have been accepted in a half hearted manner. The villagers generally do not like innovative agricultural practices mainly because of their traditional faith in the God of cultivation who may be displeased if new methods are used. People are not ready to give up their age old practices and traditions.

The literacy rate is very low amongst the Garo. Illiteracy is a cause of their economic under-development in every village. Due to the lack of education they do not have any idea about modem equipment of cultivation and modem varieties of seeds. Their economy is kin based economy. All of the family members do engage in agricultural operations. Generally parents cannot afford the educational expenditure of their wards. Rather they are compelled to engage them in agricultural and domestic works. Population explosion is another cause of their economic-underdevelopment. They believe that the children are the gift of God and having more children means more helping hands in their agricultural works. This type of belief has an impact on the population explosion. It is found somewhat true in the case poor families. Because, the poor families cannot afford wage labourers for work in the agricultural fields. Rather they are dependent on the kin based economic activities. There is a division of labour based on gender in agricultural and domestic works. Men take the responsibility of the outside work such as ploughing, harvesting the paddy, carrying the paddy to home, fishing, basketry and looking after domestic animals. Women take the responsibility of all the domestic chores as well as planting and harvesting, fishing, and take care of the children so on and so forth.

Case study: Mrs Sangma, aged, 48, of Pillangkatta village, work in Garo family for twenty years as helper in household duty for Garo community. The owner of the house was a teacher. She was very small when her parents send it to the Pillangakatta village to work with them. She was very happy to work with them and she formed strong relationship with their family. She said that economic status also decides the relationship of the groups. As she is belong to a poor family background so their have no such option to work in that particular family.

The introduction of formal education and prove of higher educational institutions have strengthened the socio-economic chasing of Garo, with better understanding and showing their outward attitudes towards change. Now a days educated women are becoming aware of possibilities and equality for their better life. The educational system has given better opportunity of women to get higher education so that they can achieved better status in the society. In fact, recognition of the significance and diversity of the interactive relationship of the forces of stability and change in the Garo community has become a very important today. Education has play a vital role in changing the economic status of the Garo community. Education has contributed to an overall development particularly among the Garo community in the study village.

Government polices

At the present day all the forest areas of the state have been brought under the forest laws and rules. The important ones among these are Indian Forest Act, 1972; Meghalaya Forest Rules; Forest (Conservation) Act, 1980; Meghalaya Forest (Conservation) Rules (Bera, ibid.).These have accelerated the process of getting the Government forest land for serving the inhabitants in public interest. There is a remarkable development in this arena, which aims to look into a wider network of tribal habitation keeping in view their traditional rights over forest. Naming it as The Scheduled Tribes and Other Traditional Forest Dwellers (Recognition of Forest Rights) Rules, 2007 were promulgated for implementing the provisions of the Act notified on 1st January, 2008.

The major legal rights recognized under the Act were:

1. Right to cultivate forestland to the extent under occupation, subject to ceiling of 4 hectares.
2. Right to collect, use and dispose of minor forest produce.
3. Right inside forests, which are traditional customary e.g., grazing.

The persons who will get the right are:

1. Scheduled tribes who have been living in and depending on forests for their livelihood prior to 13th December, 2005.
2. Other traditional forest dwellers that have been living in and depending on forests for their livelihood, for three generation (i.e.,75 years prior to13 December,2005).

The right holders had the duties to ensure sustainable use, conservation of bio-diversity, and maintenance of ecological balance and thereby strengthening the conservation regime of the forests.

Developmental programmes

The shift from rural to predominantly urban society brings about profound changes in every walk of social life (Michael, 1989; Sandhu, 2003). The growth in urbanization has accelerated the significance of education in their life. The tribes have become more open to the need of education which they consider as an important agency for social change. The change in social, economic, political, religious and educational field has brought about remarkable transformation among the tribal particularly among the Garo. These days, the Government is taking many steps to bring Garo into the main stream of development. Government has particular department to take care of the different welfares of the Tribes called Department of Tribal affairs. This department is involved with administering various developmental schemes, formulation, implementation and monitoring various schemes. The Director of the department will be the supervising authority over the tribal development activities.

Changing role of women in economic activities

Men and women are two equal components of the human society and are considered complementary to each other in all aspects of life. But the role and status played and enjoyed by these two components are not same in every human society. Women have different role and status in a society according to its social norms. Garo women have also different role and status in their family economy which is based on division of labour. Their roles in family economy can be discussed as follows:

In the field of agriculture: Without participation of womenfolk, agriculture is not possible for a Garo family. The female members of every household work hard during the time of planting and harvesting the paddy.

Custody of granary of the family: It is a common practice of the Garo society that the granary of a family is kept under the custody of the wife. Her husband cannot dispose of paddy without prior discussion with her.

Weaving: Every indigenous community in this region, tribal or non-tribal, in the hills or in the plains has their own range of textiles produced by the women in their traditional looms. Weaving is compulsory activity of Garo women. Hence, every Garo girl is bound to weave her traditional dresses herself. It is observed that women earn good amount of money by selling cloths woven by them and thus provide financial help to the family.

Self-help groups among Garo women: Nowadays, weavers' association is established in Garo villages with the view to weave cloths in community basis. The weavers are self employed and get financial benefits from the weavers' association. The self-help groups also earn money from poultry, pigs and cattle rearing in community basis. The purpose of self-help groups is to help the members during the time of distress or hardship. Self-help groups have gone a long way in providing sustenance to otherwise unprivileged underdeveloped needy families.

Changes in the fields of animal husbandry and handicrafts: Animal husbandry and handicrafts are two spheres that help in economic upliftment of the Garo. Pigs, poultry, and cattle rearing are common practices for many families. Pigs are reared for sale. They earn good amount of money by selling pigs. Poultry is reared for selling of eggs and meats. Goat and buffaloes are common animals reared by them. Milk produced from these animals is another commodity to be sold in market. Generally cow and buffaloes are reared for the dwell purposes of engaging them in agricultural work as well as selling. Garo women take the main responsibilities in this task. Garo males are expert in bamboo and cane work. The bamboo and cane items produced by the Garo men are popular among all of the rural people of Meghalaya.

Impact of economic development on their culture

In the present era of globalization, no ethnic communities are remaining isolated. Basically globalization is an economic process but it includes mass communication, culture, politics, and many other human endeavours. Globalization is worldwide phenomena; the impact of globalization can be felt in every part of the world. Globalization has been made possible through the establishment of worldwide, information and communication network. New telecommunication and computer networks have overcome the barriers of time and space. In the present era of globalization, the whole world has become a "global village". The small places have been exposed to the wider world. Hence, the tribal homelands are linked with the regional state, nation and the world. Therefore, no group even tribal communities are remaining isolated and they have been influenced by the process of globalization and so also the Garo.In the case of economy, the

Garo now, have developed their agricultural practices. They have adopted improved agricultural practices like use of tractors, power tillers, for tillage the paddy field; high yielding varieties of seeds, chemical fertilizers and pesticides. Of late, the Garo are more exposed to modem education and technology particularly the ones used in agriculture. Now, they do not hesitate to use modem technology and method in agricultural activities. Such shifts have yielded well. And this knowledge provides them good result in their agricultural production. Educated Garo take up different types of jobs. This has enabled them to take up any occupation they may find suitable. It is found during the field work that the new generation of the Garo is reluctant to agricultural works. Rather they prefer to work in towns and cities no matter what type of work. Industrial workers have been increased amongst them. And in this way economic condition has improved to a great extent. Due to the increased purchasing capacity most of the Garo families now have Television, Music system, Motorcycle, Mobile phone and other Electronic gadgets. These things have influenced their traditional lifestyle and practice. For example, the main agricultural operations like sowing, planting, weeding and harvesting are quite laborious jobs. Their folk songs reflect the social customs and traditions of their society. But at present instead of singing the communities own traditional songs people show interest in playing modern filmy Garo, English or Hindi popular songs. Leisure time recreation in the past consisted of traditional games or performances, but nowadays they prefer to go for movie or watch television or listen to the music. As a result their own culture has become a casualty. On the contrary, improved economic condition has enabled the Garo to use still camera, video camera while celebrating their traditional festivals and ceremonies. Nowadays it has become a regular practice with all to document the events like marriage and other cultural ceremonies. This kind of documentation of people's cultural activities might be helpful in research on such activities. This kind of documentation of their culture can provide knowledge about their cultural and social systems. Due to the increasing purchasing capacity through the sale of cash crops and the access to markets, the consumption of manufactured consumer goods have increased gradually. This has brought the Garo community into close economic co-operation with their neighbours. From the above discussion it is found that the Garo economy has undergone many changes. Their living condition has also undergone change. Their economy or agricultural operations are influenced by their cultural system. Similarly, culture is also influenced by their economic condition. Prof. Arthur Lewis, a distinguished Economist writes: Economic growth depends on attitude to work, to wealth, to profit, to having children, to invention, to strangers, to adventure and so on, and all these attitudes flow from deep springs of human mind." [qtd. ill Madhab,2000]. Human mind set is designed according to the culture and the working attitude of people. Again the working attitude of the people is regulated by cultural setup. Cultural set up depends on different factors such as traditions, customs, religion, geographical environment, physical strength, education and so on and so forth. On the contrary economic condition has a great impact on the cultural continuity. Hence both are inter-related and influenced mutually.

Conclusion

Garo economy falls under the broad category of production-consumption type, where any kind of production is only for their self consumption. Hence, it is still in subsistence level, although a minority of the Garo enjoys a high economic status. As of now, the economic condition of the Garo has been improved in comparison to their earlier condition. But in comparison to other societies, their economic growth rate is low. Illiteracy is one reason of that. They are not that sharp in adapting new technology nor are they innovative. Entrepreneurship is still not a forte for the Garo. Some of them are petty businessmen but successful professionals are few and far between. Present day Garo young people are not seen to be inclined to adapt their own age old economic, social as well as cultural practices, not to speak of glorifying them. Many people Garo community, both male and female, are seen working in unorganized sectors as manual workers. Lack of interest in accepting new business for their economic development is also a factor of economic backwardness. But nowadays, their outlook towards life and other things has changed. Boys and girls get themselves admitted in schools. Literacy rate is increased gradually. Young boys have shown interest in joining industrial work. Kin based economy is still going on in their society where women play an important role. The economic problems of plain Garo are not different from the economic problems of the Indian peasantry in general. They have faced the problem of landlessness, land alienation, indebtedness, and fragmentation of holdings, backward agricultural practices etc., Among these, landlessness, and backward agricultural practices are the main problems encountered by them. During the field work it was observed that most of them have been engaging in cultivation on such land which is in fact owned by rich people. They take lease of the land for some years in return of rent or products.

This system is locally known as *Adhi lowa or Adhi diya* system where the farmers have to offer half of their production to the owner of the land. Frequent landslide in Meghalaya during the last two decades has also badly affected their economic condition. Production rate is not too high due to the adherence to the age old agricultural practices. The number of some families who have adopted modem agricultural practices is quite negligible. Their culture and economy bear a close relationship. Every kind of agricultural operation is associated with cultural and religious celebrations. It can thus be concluded that the culture, economy and geographical environment are always interrelated. Geographical environment give's shape to the culture & economy of a particular group of people. Economy depends on the ideology of a group of people which is also a product of their cultural system. The economic activities, working attitude, food habit, and dress pattern are depended on culture, religion and climatic condition. On the other hand, the economic development or economic conditions also have an impact on particular culture. Because the continuity of cultural tradition and cultivation of cultural practices depend on economic condition of the people. Hence, the relationship between culture and economy can be described as a two way process and both are influenced by each other as seen in the case of the Garo.

References

Ali Irshad, A.N.M. (1974): *Social Relations among the Assamese Muslims in Rural and Situations*, Unpublished PhD Thesis, pp. 99, 224. Gauhati University, Guwahati.

Ali, M.I. (2012): *A brief Description of the Morias of Kaliabor* (Kaliaboror Moria Janagoshthir Chamu Itibritta, pp. 248.

Baruah, G.C. (1930): *Ahom Buranji, Assam Administration*, pp. 68-73, Calcutta.

Baruah, G.C. (1972): *Axom Buranji*, Assam PrakashanParishad, pp. 75-76, Guwahati.

Baruah, K.L. (1966): *Early History of Meghalaya*, Dutta Baruah Publication, Guwahati.

Bhuyan, S.K. (ed.) (1960): *Satsari Axom Buranji,* pp. 69, Publication Department, Gauhati University, Guwahati.

Bora, A. (2008*): Nere Bhere Moria, Budhbaria, Axomiya Pratidin Chambers, R*. and Conway, G. (1991): *Sustainable Rural Livelihoods: Practical Concepts for the 21st Century,* February 3rd 2010 from http://www.smallstoch.info/reference/IDS/dp 296.pdf

Das, G. (2003): *Madhyabhugir Kobolot Hajor Aitihyamandita Pital Xilpa, Dainik Janambhumi*, p-1, 19th October.

Das, P.C. (1984): *Hajo-a Socio Cultural Study,* Unpublished PhD Thesis, Department of Anthropology, Guwahati University, Pp. 25-27.

Gait E.A. (1898): *Manufacture of Pottery in Assam*, Indian Art and the Industry.

Majumdar, D.N. And T.N. Madan, 1986. *An Introduction to Social Anthropology.* New Delhi: National Publishing House.

O'Neil, D. (2006*): Processes of Change, New World EncyclopediaCensus of India* (1961)

Singher, M.ed.1959. *Traditional India: Structural and Change. Philadelphia: American Folklore society.*

Singh, T., 2002. *Cultural Change in India.* New Delhi: Rawat Publications.

Steward, J., 1995. *Theory of Cultural Change: The Methodology of Multilinear Evolution. Urban*: University of Illinios Press.

Vidyarthi, L.P. And B.K.Roy, 1985. *The Tribal Economy of India. Bombay: The All India Manufactures of Organisation.*

Young, P.V., 1961. *Scientific Social Surveys and Research. Tokyo*: Charles E. Tuttle Company.

Culture

Chapter - 11

Traditional Religious Beliefs and Practices of the Sonowal Kacharis of Tinsukia District of Assam

— ***Biswajit Kumar Singh***

The Sonowal Kacharis is one of the indigeneous tribe of Assam. They are predominantly found in Dhemaji, Dibrugarh, Golaghat, Jorhat, Lakhimpur, Majuli, Sivasagar, Tinsukia districts and some other parts of Assam. They show mongoloid racial traits and belong to Tibeto-Burman linguistic group. There are not any definite written records of the origin of these people. There are various sources which throw some light about their origin particularly the oral tradition among the people is more prevalent among them which is passed down from generation to generation. Those legends and myths also did not show any similarities. The elderly people took under consideration those stories and trace their origin. They relate themselves with *Hiranyakashapu, Prahalad* and *Bali*. They regarded *Bhim* and *Hidimba* as their ancestors.

The Sonowal Kacharis are mainly cultivators. They cultivate paddy and various types of vegetables. Rice is their staple food. The inheritance pattern of these people is patriarchal. They follow monogamy as their marriage system. Among them four types of marriage is prevalent, viz., *Nowai Dhowa (Bor bia), Hom diya* (traditional Hindu marriage by employing Priest and by performing Hom), *Gandharba Vivah* (Marriage by Elopement) and *Sursuria or Rabha Surokia* (Marriage by running away in unceremonious feast is given to some elders for legislation of the Marriage). They perform the crises rites, during the time of birth, onset of puberty (in case of females) and at the time of death. Notion of purity and pollution is also seen among them.

Religion can be defined as the belief in the supernatural beings. The most important element of religion is beliefs. The religious performances are depicted through rituals. All the people of the world have their own religious beliefs and practices. The diversity of religion is the centre of attraction of many scholars from different disciplines like Anthropology, Sociology, Philosophy etc. Religion influences the way of life of the people due to this it becomes important from scientific point of view to understand how it has influenced the people throughout the ages. Religion is one of the strongest cords which bind the human relationship thereby maintaining the social structure of every society. It is one of the mechanisms which maintains orderliness among the human society. The anthropological study of religion is an important aspect and it aims to understand how different religious domains operate the minds of the people and their activities. Anthropologists study the diversity of religious systems, present and past, in order to understand, what is common to humanity?

Various scholars have worked among different religions considering the different aspects of religion. Ramya, (2012) studied the traditional religious beliefs and practices and impact of Christianity among the Nyshis. Religious practices was also studied by Rooij (2016), Oxhandler et al., (2017) studied the religious and spiritual beliefs and practices among practitioners across five helping professions.

In this paper an attempt has been made to portray the traditional religious beliefs and practices of the Sonowal Kacharis of Rangagarah Village, Dangori of Tinsukia District, Assam. For the collection of data standard anthropological methods like observation, interview methods were employed. The secondary sources were also employed. The information collected was also cross checked.

Among the Sonowal Kacharis one can find the mixture of religious beliefs that is their traditional tribal religion *(Shakti Cult)* and *Vaishnavism.* It has been found that in the traditional religious beliefs and practices of these people they do animal sacrifices, bloodshed is there, they also offer the *Madhopurukh* (local liquor) to their Gods. It was during 1903 when *Auniaiti Shatra's* head priest Shri Keshabdev Mahanta spread Vaishnavisim among them. Since then many people became devotees of *Vaishnavism.* Due to these two major factors one can see both the traditional as well as Hindu religious beliefs and practices among them.

Some important traditional religious rituals are *Baithow puja, Baghdeo puja, Gatigiri puja, Gojai puja, Xhorogdeo puja, Jolkhai puja, Kula Samon puja, Ronga Samon puja, Bor Samon puja, Khatriya puja, Khin Vonga Puja, Tapsiling puja, Gukalika puja, Burha bhuri, Kesaikhati, KoliAai Than* etc. They also celebrate *Krishna Jhanmashtami, Shivratri, Lakshmi Puja* etc. These religious festivals are done at individual level and at community level. Some of the important traditional religious festivals are:

Baithow Puja: This is one of the main puja of the Sonowal Kacharis. It is celebrated in the month of *Phagun* (March/April) of the Lunar fortnight. Earlier this puja was done in the forest. In this puja a small bird is sacrificed and it is cooked which is then shared among them.

Baghdeo Puja: Next day after the *Baithow Puja, Baghdeo Puja* is performed in the jungle near the village. There the *Gatigiri* and *Baghdeo* Puja is performed by facing towards north and south directions respectively. In this puja birds are also sacrificed. Divination is also done to foretell their future.

Gatigiri Puja: They believe that certain invisible power is controlling their society which they called them *Gatigiri*. In order to seek blessings for their village so that nothing harm can happen they do this puja.

Gajai Puja: Among the Sonowal Kacharis *Gajai Puja* is the other important puja next to *Baithow Puja*. It is believed that *Gajai Deo* was their Dharma Guru (Religious Head) and the ideal person of their society.

Xhorogdeo Puja: This puja is also known as *Indra puja*. In this puja a pair of Cock is sacrificed. Then 120 Gods are also offered puja. After this puja they believe that Goddess *Lakshmi* will enter their granary.

Many religious beliefs and practices are prevalent among the Sonowal Kacharis of Assam. Through such beliefs and practices we come to know about the customs, traditions as well as socio-cultural scenario of the Sonowal Kaharis of Assam. Now a days the Sonowal Kacharis are gradually becoming Hinduised, especially the *Vaishnavism* and *Tantricism*. Besides their traditional religious rites and duties most of the Sonowal Kacharis arrange the recitation of *Kirtana* and *Bhagawata* in the *Namghar* (Prayer Hall) in the name of Lord Krishna. Moreover, individual families also arrange such *Nam Kirtan* casually for remedies for the ailing persons. It is seen that the Sonowal Kacharis are able to preserve their traditional religious beliefs and practices in the contemporary period also. One cannot ignore the impact of *Vaishnavism* on them. Moreover due to conversion of religion their traditional practices are becoming less prevalent. In the present day context the younger generation shows less inclination towards their traditional religious beliefs and practices.

References

Kachari Nandeshwar, (2011) Sonowal Kachari Samaj-Sanskriti aru Bhasar Parishay, Sonowal Kachari Autonomous Council, Dibrugarh.

Oxhandler, Holly K., Edward C. Polson, Kelsey M. Moffall and W. Andrew Achen Baum. 2017., The Religious and Spritual Beliefs and Practices among practioners across five helping professions., www.mdpi.com/Journal/religion.

Rooij, Laurens de. 2016., Religious Practice., https://www.researchgate.net/publication/312292863.

Tame, Ramaya. 2012., Traditional Religious beliefs and practices and impact of Christianity among the Nyshis., https://www.researchgate.net/publication/229087949.

Villegas, D.L., 2018, 'Spirituality and belief: Implications for study and practice of Christian spirituality', HTS Teologiese Studies/Theological Studies 74(3), 5037.https://doi.org/10.4102/hts.v74i3.5037.

Chapter - 12

Sacred Place and Its Rituals: Beliefs and Practices of the Deoris of Dhemaji District, Assam

— ***Humen Chutia***

The Deori is one of the prominent plain tribe of Assam and they belong to Indo-Mongoloid group of people. The Indian constitution has regarded the Deori as a Scheduled tribe of Assam. The present inhabitations of the Deoris are spread in different districts of Upper Assam but they are mostly distributed in the districts of Lakhimpur, Dhemaji, Sibsagar, Jorhat, Sonitpur, Dibrugarh and Tinsukia. As per semantics the word 'Deori' means the off springs of God and Goddess. According to Deori language *'Den'* means great or wise and *'O'* and *'Ri'* denotes male and female respectively. Hence, the meaning of '*Deori*' is the great or wise male and female being. On the other hand, the Deori are believed to be priests or worshippers of God and Goddesses. Sir Edward Gait wrote that the "Deoris are the priestly section of the Chutiya kings of Sadiya Dynasty who worshipped the Goddess *Tamreswari (Kechaikhati)* and *Sri Sri Baliababa* at the Copper Temple at Sadya. Even after the annexation of Chutiya kingdom by Ahom king in 1523 A.D., the Deori priests continued their worship at these shrines under the auspices of the Ahom kings." According to W.B. Brown the Deoris are a small and scheduled tribe of Upper Assam; and as the name implies, they are the representatives of the priestly or Levite class among the *Chutiyas*, who are one of the most numerous castes of Upper Assam; and whom it is known from history to have been the ruling race in Upper Assam before the *Ahom* invasion in the fifteenth century.

In every human society Temple or Shrine is considered as a sacred place and worship is performed with traditional rituals for well-being. Many tribal communities preserve their tradition through folklore and worship their deities' right from the occasion of birth to mourning death and they perform with some specific worship and offerings. Tribal societies are very rich in magico-religious beliefs and taboos. The socio-cultural norms as well as religious purposes of the tribal community help to live a peaceful life among them. Like the other tribes and community, Deori also believed their traditional religious beliefs and practices and keeping these as much as possible in their traditional way. The Deori of Dhemaji district is no exception to this role. Thus, the paper emphasizes on the religious beliefs and practices of the Deoris with the following objectives.

1. To explore the forms of worshiping and propitiate system to the deities of sacred place of the Deoris.
2. To study the rituals associated with the village shrine.

Materials and methods

The data for the present study were collected from the two typical *Dibangiya* Deori villages namely- Bamchenia Deori gaon and Borbam Deori gaon under the Bordoloni Block of Dhemaji district, Assam. The primary data were collected through in-depth interview with religious specialists and persons having knowledge about the rituals which are perform at their village sacred place. There are 24 respondents were covered from the studied villages for the present study. Besides these, participant observation was also done during the time of field investigation. The secondary data were collected from various documents, journals, articles, books etc.

Results and discussion

The Deori of Dhemaji district has been maintaining their traditional socio-religious organization along with their language. Agriculture is the primary livelihood and as such, excepting the beliefs of supernatural origin, the religious rites and rituals seem to be performed mainly for ensuring better agriculture. The Deoris worship different Gods and Goddesses at their village sacred place (*Midiku* or *Deoshal*).

Midiku or Deoshal

The sacred place of Deori is known as *'Midiku'* where *'Midi'* denotes God or deity and *'Ku'* means abode. In some Deori villages the *'Midiku'* is popularly known as '*Deoshal*' or '*Deoghar*'. It is a public worshiping place and set up for each villages or a group of villages. A *Midiku* or

Deoshal is generally located in the eastern side of the village or in the centre of the village. It consists with three houses and the location of houses relates to the hierarchical of the deities; these are known as (1) *Kundimama-yan* (2) *Chunketeri-Numali Kunwari*, (3) *Jakarua-yan*, (4) *Niyacha-yan*, (5) *Medera* and (6). *Morong-Achan*

Niyacha-yan is the kitchen of the temple which is situated in the south-western side of the compound facing the north direction. The votive offerings are cocked in this house by the '*Bhug-Ladani*' (special cook). It has been observed that the items cooked outside of the shrine are not offered in any case to the deities of the shrine because these foods are said to be not ritualistically pure to offer the deities. The '*Medera*' (store house) is observed in few villages where all religious paraphernalia relating with rituals of the shrine are store in a systematic way. These paraphernalia are carefully preserved in their respective places after use. These items are not allowed to use in their private rituals and even not generally use in public rituals also performed outside the shrine.

There is another kitchen '*Morong Achan*' which is situated in a long distance from the shrine. In few Deori villages this *Morong Achan* is situated outside the compound of the shrine. *Morong Achan* is use for community feast where all the sacrificial animals and birds, rice, vegetables are cooked and consumed by the priests along with their villagers just after the performed of the community ritual.

Types of Pujas

It has been observed that though the Deoris are known to be the worshippers of the *Sakti* cult (worshippers of power), their religion can't be regarded entirely as *Saktas*. There are three types of *pujas* are observed among the Deoris relating with the shrine, these are:

***Sattik Puja*:** *Sattik puja* is the first phase of *Deo-Puja* where the priest ignite a lamp wick inside the altar of shrine and offers betel nut and betel leaf with a *Sarai* of *Mah-Chaul* which is consist of pea, banana, sugar-cane, coconut, fruits etc. and some raw materials like *ranga chandan, tanglati, leafs of flowers etc.* The priest also chants the particular incantations for invitation the deities.

***Rajashik Puja*:** Worshiping by sacrifices is known as *Rajashik Puja.* After presenting the aspirations of all the attendance of the deities, the priest pure all the '*Bhetuwas*' (Offering birds and animals for decapitation) by sprinkle of '*Suchi-ji*' (pure water). It also marked in their foreheads with *ranga chandan* and offer *prashad* to eat them. The priest explains the purposes of the ritual along with the sacrifices of *Bhetuwas*. The *Bordeori* decapitated heads and offers their blood to the deities of shrine. He also prays to the deities for the welfare of the villagers as well as the persons or family who offered *Bhetuwas*.

***Tamashik Puja*:** In the *Tamashik Puja* they offered cooked foods and rice beer to the deities. The foods are cooked by '*Ladanes*' with the decapitated flesh of *Bhetuwas*. They have a customary role that they can use only the leaves of banana, *torapat, ko-pat* (wild plant leafs) for offering the foods to deities.

Sacrifices

The main objective of sacrifices is to placate their deities and prevalent spirits who they believe are responsible in affecting human life in many ways and to bring them to terms so that do not cause harm. The main sacrifices are pigs and fowls, the numbers of which vary according to the importance of the occasion and in its aftermath cooking its flesh and partaking of it along with rice and rice beer is a common feature. Sometimes they also offer and sacrifice black goat according to the importance of rituals. Human sacrificed was also performed by the Deoris in the past. In the present day, the sacrifice of pigs, fowls and goat are still prevalent among them. After a sacrificed is performed, their blood and decapitated heads are offers to the deities of shrine.

Ritual sacrifice of animals or bird is found to be performed among the Deori societies in the following four manners:

1. Decapitate with one stroke at the neck of the victim by a sharp cleaver.
2. Serving of the head of victim by repeated to-and-fro movement of a cleaver in the underside of the neck, i.e. the system of killing a victim by cutting its clavicle.
3. Stunning the victim with strokes of a club on its head, and
4. Staking the victim by piercing it's by a pointed bamboo stake.

Pujari

There are two sets of religious functionaries for conducting the rites and rituals among the Deori villages. One set is called '*Chari Deori*' and it consisting of '*Bordeori'or 'Boderi'* (chief priest), '*Sarudeori*' or '*Saderi*', '*Borbharali*' and '*Sarubharali*'. Among the '*Chari Deori*' only *Bordeori* and *Sarudeori* are entitled to performed sacrifice and worship and enter into the main temple. The *Bordeori* is the most respected person of the village and he acts as the judge of the crimes committed by the villagers. When the *Bordeori* becomes unfit for his work due to old age or any other reason, people of the village select another suitable man for the post of the *Bordeori*. The person must be of good health and from the clan of the *Bordeori*. There is some eligibility or qualifications for the post of *Bordeori* and it is minutely observed during the time of his induction. According to their customary role, he should be a person of good character and should not be mauled by a tiger or bitten by snake nor have excreta of a vulture or crow fallen upon him. If, somebody faced these incidents but tries to hide these incidents and aspire to become a *Bordeori* in such case, it is believed that his defects are easily detected by the '*Midi-Girachi*' or '*Deo-dhani*' in course of time. At the same time, it is also believed that the offerings to the deities made by such priest become fruitless which leads to downfall of the society.

The *Sarudeori* works as assistant of the *Bordeori* and during the absence of the later he performs his works. On the other hand, the *Sarubharali* works as assistant of *Borbharali* during the performances of the rituals. It is duty of *Borbharali* to collect the dues of the temple and to provide animals for sacrifice; he is privileged to hold the head of the sacrificial birds or animals. He also collects its blood for offering to the deities.

Except the *Chari-Deori*, some bearers are also engaged for assist the priests on the occasion of the ritual viz. '*Barik*' who announces to villagers of the ritual date one or two days before and also he assist the priests on the occasion of the ritual. Another duty of the *Barik* is to collect rice beer, rice, fowls etc. from the village household for the ritual and community feast. '*Bora*' employs special worker to the clean the compound of the temple and also supervises the public feast. The '*Ladani*' works as a cock man, he prepares the ritual foods. The '*Telia*' and '*Dupia*' are engaged to oil and incenses respectively at the time of ritual in the temple.

Mantras

The incantations or *mantras* (religious utterance) are very secrecy. These incantations or *mantras* are unwritten but have been handed down orally from one generation to next. Different incantations or *mantras* are chanting to appease different deities during the ritual period. The Deori do not have or follow any sacred text.

Religious beliefs and Chief Deities of Deoris

The Deori pray great reverence and homage to the village shrine and worship the deities according to their traditional calendar year. There are altogether fourteen principle deities in the shrine. The deities are resides in their respective houses according to the hierarchy. The houses are namely- *Kundimama-Yan or kundi-Kon*, *Chunketeri-Numali Kunwari-Yan*, and *Jakarua-Yan*.

Kundimama-Yan or kundi-Kon: It is the main house and situated on the eastern side of the *Midiku* compound and facing into the west direction which is the abode of five principal deities, viz. - (1) *Kundigira* (2) *Mama* (*Girachi)*, (3) *Aborchi,* (4) *Kundiyo-Pisa oaiguru Kundi* and (5) *Kunwar Kundi*.

Chunketeri-Numali Kunwari-Yan: It is an abode of *Chunketeri* (elder daughter of *Kundimama* and *Numali Kunwari*, (younger daughter of *Kundimama*) which is situated in the northern side facing into south direction. Sometimes *Chunketeri* is also referred to as *Tamreswari Mai* and she is the supreme deity and worshiped by the *Borganya* group.

Jakarua-Yan: *Jakarua-Yan* is the abode of seven deities; these are known among the Deoris as (1) *Gailurung Kundi* (*Baliababa*), (2) *Gailutang Kundi*, (3) *Disachi Kundi*, (4) *Korchi Raja Kundi*, (5) *Achipatala Duyan Kundi*, (6) Memeduriachi Kundi, and (7) *Talbal Kundi*. The deity *Gailurung Kundi* (*Baliababa*) is again worshiped by *Tengapaniyas* group.

It has been observed that the supreme deities' viz., *Kundimama* or *Gira-Girachi* (*Bura-Buri*), '*Pisa-Dema*' (*Baliababa*) and '*Pisachi Demasi*' (*Kechaikhati* or *Tamreswari*) worshiped by the *Dibangiyas*, *Tengapaniyas* and *Borganyas* respectively. Beside these chief deities of shrine, they have also a good number of household deities which have been propitiated by the villagers individually as well as collectively in their respective households or public places or shrine.

Procedure of propitiation at *Midiku* or *Deoshal*

All the priest of shrine first takes bath and put on new or cleaned sets of dresses before starting the ritual in the shrine. *Bordeori* sprinkle purified water from his jar to the assistant priests. He also sprinkles purified water to all the articles of the ritual. He spread some bananas leaves on the altar of the shrine for offering to appease the deities and distributes all the sprinkle purified water. After that he starts recites incantations in praise of the deities.

The *Midiku* or *Deoshal* and its rituals according to their annual calendar

The traditional religious beliefs and practices performed and observed throughout the year by publicly in their village sacred place. The rituals are performed at their sacred place among the Deoris of Dhemaji district and these are listed here in the month wise (Table 12.1).

All the mentioned forms of rituals have been performed almost by all the three section of the *Deoris* viz. *Dibangiyas, Tengapaniyas* and *Borgayans* for the welfare of the villagers, domesticated birds and animals and for better production of crops. But minor deviation in the propitiation system from village to village and section to section cannot be ruled out. Some additions as well as omissions in the propitiating systems in various rituals are also observed in the greater Deori society.

The shrine and its rituals

Among the Deoris, a new year is starts from the month of *Bohag* (Mid-April). *Bohagia Bisu puja, Raj-Kebang* or *Midi Deruruba* and *Metua* are three primary rituals performed in the month of *Bohag*.

Bohagia Bisu puja: *Bohagia Bisu puja* is a socio-religious festival which is performed on the first Wednesday of the month of *Bohag*. To perform this ritual, the priests take bath, put on new white set of dresses i.e. - *Iku* and *Cheleng*. The *Bordeori* (chief priest) first offers articles like '*Yam*' (a kind of food), '*Merku*' (fried rice), *Tiri* (bananas), *Guin-Pemchu* (betel vine leaves-areca nuts), *salita* (lamp wicks) etc. to each deity of the shrine. Then he invokes the deities and sacrifices chickens and offers their blood to each deity of the shrine. He also prays to the deities for welfare of the villagers and for successful celebration of the *Bisu* festival.

Raj-Kebang* or *Midi Deruruba: The *Raj-Kebang* ritual is also popularly known as *Midi Deruruba*. This ritual is considered as the most important and significant ritual among the Deori society. It has been observed that *Raj-Kebang* ritual is performed especially on Wednesday where sixty four numbers of deities are worshipped collectively in the month of *Bohag* (April-May) at the village sacred place. To perform this ritual a large number of articles are necessary and the required articles are collected from each family of the village without any consideration. The *Boedeori* (chief priest) offers lamp wicks as well as betel nut and betel vine leaves and large number of pigs, sixty chickens, ducks, pigeon, eggs etc. to the deities and pray them for the welfare of the villagers and for better production of crops. Later on, the sacrificial meats are cooked by *Ladani* (special cook) for feast which is consumed by the villagers as a token of social unity in the *Morong ghor*.

Metuwa* and *Bor Metua: *Metua* ritual is performed thrice in the month of *Bohag, Ahin* and *Phagun* annually. While Bormetua ritual is performed in the month of *Jeth*. They believed that people are suffers various illness and diseases along due to the change of seasons and climate in the month of *Bohag, Jeth, Ahin* and *Phagun. Metua* and *Bormetua* are performed during these months at the shrine to get rid of the physical calamities. To performed and worship *metua* ritual, one non-castrated he-goat (white or black colour) is necessary for sacrifice. But a large number of goats and fowls are essential for performing *Bormetua* ritual.

The priestly council along with their villagers performed in a systematic manner and accordingly sacrifices are made by *Bordeori* (chief priest) with the help of his assistance priests. The *Bordeori* uttered incantation in praise of Chief deity and their associates and prey for an auspicious summer as well as for good health and good production of crops. Later on, the sacrificial meat and rice are cooked by *Ladani* in the *Morong ghor* and consumed with *suje* (rice beer).

Sat Labiruba: This is the ritual performed during the month of *Ahar* (June-July) to purify the shrine polluted due to '*Sat*' (*Ambubachi*). It is believed that mother earth temporally polluted during the month *Ahar*. So, they performed this ritual to purify the shrine. This is comparable to the ritual impurity during *Ambubachi* of Hindu calendar. The functionaries prepare the offerings and later on, such sacrificial foods are consumed similarly.

Sauna Puja: This ritual is observed during the month of *Saun* (July-August) by the priestly council of the village. The priests first dig a ditch within the compound of the shrine and introduce a bunch of green bananas and cover the ditch with loose earth for ripening. It is observed that, the *Bordeori* offers '*Ewan*' such as bananas, areca-nuts, betel vine leaves, incenses etc. at the altar of the shrine. After that he sacrifices chickens and offers their blood to deity and praying for welfare of the villagers as well as for a successful harvesting of *Ahu* paddy. Later on, the villagers arranged a feast and consumed in the *Morong Ghor*.

Makan Chiban: *Makan Chiban* ritual is performed collectively at the shrine, especially by the priestly council in the month of *Bhado* (August/September). In this ritual seven pair fowls are collected from the villagers and these are sacrificed later. It is obligatory to perform *Makan Chiban* ritual before taking the newly harvested *Ahu* rice (*Ahu*-a kind of seasonal paddy) by all the general people of a village. Later on a community feast is organized at the *Morong* precincts with the meat of sacrificed fowls.

***Bhakat Makan hareba*:** The *Bhakat Makan* ritual is performed during the month '*Aghun*' (November/December) at the village sacred place in every year. After performing this ritual, each family of the village can consume the new *Sali* rice. It is the meant for offering the first fruit to the deities of the shrine. The chief priest *Bordeori* sacrifices chickens and offers their blood and decapitated heads to the deities of the shrine. He prays to the deities for the well-being of the villagers and successful harvesting. The cook prepares the meat of the sacrificed chickens and rice in the '*Morong*'. The villagers consume the feast with chicken, newly harvested rice and rice-beer.

***Maghio Bisu Puja*:** The Deori *Magh bihu* is a socio-religious festival and it start on the first Wednesday of *Magh* (January). It is their customary role that the villagers can celebrate the *Magh bisu* after performing the *Maghio Bisu Puja* at the village sacred place. To perform this ritual, the chief priest along with office bearers take bath, put on new or clean dresses i.e. - *Iku* and *Cheleng*. The *Bordeori* (chief priest) first offers articles like '*Yam*' (a kind of food), '*Merku*' (fried rice), *Tiri* (bananas), *Guin-Pemchu* (betel vine leaves-areca nuts), *salita* (lamp wicks) etc. to each deity of the sacred place. He invokes the deities and sacrifices chickens and offers their blood to each deity of the shrine. He also prays to the deities for welfare of the villagers. After performing the propitiation the villagers excluding womenfolk consume a feast with sacrificial meat of fowls, cooked rice and suje (rice beer) in the *Morong*.

Conclusion

The Deoris are very God fearing people. Therefore, the village sacred place and its rituals have been playing a significant role among their society. The Deoris have a deep faith in their traditional way of worshipping and perform each and every rituals very deeply and hearty of their respective deities. They have a good numbers of Gods and Goddess associated with their total way of life. The Deori society believes in appeasing the deities in order to maintain a good relationship with them. Among them, some of the significant rituals are associated with their shrine and these rituals are performed to appease the deities showing gratitude towards the almighty in order to gain their blessings in every steps of their life. These rituals are still maintaining as much as possible by all the Deori villages especially in the rural and peasant Deori society of Assam.

References

Deori. N. (2009) Deori Loka-Sanskritir Ruprekha, Kiran Prakashan, D.K. Complex Market, Dhemaji, First edition.

Deori, P. (2011) Deori Sanskritir Itihas, Kiran Prakashan, D.K. Complex Market, Dhemaji, First edition.

Deori, S. (2002) Religious Practices of the Deoris, Bina Library, Panbazar, Guwahati, First Edition.

Deori, S. (2015) Glossary of Deori Language (English-Assamese-Deori), Ajeevan Printers, Beltola, Guwahati-781028, Assam.

Deori, S. (2013) From Tradition to Transition: A glimpse of Deori in Assam, Assam Institute of Research for Tribal and Scheduled Caste, Jawaharnagar, Guwahati-22.

Kaman, R. (2013) Religious Beliefs of Tribes of Assam: with special emphasis on the Mishing Tribe", in Blue Ocean Research Journal (JBM & SSR) volume 2, No. 9, Sept, pp. 120-126.

Table 12.1: *Midiku* or *Deoshal* and its Rituals according to their Annual Calendar

Deori Calendar (Months)	*Assamese Equivalent months*	*English Equivalent Months*	*Ritual Performed*
Amechu	*Bohag*	Mid-April—Mid-May	*Bohagia Bisu puja, Raj-Kebang* or *Midi Deruruba', Metua*
Asandu	*Jeth*	Mid-May—Mid-June	*Bor Metua*
Ajuron	*Ahar*	Mid-June—Mid-July	*Sat Labiruba*
Agiring	*Saun*	Mid-July— Mid-Aug.	*Sauna Puja*
Asereng	*Bhado*	Mid-Aug—Mid-Sept.	*Makan Chiban*
Alibaji	*Ahin*	Mid-Sept—Mid-Oct.	*Metua*
Achutu	*Kati*	Mid-Oct—Mid-Nov.	Nil
Amili	*Aghun*	Mid-Nov.—Mid-Dec.	*Bhokat Moko Hareba,*
Akenma	*Push*	Mid-Dec.—Mid-Jan	Nil
Ahachu	*Magh*	Mid-Jan.—Mid-Feb.	*Maghio Bisu puja*
Abenma	*Phagun*	Mid-Feb.—Mid-March	*Metua*
Yajam	***Choat***	**Mid-March—Mid-April**	**Nil**

Chapter - 13

Ke-che-cham or Lord Shani Puja among the Hill Karbis of East Karbi Anglong District, Assam

— *Leena Laskar*

Ritual is a religious ceremony and social behaviour. In Anthropology, it is an action with intentional symbolic meaning undertaken for a specific cultural purpose, such as a rite of passages from childhood to adulthood.

Rituals may be prescribed by the traditions of a community, including a religious community. Rituals are characterized, but not defined, by formalism, traditionalism, invariance, rule-governance, sacral symbolism, and performance (Bell, Catherine. 1997, pp. 138-69). Rituals are a feature of all known human societies (Brown, Donald. 1991, pp. 139).

The Karbis are the principal indigenous community in the Karbi Anglong district of Assam. Besides Karbi Anglong district, the Karbis are also inhabit in the districts like Dima Hasao, Kamrup, Morigaon, Nagaon, Golaghat, Karimganj, Lakhimpur, Sonitpur and Biswanath Chariali of Assam. Apart from Assam they also inhabit in Papumpare district of Arunachal Pradesh, Jaintia Hills, Ri Bhoi and East Khasi hills districts of Meghalaya and Dimapur district of Nagaland. The Karbis belong to the Mongoloid group and linguistically they belong to the Tibeto-Burman group.

The Karbis are Mongoloid in origin and speak a local dialect 'Karbi', a Tibeto-Burmese, more particularly the Kuki-chin sub-group of languages. Opinions of learned and elderly persons and excerpts from folklores suggest that the Karbis have migrated from the Kuki-chin area in and around the Chindwin river valley in western Myanmar. The Karbis are basically hill tribe and their main agriculture is still the traditional *Jhum*, at least in the hills (Teron, Rabindra. Vol. 5(5), 2006, pp. 377-381).

Traditionally, Karbi religion is basically animistic. Nowadays, they are following Christianity and Hinduism too. Most of them still practice their traditional belief system or animism. The practitioners of traditional worship still believe in reincarnation and the immortality of the soul. They believe that all the diseases are associated with a presiding deity.

Chomkan is a death ritual among the Karbis. During *Chomkan* they have been erecting megaliths in the memory of dead ones. Among the Karbi people there is a folk belief that if they erect megaliths for their forefathers, then their forefathers protect them from the dangers in life, increase the happiness of the family and pardon the convicted one.

Chomkan is often celebrated for natural deaths. The *Chomkan* for unnatural deaths cannot be celebrated until and unless the *Ke-che-cham* or Lord Shani Puja is performed. *Ke-che-cham* is performed only for those who receive death unnaturally. *Ke-che-cham* is performed to purify the evil soul of unnatural deaths.

Objectives

The main objectives of the study were:

1. To document the existing culture.
2. To identify the associated socio-cultural practice.

Methodology

The study is an attempt to present such an interesting aspect to the readers especially through a succinct account of the study area. The study was conducted among the Hill Karbis of *Thero Bey* Village of East Karbi Anglong District, Assam in the month of February, 2018. The data was collected through primary data collection among the Karbi people of East Karbi Anglong District. Another methods used during data collection were Interview method, Observation method and Photographic method.

Study Area

The study was conducted in *Thero Bey* Village of East Karbi Anglong District, Assam. The village is named after the name of first *Gaonbura* or headman of the village. The inhabitants in the village are Hill Karbi community. It is located in the Howraghat sub-division of East Karbi

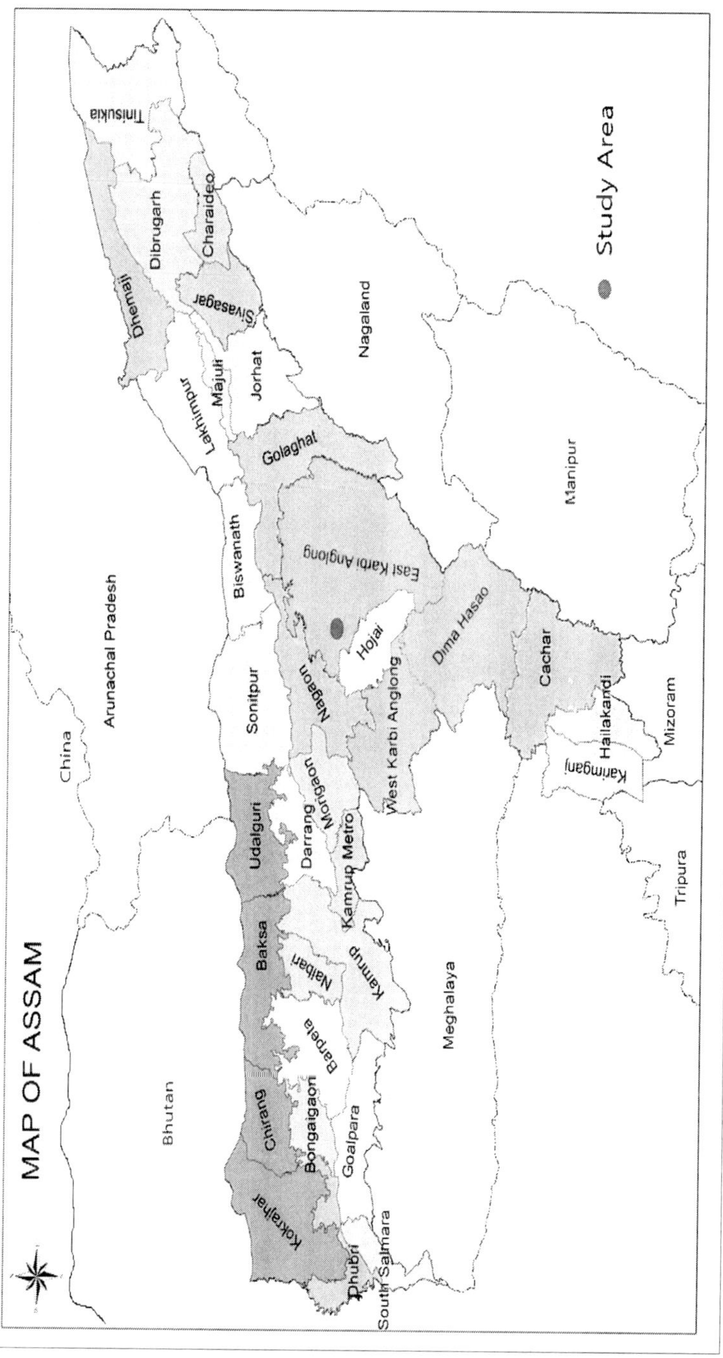

Map 13.1: Map of Assam.

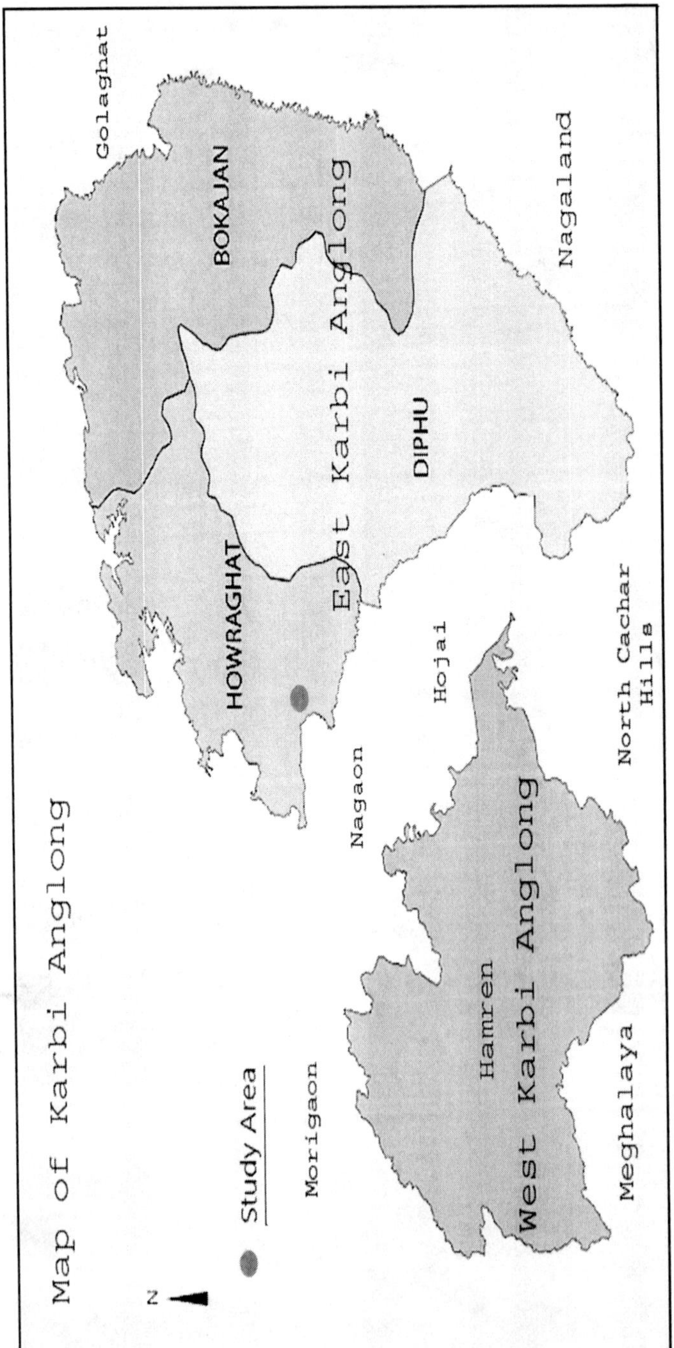

Map 13.2: Karbi Anglong district.

Anglong district. According to the villagers, it was established more than 140 years ago. It is about 70 kilometers away from the district headquarter Diphu. It consists of 185 households. Its area is about 3 sq. km. It is surrounded by *Hatipara Basti* and *Meteka* village in the East, paddy field, *Mistribali* village and *Jamuna* Gaon in the West, paddy field and *Dighali Ati Gaon* in the North, paddy field and *Panditghat* village in the South. The houses of the village are mostly of Assam type and some are bamboo houses with mud plaster. The river *Dighalpani* flows a bit far from the village. The climatic condition of the village is same as the hills district.

Due to variation in the topography, this hill zone experiences different climates in different parts. The winter commences from October and continues till February. During summer, the atmosphere becomes sultry. The temperature ranges from 6° to 12° in winter and 23° to 32° in summer. The average rainfall is about 2416 mm.

Results and discussion

Among the Karbis the death ritual is performed by the individual families. It is an inevitable part of their society. This death ritual is known as *Chomangkan* among them. It was known as the *Thi-karhi* in earlier days. However, the term *Chomangkan* is replaced by the term *Chomkan* at present days. Among them, there are three types of *Chomkan* namely *Kanphila-phila, Langtuk,* and *Harne*. Karbis have a folk belief that if they do not perform death ceremony or *Chomkan* for forefathers, then their forefathers would not get redemption from the world and they would have to rest at the *Jhum* or Slash and burn cultivation site or *Englong-Arit*. Only after the celebration of *Chomkan* the souls will get place in the heaven.

The death ceremony does not require any formal invitation to join and all are welcomed. It is the most expensive and widely celebrated socio-cultural ceremony of the Karbis, which lasts for four days and four nights. But some family celebrates this for five days and four nights. This ritual is performed for the soul of dead members for their peace and safe passage who has died recently or previously. Traditionally, the Karbi people use to burn corpse. They do not cremate the corpse just after the death, however they cremate after three days.

To perform *Chomkan* for unnaturally dying people first have to perform *Ke-che-cham*. They believe that people receive unnatural deaths due to wrath of Lord Shani. *Ke-che-cham* is performed only for those who receive death unnaturally because of suicide, murder, accident, wild animal bite etc. Usually, *Ke-che-cham* is performed at the River bank or Stream bank. It is important to mention that the place where *Ke-che-cham* is going to perform must have water source near. In some cases, when there is no River or Stream near, then the edge of the pond is selected as an alternative place to perform *Ke-che-cham*. The selected River, Stream and Pond should be a bit away from the village.

The clans and the families of the deceased go to the river bank to perform *Ke-che-cham* accompanied with the *Khakhre* or Priest, *Lunsepi* or weeper and the villagers. However, the villagers remain seated and take part in the feast which is the last part of the ritual. At the river bank the haystack idol making begins. They make this as the replica of unnaturally dead person. Only the Priest, *Lunsepi* and the families of the deceased can involve in idol making. When the idol making is over, the idol is laid down on a new bamboo bed. The idol is carried by four people to other bank of the river on their shoulder. In this way the idol crosses river accompanied with the Priest, *Lunsepi* and the families. This part of ritual by which the idol crosses the river is known as *Lang-kechang-lo* or crossing the water.

On the other bank of the river, the Priest chants some traditional Karbi incantation in order to call the evil soul of unnatural dead to take shelter in the idol. Then, they worship to purify the evil soul of the idol.

The idol is carried back from that bank of the river. After that the idol is carried to the burial ground or *Thiri* or *Tipit* and is burnt by one of his or her close relatives in the presence of Priest and villagers. Thus the ritual of *Ke-che-Cham* completes and provides clearance to perform *Chomkan*.

Lunsepi, also known as *Charhepi* is an experienced professional weeper. She plays key role in *Ke-che-cham* ritual, because the ritual progresses with her cries and songs. She sings and cries throughout the whole ritual. In her songs, she requests their beloved dead ones to take rebirth in their own clan. Only *Lunsepi* is allowed to sing melancholy songs called *Sarhe* during *Ke-che-cham* and *Chomkan*.

Associated ritual

Ke-che-cham is performed either on Tuesday or Saturday. During *Ke-che-cham*, Priest or *Khakhre* offers four chickens to their Gods. The Gods are *Hempho* or *Champutho*, *Mukrang*, *Rasingja* and *Hempho Chinthong*.

He also offers a hen and four chickens to their five clans. The five clans are namely *Ingti*, *Inghi*, *Terang*, *Timung* and *Teron*. Together, they are known as *Karbi Kurpho*.

Associated taboo

In the Karbi society, there are some taboos associated to *Ke-che-cham* ritual. Karbi clan system is composed of five major clans or *Kur*. Only the members of the same clan can participate during *Ke-che-cham* ritual. Even the cremation ground is also kept demarcated for each clan. *Kurkepon* is an important ritual of Karbis by which the non Karbis can be converted to Karbi tribe.

Conclusion

Ritual is a religious ceremony and social behaviour. Rituals are features of all known human societies. The Karbi religion is basically animistic. Nowadays, they are following Christianity and Hinduism too. Most of them still practice their traditional belief system or animism. Death ritual is known as *Chomkan* among Karbis. *Chomkan* is often celebrated for natural deaths. The *Chomkan* for unnatural deaths cannot be celebrated until and unless the *Ke-che-cham* or Lord Shani Puja is performed. *Ke-che-cham* is performed only for those who receive death unnaturally. *Ke-che-cham* is performed to purify the evil soul of unnatural deaths.

From the study it has been found that the *Ke-che-cham* ritual is an inevitable part of Karbi society. *Ke-che-cham* is performed either on Tuesday or Saturday. *Lunsepi* plays key role in *Ke-che-cham* ritual, because the ritual progresses with her cries and songs. She sings and cries throughout the whole ritual. In her songs, she requests their beloved dead ones to take rebirth in their own clan.

In the Karbi society, there are some taboos associated to *Ke-che-cham* ritual. Karbi clan system is composed of five major clans or *Kur*. Only the members of the same clan can participate during *Ke-che-cham* ritual. Even the cremation ground is also kept demarcated for each clan.

Acknowledgement

It is an immense privilege for me to convey my thanks to those who helped me during the course of research work. My special thanks goes to the people of *Thero Bey* village and the family who performed this ritual for their endless help, co-operation and warm hospitality, without which my mission would not have been possible. Last but not the least I take this opportunity to thank my parents for their financial help and co-operation.

References

Bell, Catherine. 1997. *Ritual: Perspectives and Dimensions*. New York: Oxford University Press.

Brown, Donald. 1991. *Human Universals*. United States: McGraw Hill.

Government of Assam, Karbi Anglong. Government of *Assam*, Retrieved 18 September, 2019.

Teron, Robindra. 2006. *Hor, the traditional alcoholic beverage of Karbi tribe in Assam*. Natural Product Radiance,Vol. 5(5).

Plate 13.1: A view of* Ke-che-Cham *or Lord Shani Puja.

Plate 13.2:* Hor-Lang *or Rice Beer,* Arak *or local liquor and food cooked in bamboo tubes.

Plate 13.3: Sacrificed Piglet Head.

Plate 13.4: The River Bank where Ritual was performed.

Plate 13.5: Bamboo bed for carrying Haystack Idol.

Plate 13.6: Carrying Haystack Idol to burial ground.

Plate 13.7: Burning Haystack Idol.

Plate 13.8: Preparing food for feast.

Plate 13.9: Preparing food for feast.

Plate 13.10: The Family of the Deceased.

Plate 13.11: The Priest and the Weeper.

Chapter - 14

Role of Ethno-Medicine in the Provision of Primary Health Care among the Ahoms of Chiring Chuk Village of Lakhimpur District, Assam

— *Pallabi Gogoi*

Indigenous Knowledge can be broadly defined as the knowledge that an indigenous community accumulate over generations of living in a particular environment. This definition encompasses all forms of knowledge like technologies, skills, practices and beliefs that enable the community to achieve stable livelihoods in their environment. The indigenous communities have always generated, refined and passed the knowledge from generation to generation. Such "traditional knowledge" is an important part of their cultural identity.

Traditional medicine or ethno medicine refers to the procedure of protecting and restoring health that existed before the existence of modern medicine. The name traditional implies the approaches to health belong to the traditions of indigenous people, which have been handed down from generation to generation. Traditional knowledge includes mental inventories of local biological resources, animal breeds, and local plant, crop and tree species. Traditional knowledge is dynamic by nature and includes experimentation in the integration of new plant or tree species into existing farming systems or a traditional healer's tests of new plant medicines. The term "traditional" used in describing this knowledge does not imply that this knowledge is old or Non-technical by nature, but is rather "tradition based". It is "traditional" because it is created in a manner that reflects the traditions of the communities, therefore not relating to the nature of the knowledge itself, but to the way in which that knowledge is created and preserved. Thus, traditional knowledge is collective by nature and is often considered the property of the entire community, and not belonging to any single individual within the community.

The present paper deals with the role of ethno medicine among the Ahoms of Chiring chuk village of Lakhimpur district, Assam. In Chiring Chuk village, the villagers have good knowledge of common diseases and their remedial response in the form of herbs, roots, and shoots of plants. They are confident to treat the patients suffering from fever, cold, cough, headache, stomach disorder, injuries, etc. Beliefs in Mantras are important aspects of traditional health care system of the village. When somebody fall in ill which is not cure by the doctor then they contacts the *Bej* (medicine men) for help. He diagnoses the cause of the illness through divination. At the time of divination he invokes the dead ancestors and gods, through appropriate spells and incantations.

Objectives

In the Study an attempt has been made to understand the socio-cultural dimension of the health as well as the natural and extent of interaction between the traditional health practices and the modern medical system. The main objective of this paper is to get an idea about the traditional preventive and curative health measures prevalent among the people of that study area.

Methodology

Various method and technique were applied depending on the nature of enquiry. The relevant data for this study were collected from Chuuring chuk village of Lakhimpur district of Assam. Besides the surveys, the other method and technique in the research work are observation, interviews, collection of concrete case and informal discussion, group discussion etc. Based on this specific nature of data some relevant persons and sources were also contacted. To acquire data on their traditional medicare system extensive interviews and observation were undertaken. Selection of informant was the most important part of field investigation. To get information regarding the uses of different plants, personal interviews with the village people like herbal healers, elderly persons, housewives, etc., were made. Two local medicine men of that locality are structurally interviewed. For verification of information, 5 to 7 users are interviewed. Photographs of few plant species had also been taken during field investigation.

Results and discussion

Every human community has it owns nation regarding health and health seeking behavior which is referred to as health culture. The Ahoms of Chiring chuk village practiced both modern and indigenous health care systems. But there is a common belief that they are inclined towards traditional medical system. This inclination, it is said, is existent even in the presence of modern medical facilities. Among the people of that area have been found to suffer from disease like dysentery, diarrhea, cholera, general weakness, chicken pox, malaria, jaundice, paralysis, pneumonia, gastric, indigestion and vomiting, etc.

The villagers have their indigenous method of treatment of different kinds of disease with the help of local herbal medicines. The earliest mention of use of medicinal plant is found in "Rigveda", the holy Hindu epic, which happens to be the oldest Indian scripture. The people of the village use and gives valuable position to the flora and fauna for their basic needs, sustenance and livelihood.

In the Chiring Chuk village there is one herbal medicine man so, the people relies on him who gives his services to the entire village and also the other neighboring villages. While curing the patient he does not demand any money. But after gives his best, whatever is provide by the affected patient he received. He considered this expertise as a gift of the almighty as well as their forehead. Some of the disease that is cured by herbal medicine is as follow:

Cough: To get reliefs from cough, honey (*Mou)* is used extensively. It is said to be more useful in the cough of the babies and the minors. The adult take it in the form of a paste made out of ginger (*Ada*) and Basil leaves (*Tulokhi*).

Fever: In common fever, water boiled with coriander seeds or Coriandrum sativum (*dhania*) is taken as a medicine for two or three times a day for one to three days. They also used mustered oil (*horiyoh tel*) with garlic (*naharu*) and massage it on the feet and body.

Diarrhea: Intake of lemon juices in believed to bring relief from diarrhea. The wild herbs locally known as *Durun-bon (Leucas aspera)*, *Mani-muni (centella asiatica)* and *Mosundari (Houttunia cordata)* are also taken as leafy vegetables for the purpose. Some people also used young shoot of *Joba* or china rose (*Hibicus rosa-sinensis*) and guava or *modhuri aam (Psidium guajava)* as a medicine for diarrhea.

Pneumonia: Medicine for the disease is prepared from by grinding the *leta guti (Caesalpinia bonducella)* and *jaluk (Piper nigrum)* is mixed with a glass of warm water along with pinch of salt which should be take in empty stomach for cure.

Lever Disorder: Pain in the upper portion of the stomach along with digestive complaints is considered to be the symptoms of liver disorder. The people used wild herbs such as *manimuni or centella asiatica* and *durum-ban or Leucas aspera*. The continuous use for these herbs at least once a day for a week is required to get positive result.

Gastric: The medicine is prepared from particular varieties of *halodhi* or turmeric (*Curcuma longa)*, *ada* or ginger *(Zingiber officinale)*, clove or *laung* (*Syzygium aromaticum)* and bay leaf or *tejpat (Laurus nobilis)*. These are pounded into a paste from which pills are made. One or two pills are administrated early morning in empty stomach. The course needs to be continued for one week.

Menstrual disorder: The abnormalities in menstrual discharge of the females is also treated by some herbal medicinal plant like *jetuka (Lawsonia intermis), keharaj (Eclipta prostrate), manimuni (centella asiatica , etc.* to be mixed to make a juice which should take at the time of Menstruation time.

Urine trouble: Urinal trouble is common health problem in the village. The ailment is cured by drinking juice extracted from the leaves of *dupor tenga (Bryophyllum pinnatum)*.

Vomiting: To prevent from vomiting the people generally use ginger or *ada* (*Zingiber officinale)* and leaves of lemon (*Citrus limon)*.

Piles: Medicine for the disease is prepared by consumes tablet from *bon jaluk (Oldenlandia diffusa), huhwani, kheharaj,* and *manimoni,* etc which take with empty stomach for three days. Moreover for curing piles, the worm cast is dried up and mixed with water. The water is administered to the patient once a day in empty stomach and also used to eat papaya regularly one to two week.

Inadequate breast milk: A lactating mother who does not have sufficient breast milk to feed her baby, then the mother is given the medicine prepared from the barks of jackfruit tree and black pepper. These ingredients are grinded and the paste in administered to the mother twice a day.

Jaundice: Jaundice is another acute health problem. The basic symptom is yellowish pigmentation of the skin. In this regards intake of sugarcane juice is better for recovery of the patient. Again the juice from the medicine plant like *gorukhia* or mock strawberry (*Duchesenea indica)* and the insect that found in only banana trees is used to grinding and mixed with the juice which should take once in empty stomach in morning. Again this medicine is also prepared by consume juice from *gorukhia* which mixed with curd and take with empty stomach for cure.

Headache: Herbal medicine for headache is prepared from *Dorunban* (lucas liniflia) and a wild vegetable locally known as *tengashitenga* (oxalis cornicalata) all these ingredients are pounded and juice applied at the nose and also used to paste of coconut, Dalseni and sun flower.

Eyes infection: To get relief from the eye problem, a kind of wild herbs known as *Konaihimola* (Commelina diffusa) should apply as an eye drops.

Facture: The gum of *Dimoru (Ficus glomeratal* is applied in the affected area and then banded till 3-7 days.

Tonsil: It is treated with local medicine prepared by Jaluk (black pepper) and bark of kathana (ervatamia coronaria) all these ingredients are pounded and then boiled in water to get the extract. A cup of extract is administered after the dinner for two or three days to the patient.

Joint Pain: If a person suffers from joint pain, treated with traditional medicine leaf of harjora lata (cissus quadrangular) and a particular variety of kulahaladhi (turmeric), garlic, tulshi (*Ocymum santum)* all these ingredients are grind to make a paste and apply in perspective areas for a week.

Stomach pain: The stomach pain is treated by locally available medicine prepared by bark of *aam* or mango *(Mengafira indica)*, *kal* or banana (*Musa)* and barck of a*mara* or hog-plum tree *(Spondias mombin)*. All these items are pounded and then administered in empty to the patient for a week or so.

High blood pressure: The local medicine man prepared medicine for high blood pressure from the root of *Satmul* (Asparagus raecmosus) and the root of *tamul gas* (bettle nut tree), *Debodaru* tree (a kind of pine tree). The ingredients are pounded and a few tablets are prepared and administered twice daily for three five days to the patient and regularly used to *nefafu* leaf (calorodendro).

Ear pain: The local medicine man prepares for ear pain using a plant known as *Ramtulokhi*, *Dhatura* and sesame oil. The liquid extract of the leaf of this plant is given as ear drop against ear pain, and sajina leaf (morninga pterygosperman) liquid is given as ear drop.

Rickets: When a child suffer from ricket disease, then local medicine man prepare medicine for *Ashwa gandha* (*withania somifera*) power and cow's milk or ghee boiled in water. The milk paste containing the extracts of ingredients is only orally administered to the child one to two week and so.

Socio-religious practices

There are some symptoms (via, pain in the neck region, one-sided headache, sudden pain in the stomach, pox of various types, paralysis, miscarriage, indigestion and vomiting, etc) that are believed to be caused either by wrath of some deity or due to the influence of some evil spirit and evil eyes. These diseases are treated by socio-religious method.

Pox (*aie*): Pox is believed to be act by deity *aie*. To get relief from the suffering the individuals should be worshipped and appeased. Here the medicine man performs a vital role by doing some rituals on the name of deity. A pair of betel nut is offered to appease the deity. After cure the affected family member offer a small feast to the neighbor which contain, sweet rice made of milk, fruits, etc.

Influence of evil eyes (*mukh-loga*): There is belief among the people that some individuals have some evil powers. Hence, if he or she watches someone with evil motives, it may cause illness. Generally, the minors and the beautiful girls easily become the victims of such persons. This is popularly known as evil eyes (*mukh-loga*). Generally, it causes indigestion, diarrhoea, fever and vomiting, etc. So in this regards the medicine man use betel leaf which ripped with mustard oil and chants some mantras and rubbed the betel leaf all over the body of the affected person and then the leave is to be burned to get relief.

One sided headache (*huruj kopali*): The people have the belief that half headache is caused due to the sun deity (*donyiaie*). But, the nature of the fault that results in his ailment is not known to them. They considered that the fault may be done ignorantly by them during their day to day life that makes the deity annoyed. They preferably consult the socio-religious or magical practitioner *(bej)* for curative measure. The medicine man usually chants some mantras on a small quantity of water and provides the patient for taking at regular interval for a specific period.

Conclusion

The findings of the present populations under study indicate that the Ahom of that study area have deep faith on ethno-medicine. They seem to depend upon the plants for curing various diseases including stomach pain, liver disease, menstruation troubles, etc. Apart from the modern health care system, the Ahoms under investigation have their own traditional measures with regard to the health care. The traditional Medicare system of the people broadly belongs to two types, namely, Magico-religious and Herbal medicines. As matter of fact, in their traditional system, they take not only to curative measure but also to preventive health care measure. The life histories of the traditional medicine man have also incorporated for a relative understanding of the system. Spreading and preserving this knowledge on medicinal plant and their use become important for human existence and welfare. Thus a detailed scientific study is necessary.

References

Chopra, R.N., Nayar, S.L and Chopra, I.C., 1956, *Glossary of Medicinal Plants of India*. CSIR, New Delhi

Jain,S.K.1998, *Tribal Medicine*, Naya Prokash, Calcutta

Kar, R.K. 1993, Health behaviour among the tribes of North East India: A *Profile Journal of Indian Anthropological Society*, Calcutta 28(2). pp. 156-164

Valorie, A. Crooks and Gavin. J. Andrews, 2009, *Primary health care: People Practices, Place* Ashgate Publication Limited

Winkelman Michael, 2009 *Culture and Health, Appling Medical Anthropology,* U.S.A. John Wiley and Son Publication

Yesudian, C.A.K. 1991, "Introduction *in Primary Health Care"*, Edited by C.A.K, Yesudian Bombay: Tata Institute of Social Science. pp. 1-10

Zaman, A, 2009, *Continuity of Traditional Health Care System among the Rural Tiwas of Assam, in the journal of Politics, Dibrugarh University,* Vol: 14:92-102

Table 14.1: Medicinal plants used by the Ahoms of Chiring Chuk Village

Sl. No.	*Local Name*	*Scientific Name*	*Part Used*	*Ailments*
1.	Ada	Zinziber officinal	Rhizome	Cough
2.	Bor manimoni	Centella Asiatic	Whole plant	Stomach disorder
3.	Bikholyakoroni	Helitropium indicum	Leaf	Septic
4.	Dimoru	Ficus glomerata	Gum	Fracture
5.	Dupor –tenga	Bryophyllum pinnatum	Leaf	Urinary trouble
6.	Drun-bon	Leucas Linifolia	Leaf	Stomach pain and indigestion
7.	Gorukhia	Duchesenea indica	Leaf	Jaundice
8.	Halodi	Curcuma longa	Rhizome	Gastric
9.	Jaluk	Piper nigram	Seeds	Pneumonia
10.	Konaihimala	Commelina diffusa	Gum	Eye infection (asina)
11.	Keheraj	Eclipta prostate	Leaf	Eye injuries
12.	Leta guti	Caesalpinia bonducella	Fruits	Cough & Pneumonia
13.	Modhuleng	Polygonum Chinese	Leaf	Toothache
14.	Paan	Piper betel	Leaf	Pneumonia
15.	Sirata	Andrographis paniculata	Leaf	Pneumonia
16.	Tulsi	Ocymum santum	Leaf	Cough
17.	Tubuki lota	Stephania elegans	Leaf	Menstrual pain

Chapter - 15

Ancestor Worship among Ahom Community

— Prasanna Bharali

The Ahom is the descendants of the ethnic Tai people who accompanied a Tai prince, Sukaphaa, in his migration from what is now the frontier regions between Myanmar and Yunnan Province in southwest China into the Brahmaputra valley in 1228. Sukaphaa and his followers established the Ahom kingdom(1228–1826), which controlled the Bramhaputra Valley and the territory of modern Assam until the British gained control of the region through the Treaty of Yandabo after their 1826 victory in the First Anglo-Burmese War. In the early days of the Ahom kingdom, although the Ahom made up a relatively small portion of the kingdom's population, they maintained their original Tai language and practiced their traditional religion. Over time however, the kingdom adopted the lingua-franca of the region the Assamese language as their mother tongue, and the royal court eventually converted to the dominant local religion, Hinduism.

The modern Ahom people and their culture are a syncretism of their original Tai culture and the cultures they interacted with in Assam. Some local ethnic groups, including the Tibeto-Burman speaking Borahi, were completely subsumed into the Ahom community, while members of other communities, based on their allegiance to the Ahom kingdom or the usefulness of their talents, were accepted as Ahom. Currently, they represent the largest Tai group in India, with a population of nearly 4 million in Assam, and are the majority ethnic group in the North Bank and Upper Assam Division.

The name "Ahom" is an exonym applied by local Tibeto-Burman groups to the Ahoms. In the early 13th century, *Mong Mao* was a small kingdom of Tai people, related to the Shan, along the borders of Myanmar and Yunnan Province, China. In 1228, the *Mong Mao* prince Chaolung Sukaphaa began a journey to the Brahmaputra Valley with about 9000 followers, mostly men. He crossed the Patkai Hills and reached the Brahmaputra valley in 1228. He moved from place to place, searching for a seat. He made peace with the Borahi and Moran, and his depleted followers married into the. The Borahis, a Tibeto-Burman people, were subsumed into the Ahom fold, though the Moran maintained their independent ethnicity. Sukaphaa established his capital at Charaideo near present-day Sivasagar in 1253 and began the task of state formation.

The Ahom kingdom then consolidated its power, building their kingdom for the next 600 years. The first major expansion weakened the dominant power in the Bramhaputra valley, the Chtiya kingdom, which was partially annexed in 1524 under King Suhungmung. The conquest reflected changing cultural norms within the Ahom kingdom. Suhungmung was also the first Ahom king to adopt a Hindu name: 'Swarga Narayan', and he and his successors were named 'Swargadeo,' meaning 'Lord of Heaven in Assamese, and were crowned in the Singarigharutha ceremony. In 1536, they took over the Kachari capital of Dimapur, thus giving them control of all of present-day eastern Assam. The late 17th century saw another expansion of Ahom territory. After the 1682 Battle of Itakhuli, that marked the end of the Ahom-Mughal conflicts, much of the control of Koch Hajo fell into the hands of the Ahoms. By bringing the various indigenous Assamese ethnic groups and regions under one ruler and one governing polity the Ahoms are considered the architects of modern Assam.

However, the Ahoms gradually mixed with various other indigenous Assamese communities. Their rulers converted to Hinduism and spoke the dominant local language of the region, Assamese, instead of their native Ahom language.

In 1769, various marginalized ethnic groups like the Moran, Motok, Bodo, Keot (Kaibarta) etc who were resentful of the Paik labor system and the persecution of followers of Mahapuruxiya Dharma, launched the Moamoria rebellion against the Ahom kingdom, and from 1788 to 1794, the rebels took over and administered the Ahom capital of Rangpur (now Sivasagar). It was only with the help of the East India Companythat the Ahom king was able to take back his capital and defeat the rebels in 1805. The Moamoria rebellion left Ahom severely weakened and vulnerable to invasions, and due to the rebellion, the Ahom king moved the capital from Rangpur to Jorhat in 1794. In the first part of the 19th century, the Burmese army invaded the Ahom kingdom, took over the capital and set up a puppet Ahom king. The Burmese were defeated by the British in the First Anglo-Burmese War resulting in the Treaty of Yandabo in 1826, which paved the way for the British to convert the Ahom kingdom into a principality, marking the end of the Ahom rule. Assam was then annexed by British India as part of the Bengal Presidency, and would later become a state as the Ahom were gradually subsumed by the dominant Assamese culture.

Ancestor worship is often referred to as the ancestral cult, namely, a set of religious beliefs and ritual practices that commemorates the continued existence of the deceased ancestor beyond death. The rites of this cult are meant to cater to the needs of the diseased in the afterlife. The beliefs of this cult centre on the ability of the dead to protect kinsmen in return for worship from them. Reciprocity between the living and the dead is the key to ancestor worship (Freud 1950; Opler 1936; Gough 1958; Fortes 1965).

Two forms of ancestor worship can be identified in the anthropological literature. One is a domestic cult, which is observed by the family in dedication to its recent ancestors rather than remote ones. The other is observed by the descent group in dedication to its common ancestors in the remote past. As a cult of the descent group, ancestor worship functions to prescribe the principle of rights and obligations and the rules of conduct for the living, who form a property-holding corporate group. Not only are these rules and principles institutionalized in social structure and organization, but they also regulate individual access to the benefits of the corporate property. In short, they serve to keep up the social relations of the living world. Members of the descent group venerate their common ancestry communally, in addition to individual observance of ancestor worship as a domestic cult.

Ancestor worship, or "the worship of the Manes," is no ordinary cult of the dead. It is, for example, not applicable to children who die young or to dead elders who belong to a different kin group, because neither qualifies as ancestors. Demonstrative ancestry is the litmus test for such worship. The deceased must stand in a line of identified human progenitors to the living in order to receive ancestor worship from them. It follows that the mythical beings or animals revered as totemic forebears by the aboriginal clans in Australia are not receivers of "ancestor worship" in the proper sense of the term (Fortes, 1949).

The concept of ancestor becomes more complicated when parenthood is not based on natural conception and gestation (Baker, 1979). In adoptions, ancestor hood is created by jural action where natural offspring are lacking. Chinese parents, for example, have the right to manipulate the filiations of their children jurally and put them up for adoption by either partner's patrilineage in case its continuity of succession and inheritance is tenuous or in danger of a breakdown. It enables close relatives without biological heirs to receive ancestor worship after death and avoid becoming "orphaned ghosts" that would harass the living. In all adoptions, ancestor worship is made to continue on the jural manipulation of filiations.

Ancestor worship

The Tai Ahom worships their deceased forefathers as they are the guardian deities of the house holders. They believe that their ancestors must be duly worshipped so that they being satisfied and keep them safe. There is a saying among them that "Neither the wall nor the roof, no other gods can protect the house holders, if the god of the household do not. Neither the serpent bites, nor the tiger eats, even the god of death is afraid when the household's dead protect,"

The Tai Ahoms worship their ancestors within the family as well as in community. The Tai Ahom families worship their dead ancestors in the occasion of marriages; festivals like Bihu, before and after harvesting, feast of new paddy, birth and death ceremonies etc.

For the purpose of the present study I selected Na-pam village for collecting data, as the village have majority of Ahom families. The Ahom people of the Na-pam village are found in two different group and they follow their own way of ancestor worship. They have their own constitution, and each group follow the constitution during every ritual. The present study found two groups of Ahom people and these were:

1. *The Kal-Honghoti Ahom.*
2. *The Phualung Ahom.*

Anestor worship among Kal-Honghoti group

The Na-pam village has twenty three family of Ahom which follow the Kal-honghoti rule of Ahom community. The Kal-honghoti is an Ahom organization which is formed in the year of 2005 to maintain the tie between the Ahom people of Assam. The organization has their own constitution and all the member of the organization follow all the rules and regulation of the constitution.

The Kal-honghoti included family of Napam village has been following the way of ancestor worship as per the constitution of Kal-honghoti.

The particular group of Ahom doesn't have any separate language for communication among themselves. They use the Assamese language as the main communication language. In earlier days they have the Tai language but in present scenario they do not know to speak or write the Tai language.

The Kal-honghoti Ahom has many rituals among themselves and they practicing it in both home and community level. They follow the Assamese calendar year for fixing the date of their rituals. They have many rituals relating to paddy field and ancestor worship.

Rituals at family level

The *Kal-honghoti* group of Ahom worships their ancestor both in community and family level. In family based ancestor worship rituals they worship their own grandparents or their parents, recent death ancestor etc. They follow the Assamese calendar year for fixing the date for the rituals. In the Na-pam village I have found four number of family practicing ancestor worship ritual. Among these four rituals, three have been practicing during the three Assamese main festivals; the *Bihu*. And another one is practice in any date of the year, which is practice once in a year and this is mandatory to every family.

Among the *Kal-honghoti* Ahom they have believe that if they fail to practice the worship rituals then the ancestor will come to their dream and something will happen wrong to their family.

The following are the rituals followed by the *Kal-honghoti* Ahom in their family:

1. Bihu: (a) *Bohag Bihu* Rituals
   (b) *Kati Bihu* Rituals
   (c) *Magh Bihu* Ritual
2. *Bosorekiya* (Yearly ritual)

Ancestor worship during bihu

The Assam has three main *Bihu* festivals which are namely

1. *Bohag Bihu* (During the month of April)
2. *Kati Bihu* (During the month of October)
3. *Magh Bihu* (During the month of January)

Bohag is the first month of Assamese calendar and it is observed in the month of April. As the first month of a year the Ahom people worship their ancestor to get *Ashirbad* (blessings) from their ancestor for wellbeing and peace of their family. *Bohag* is also related to the farmer. From the month of *Bohag* the farmer start ploughing their farm for cropping seeds. They take blessings from their ancestor for the wellbeing of their crops.

Kati is the second festivals of Assamese calendar. The festivals observed during the month of October of English calendar. During the month of *Kati* the crops starts flowering and for the well harvesting of crops the people of Assam use to pray to the god. The Ahom people also worship their ancestors during the *Kati Bihu* as they believe that the ancestor will protect their farm from the bad evils.

Magh is the third and the last *Bihu* festival of Assam. This festival is observed in the month of January of English calendar. The Assamese people find this *Bihu* as the most wealthy festivals of Assam, because this festivals is start just after the completion of cutting the harvested crops from the farming field. The Ahom people use to make ***Haj*** (rice beer) from the newly harvested rice. The worship of ancestor during *Magh Bihu* is completely base on new crops. The Ahom give the rice beer to their ancestor by practicing ritual from the newly harvested rice. They thought their ancestors as their main roof of their family and so they give the first crops to the ancestor.

Process of the ritual

The process of the ancestor worship rituals during *Bihu* is same in all the three *Bihu*. The process of the ritual is start by the invitation process. The family members invite the local Ahom people of their own group to participate in the ritual. A ***Hadhu*** (the priest) is the key person without whom the rituals can't be practice.

At first the priest (*Sadhu*) takes his seat in the dice and surrounding the priest two man (*Parishad*) takes their seat. Then the other people will seat in the dice after the priest. The priest lighting the lamp (a lamp made by pottery) of mustered oil by praying to the god. Thereafter two or three man takes permission from the priest to cook the pork/ duck/ fish for the rituals. After completion of the cooking meat or fish (cooked meat or fish is called as ***Kach*** within the *Kal-honghoti* Ahom group) the family member will pray in the dice and the priest will give blessings to them.

Then the priest will make two *Thali* (*Haj* and *Kach* together) one for the ancestor and one for the priest. Then the women (women are called as ***Radha*** during the ritual) provide *Thali* to the priest by singing some traditional songs. Thereafter they provide *Thali* to the ***Parishad*** by singing different song. Here, the women play a significant role in providing *Thali* and singing traditional songs. Without women the rituals is not possible. After giving *Haj* (rice beer) to the *Hadhu* and the *Parishad* the women distributed *Thali* (*Haj* and *Kach* together called *Thali*) to other present individual (both men and women).

The process of providing *Haj* to *Hadhu*, *Parishad* and other people are repeated for three times as same as earlier. After third time distribution and finishing of the *Thali* the rituals supposed to be finish. After finishing of the *Thali* the family members takes *Ashirbad* (blessings) from the priest for the final time and this is the end of the ritual.

Goods used in rituals

The Kal-honghoti Ahom people used the following goods during the rituals, Meat/ Fish, *Haj* (rice beer), Pot lamp, Banana leaves, Vegetables, Dish of bronze, etc.

***Bosorekiya* (Yearly rituals):** The Kal-honghoti Ahom people practice a yearly ancestor worship ritual in their home for their own family ancestor in a particular day. The family fix the month of the rituals by relating to their ancestors death month. They worship their all ancestor of their own family including recent dead and early dead together in a day. They use to sacrifice as much as they can as they think *Bosorekia* is the main ritual for them. They believe that their ancestor observing them from the haven and protecting them from the bad spirits. They thought that if they fail to do the ritual then the ancestor will punish them and will not save them from the bad ones.

Process

The process of the rituals is almost same with the rituals practiced in the Bihu. Here they use three *Thali* (dish of rice beer with cooked meat/fish) for the rituals when they use only two *Thali* in the Bihu rituals. Here they use two *Thali* for the ancestor and one *Thali* for the Priest. Otherwise everything is same as the rituals of *Bihu*. Women play a significant role in this festival. Here they use materials like Meat/fish, rice beer, vegetables, banana leaves, bowl of bronze, dish of bronze, pottery lamp etc.

Songs sung during ancestor worship rituals

The *Kal-honghoti* group oh Ahom people use Assamese language for singing as they don't have any separate language. The following songs are sings during their rituals......

In bihu

When lighting the lamp

Kikoyo Tori Naame Aate Nijor Swamii""

Devata Purushe Koroni Namiche Parim Kimote Pat.........""""

(hey lord the priest preparing seat for you.)

When preparing *Thal*

Guru Churamonii Hridoyore Romonii...

Bhokot Botshol Horii..

Apunar Choronot Amii Chindii..

Adoror Mamoni Korii...

(here they recognize their ancestor as the heart beat and the other men as their body.)

When women take blessing from the priest

Heii Purna Swamii Amihe Dukanii

Purayuu Monore Kam...

Boikunthore Poraa Dhare Boi Ahise

Iitu Rokh Guno Naam.......

(hey lord please fill my desire, the songs I m singing is coming from the heaven.)

In Bosorekia

In bosorekia the other songs is same but they use different song when the priest lighting the lamp. The song is recites:

Sankardev Karanii Madhab Dev Koronii
Gopal Dev Dharmar Huut......
Krishna dev Atile Brishnu dev Bandhile
Jaduu dev Koronii Guut......

(here they recognize Sankardev and Madhabdev as the key of work and the Gopaldev as the key of religion.).

Worship of ancestor among *Phualung* Ahom

The village has only five family of *Phualung* Ahom which are mixed with other community people as their neighbour. They follow their traditional way of doing rituals which were followed by their ancient generation. These are the only group of Ahom people who use their ancient language and scripture for doing rituals among themselves. They have separate language called Tai language, but as influence of other community and as the requirement of communication with others they use Assamese language as their medium of communication language. As a result the new generation of the *Phualung* group do not know to write or speak their language. Only some priest or the priest family can read or write the Tai language. On the occasion of some rituals the priests use the original Tai language.

The *Phualung* group not only worship their own family ancestor but they also worship their community ancestors with great devotion. They have many ancestor worship rituals in which some are practiced for their own family ancestor and some are practiced for the whole community ancestors i.e., the Kings, Warrior etc., in many season.

Household level rituals

According to the belief of Ahom, there is the hierarchy of the spirit after death i.e. Dam and Phi. After death a man becomes a *"Dam",* he continues to exist and protect the living family members from all evils. In this period he is called "god of the home". After a period of time when the duty as Dam is over then he rises above Dam to be a *"Phi"*. The Phi has a duty as a god of the society. He is now "a society god" and cuts off all relations with his family. When the deity as a Phi is over then he gets reconciled into *"Kung Ing Ka Phra"* (Creator God).

The Tai Ahoms believe that after death a person becomes a Dam Phi, or a god, who goes to reside in the heaven in the same way as he was in his earthly life. He is worshipped and propitiated as a god with the offerings made by the descendants but not as a revengeful ghost.

The Tai Ahoms offer their first seasonal crops, vegetables and fruits to the ancestors and they could take these only after offering these to their ancestor gods. The priestly families worship their ancestors in a very clear way making different grades to each kind of Dam. These are:

1. *Ghai Dam*,
2. *Chi Ren Dam*,
3. *Na Dam* and
4. *Jokorua Dam*.

Ghai Dam: 'Ghai' means 'main' and 'Dam' means 'Dead', hence *Ghai Dam* means dead grandparents of the living householder. The family worship the main ancestor of their family in their home by practicing rituals and offering ***Haj*** (rice beer) with Pork or Duck in every year.

Chi Ren Dam: '*Chi*' means 'four', '*ren*' means a 'house'. Thus *Chi Ren Dam* means the fourth generation of the parents of the dead grandfather of the living householders.

Jokorua Dam: The word '*Jokorua*' is used in a collective sense to mean all the dead ones who died without having a male child, who died in childhood, who died without getting married and also who died with physical and mental abnormality. This kind of Dam is propitiated in the house of the eldest member of the living generations.

Na Dam: 'Na' means 'new'. The recent dead in the household, whether the head of the family or his wife or his parents, is called *Na Dam*.

All these kinds of Dams are altogether called *Griha Dam*, who is worship annually. The members of the family worship their ancestor in a day which is fixed by their own choice. They worship their all *Dams* (ancestors) together in specific day in every year. They believe that if they will fail to do the rituals something will be happen wrong in their family and then the ancestor can't save them from the bad.

Process of the Rituals

On the given day of rituals the family invite a priest to practice the ritual. The married man and woman also participate in the rituals. But the unmarried man and woman can't seat in the dice during the rituals. For the first the priest takes his seat by praying god. Thereafter two or three man takes permission from the priest to cook the pork or duck for the rituals. After finishing the cooking processes the main ritual is started. The women take permission from the priest to open the *Haj* (rice beer).

Women play a key role in every ancestor worship rituals of Ahom. Thereafter the women prepare *Thali* (rice beer in a bowl and pork/duck meet together in a piece of banana leaf) separately for the entire Dam's and one *Thali* for the priest.

The priest use to sing some traditional song to give the *Thali* to the ancestor in their secrete way. Then the women provide *Thali* to the priest. Once the priest used to drink the *Haj* then the other present individuals are supposed to be permitted to drink the *Haj*. The women use to sing some traditional songs of their Tai language when they providing *Haj* to the men. Providing of *Haj* with Pork or Duck is thought to be the main gifts for their ancestor.

When everyone finishes their *Thali* then the women sing the final closing songs of the ritual. At last the family members take blessings from the priest and the rituals supposed to be end.

Rituals at community levels

The *Phualung* Ahom not only practice their ancestor worship rituals in their family they also practice some rituals in community level. The community level rituals are practiced by the entire village or sometimes in large scale area too. They try to preserve their tradition for upcoming generation by showing their tradition in community level. They have many festivals but they worshiped their ancestor in the following rituals:

1. *Me-Dam-Me-Phi*
2. *Phi-Sua-Mung worship*

Me-Dam-Me-Phi: *Me-Dam-Me-Phi* is the Tai-Ahom traditional ancestor worship ritual. It is said that, this worship has been performed from the immemorial past. This festival is the festival of community; all the Ahom families practice the worship to all their ancestors simultaneously on 31st of January every year.

The meaning of the word *"Me"* is "worship", "*Dam*" means "the dead person" and "*Phi*" is referred to the higher level of "*Dam*". The Dam worshipping is observed by the sons of the Dam at their house. This ritual is called "*Lu Dam*" means "the annual worship to the Dam", hence it is to be held annually. After the sons of the Dam die, then the Dam worship comes to the end and the Phi worship begins from then.

Phi-Sua-Mung Worship: The *Phi-Sua-Mung* is worshipped among the Ahom and it is regarded as protecting deity of the country. This worship is performed on the 5th month (*Din Ha*). In the previous times of Ahom, this worship was held in full grandeur. To perform this rite, a hut, a pig, two fowl, eight baskets of rice, two ducks, fried rice, banana, sugarcane, areca nut and betel leaves, salt, ginger, oil, citrus fruits, milk, etc. will be offered to the deity by the Ahom priests.

Taboos and restrictions relating to ancestor worship rituals

The Ahom people have been practicing the ancestor worship rituals from very beginning. They follow the rules and regulation which has been provided by their constitution. They never try to break the rules as they thought that if they break the rules their ancestor will not be happy and they will be punish by their ancestor. The following are the taboos which they always try to maintain:

1. An unmarried individual cannot participate in the rituals.
2. A girl or woman during menstruation period is not allows to participate in ritual.
3. The rice beer needs to be make by a woman by praying to god. A man is not allows to make rice beer.
4. During the time of ritual, no individual can leave the dice.
5. Everyone should wear proper traditional dresses.
6. The rituals of *Bihu* need to be finish at day time.
7. No one can seat by showing back to others.
8. The rituals cannot be practice in that home where someone is dead within 6 month.
9. The men need to be clean shave when they participating in rituals.

Conclusion

The Ahom people of the Na-pam village are found in two different group and they follow their own way of ancestor worship. They have their own constitution, and each group follow the constitution during every rituals. The Kal-honghoti is an Ahom organization which is formed in the year of 2005 to maintain the tie between the Ahom people of Assam. The organization has their own constitution and all the member of the organization follow all the rules and regulation of the constitution. The particular group of Ahom don't have any separate language for communication among themselves. They use the Assamese language as the main communication language. In earlier days they have the Tai language but in present scenario they do not know to speak or write the Tai language. Among the *Kal-honghoti* Ahom they have believe that if they fail to practice the worship rituals then the ancestor will come to their dream and something will happen wrong to their family.

The Kal-honghoti Ahom has many rituals among themselves and they practicing it in both home and community level. They follow the Assamese calendar year for fixing the date of their rituals. They have many rituals relating to paddy field and ancestor worship. They have rituals such as; (a) *Bohag Bihu* Rituals, (b) *Kati Bihu* Rituals, (c) *Magh Bihu* Ritual, (d) *Bosorekiya* (Yearly ritual).

The ancestor worship rituals during *Bihu* are same in all the three *Bihu*. The process of the ritual is start by the invitation process. The family members invite the local Ahom people of their own group to participate in the ritual. A ***Hadhu*** (the priest) is the key person without whom the rituals can't be practice. The Kal-honghoti Ahom people used the following goods during the rituals such as; Meat/ Fish, *Haj* (rice beer), Pot lamp, Banana leaves, Vegetables, Dish of bronze, etc.

The Kal-honghoti Ahom people practice a yearly ancestor worship ritual in their home for their own family ancestor in a particular day. The family fix the month of the rituals by relating to their ancestors death month. They worship their all ancestor of their own family including recent dead and early dead together in a day. They use to sacrifice as much as they can as they think *Bosorekia* is the main ritual for them. They believe that their ancestor observing them from the haven and protecting them from the bad spirits. They thought that if they fail to do the ritual then the ancestor will punish them and will not save them from the bad ones.

The *Phualung* Ahom which are mixed with other community people as their neighbour follow their traditional way of doing rituals which were followed by their ancient generation. These are the only group of Ahom people who use their ancient language and scripture for doing rituals among themselves. They have separate language called Tai language, but as influence of other community and as the requirement of communication with others they use Assamese language as their medium of communication language. As a result the new generation of the *Phualung* group does not know to write or speak their language. Only some priest or the priest family can read or write the Tai language. On the occasion of some rituals the priests use the original Tai language.

The *Phualung* group not only worships their own family ancestor but they also worship their community ancestors with great devotion. They have many ancestor worship rituals in which some are practiced for their own family ancestor and some are practiced for the whole community ancestors i.e., the Kings, Warrior etc., in many season.

According to the belief of Ahom, there is the hierarchy of the spirit after death i.e. Dam and Phi. After death a man becomes a *"Dam"*, he continues to exist and protect the living family members from all evils. In this period he is called "god of the home". After a period of time when the duty as Dam is over then he rises above Dam to be a *"Phi"*. The Phi has a duty as a god of the society. He is now "a society god" and cuts off all relations with his family. When the deity as a Phi is over then he gets reconciled into *"Kung Ing Ka Phra"* (Creator God).

The Tai Ahoms believe that after death a person becomes a Dam Phi, or a god, who goes to reside in the heaven in the same way as he was in his earthly life. He is worshipped and propitiated as a god with the offerings made by the descendants but not as a revengeful ghost.

The Tai Ahoms offer their first seasonal crops, vegetables and fruits to the ancestors and they could take these only after offering these to their ancestor gods. The priestly families worship their ancestors in a very clear way making different grades to each kind of Dam. These are: *Ghai Dam*, *Chi Ren Dam*, *Na Dam* and *Jokorua Dam*.

Me-Dam-Me-Phi is the Tai-Ahom traditional ancestor worship ritual. It is said that, this worship has been performed from the immemorial past. This festival is the festival of community; all the Ahom families practice the worship to all their ancestors simultaneously on 31st of January every year. The meaning of the word "*Me*" is "worship", "*Dam*" means "the dead person" and "*Phi*" is referred to the higher level of "*Dam*". The Dam worshipping is observed by the sons of the Dam at their house. This ritual is called "*Lu Dam*" means "the annual worship to the Dam", hence it is to be held annually. After the sons of the Dam die, then the Dam worship comes to the end and the Phi worship begins from then.

The *Phi-Sua-Mung* is worshipped among the Ahom and it is regarded as protecting deity of the country. This worship is performed on the 5th month (*Din Ha)*. In the previous times of Ahom, this worship was held in full grandeur. To perform this rite, a hut, a pig, two fowl, eight baskets of rice, two ducks, fried rice, banana, sugarcane, areca nut and betel leaves, salt, ginger, oil, citrus fruits, milk, etc. will be offered to the deity by the Ahom priests.

References

Bloch, M., & Parry, J. (1982) Death and regeneration oflife. Cambridge: Cambridge University Press.

Campos; Don Jose, *"The Shaman & Ayahuasca: Journeys to Sacred Realms"*. 2011.

Ember; C.R, Ember; M, & Peregrin; P.N, *"Anthropology"* 12th Edition. Pearson Publishing.

Fortes, M. (1949). The web of kinship among the Tallensi. London: Oxford University Press.

Goody, J. (1962). Death, property, and the ancestors. Stanford, CA: Stanford University Press.

Hertz, R. (1960). A contribution to the study of the collective representation of death (R. & C. Needham, Trans.). In R.

Needham (Ed.), Death and the right hand. Glencoe, IL: Free Press. (Original work published in French, 1907)

Jha; M, *"An Introduction To Social Anthropology"* 2nd Revised Edition, Vikash Publishing.

Mohanty; P.K. *"Encyclopaedia Of Schedule Tribe In India"* Vol. 5 (2001), (Isha Books)

Newell, W. H. (1976), Ancestors. The Hague, the Netherlands: Mouton.

Owusu; Heike, *"Voodoo Rituals: A User's Guide"* (Sterling Publishing Company, 2002)

Van Gennep, A. (1960). The rites of passage (M. Vizedom & G. Caffe, Trans). Chicago: University of Chicago Press. (Original work published in French, 1908).

Plate 15.1: After lighting of the lamp.

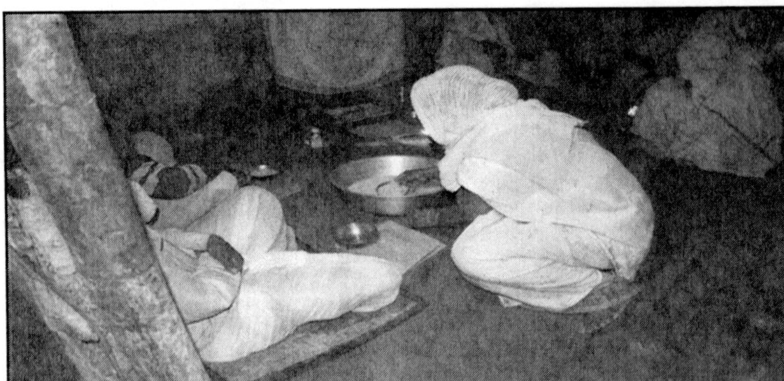

***Plate 15.2: Woman serving* Haj.**

Plate 15.3:* Haj *and* Kach *together.

Plate 15.4:* Me-dam-me-phi; *men in traditional Ahom attire.

Chapter - 16

Social Folk Customs Associated with Birth, Puberty and Death Rites of the Sonowal Kacharis of Assam

— Suravi Gohain Duwarah

The word 'Social Folk Custom' is an important area of Folklore and Folk life. According to Dr. R.M. Dorson, "It is very close to material culture and lies in between oral literature and material culture. Here the emphasis is on group interaction rather than on individual skills and performances" (Dorson, 1972, 3). The Oxford English Dictionary gives the meaning of the term 'custom' as "a traditional and generally accepted way of behaving or doing things." Thus customs are an important part of the life of each and every community or group of people living in this world. The social folk customs are based on traditional beliefs and practices. Each one of us living in the society has our own customs, beliefs, rites and rituals. The ritualistic observances differ from society to society.

Assam is a land where people from different community and tribe live together. These groups of people have their own distinctive culture, tradition and customs. Each tribe live their life carrying with them the traditional beliefs and practices. Among these the Sonowal Kachari tribe is one of the largest plain tribe of Assam. They are the offshoot off the Tibeto-Burman or Bodo group of people. At present they are distributed in the different districts of the Brahmaputra valley. The Sonowal Kacharis have their own social folk customs which is being practised till date. The topic of discussion in this paper is the Social Folk customs associated with birth, puberty and death rites of the Sonowal Kachari Tribe of Assam.

Customs associated with birth rites

The Sonowal Kacharis practise certain customs when a woman expects a baby. There are also certain folk beliefs which are usually seen in the society of the Sonowal Kacharis. When a woman expects a baby there is a custom of restricting the husband from certain activities. There is a belief that the man should not attend any death rituals and kill animals. Moreover, if the man goes somewhere during the night hours he should not enter into the room of the expecting mother. This is done with the fear of some evil spirit coming with him. This folk belief is still prevalent among the other communities of Assam also. There is a custom of keeping the twigs and branches of '*bogori*' (thorny plum tree), fishing net and '*rash*' (reed of a loom) at the entrance of the room so that no evil spirit would reach the expected mother. When a male child is born in the family the midwife announces the birth by *uruli* (shrill sound produced by women in religious or festive occasion) and when a female child is born the mid wife hits the wall of the room. There is the custom of cutting the umbilical cord of the child by a sharp '*sesu*' (thin slice of bamboo piece having sharp edges on both sides). The cord is then wrapped by a clean piece of cloth and kept safely. There is a belief that if the child undergoes any problem or trouble related to his or her health then a ritual known as '*ayush tula*' is done to make the child live a healthy life. On the third day of the birth of the child there is a custom of '*jaal khuwa*'. On this particular day there is the custom of giving the mother '*kachu saak*' (leaves of arum) cooked with pepper. This is done with the belief that the wounds of the mother would heal and her health will be appropriate for feeding the child. Several other herbal plants are also seen to be used with the belief that the mother would regain the normalcy of her health.

The Sonowal Kachari community has the custom of '*baaj uluwa*' (bringing out of the child and mother from the house) which is observed when the umbilical chord dries and falls apart from the child. The room of the mother is cleaned and her clothes are washed. On this day a '*pira*' (low wooden stool) is placed in the courtyard of the house which is covered by a clean '*gamusa*' (Traditional Assamese towel). A 'Chaki' (an earthen lamp) is lit, and a bowl of water, '*pota guti*' (stone roller used to for grinding on a flat piece of stone called '*pota*'), is placed near the stool and a '*kheror jumuthi*' (braided wisp of straw) is also burnt near the stool. The child is bathed and after wiping off with the 'gamusa' the mother circles around the stool and other articles for three times. Then the mother throws four '*thuria tamul'* (rolled up betel nut) in four directions and holds up the baby towards the sun thrice and then places the baby on the '*pira*'. Then the '*pira*' is hit gently by the '*pota guti'* and touched in the '*nari*' (naval portion of the child). Then the baby is brought over the bowl containing water and circled for three times and prays that he/she does not die falling in water. After that the baby is again brought upon the burning '*kheror jumuthi*' and circled for three times and prays God that he/she does not die due to any fire accident. Then the baby is kept on the 'pira' and to keep away all hindrances in life passes a '*bogori jeng*' (thorny branch of plum tree) under the legs of the baby and throws it away. The mother offers her prayer to 'Surya' and concludes the ceremony. The entire ritual is performed in presence of the women folk of the village.

Another custom associated with birth is 'Suddhi Hobah' (purification ceremony). When a male child is born the ceremony is observed on 14th day and in case of girl child it is observed on the 21st day. On this day the hair of the baby is shaved. Fresh cow dung is pasted on the wall of the house. Few shaved hair, '*dubori bon*' (a type of grass), rice, two pieces of betel nut, a coin and a bow and arrow is hanged upon the dung. The baby is marked on the forehead by the earth thrown out by earthworm. It is a folk belief that the mark will save the baby from any evil eyes. The Vaishnavite followers in some places invite '*bhakat*' (Satra devotees) and arrange '*naam kirtan*' (holy readings).

Customs associated with puberty rites

The Sonowal Kacharis of Assam observes the puberty rites in numerous customs and rituals. As soon as the girl attains puberty there is a custom of keeping the girl in a separate room. The family visits the astrologer to ensure if there are any hindrances. The girl is kept in the separate room for three days and male members are not allowed to seed the girl during this period. She is allowed to have fruits only. On the fourth day the girl is taken out of the house and is bathed in presence of the women folk. Several customs are practised on that day. A '*bei*' (place used for bathing of the bride or groom) is made of three reeds on the eastern directon of the back yard. A '*pira*' (low wooden stool) is placed in the '*bei*' and the girl is allowed to sit on the stool. Then 'ou tenga beez' (seed of elephant apple) is applied on her hair and '*maah-halodhi*' (paste of turmeric, pulse, oil etc) is rubbed on her body and the women folk pours five to seven pots of water to bath her along with '*uruli*' from them. Then the girl prays the sun god to forgive any fault is she has done while entering and coming out of the '*bei*'. Then she looks into the betel nut of the tree and then offers her '*sewa*' (obeisance i.e. gesture expressing respect) to her mother and the women folk. Then she ties a garland around banana tree which symbolizes to be her prospective husband without changing her clothes and applies turmeric paste by her right hand and pulse paste by her left hand for three times from bottom of the plant upwards, the women folk chants '*uruli*' and pours a pot of water upon the banana tree. Then she offers '*sewa*' by pouring '*ahkoi*' (puffed rice) and '*pithaguri*' (rice flour) near the roots of the banana tree. Then the girl is taken inside the house and after wearing a new pair of clothes, her hair is combed and vermilion is applied on her forehead. From the fourth day to the seventh day the girl is allowed to eat 'jalpan' (home made snacks) during the day and after sparkling of the moon and stars at night three handful of rice along with 'magur' (cat) fish is cooked and served to the girl. During these days oil and turmeric is not allowed to girl. If the astrologer confirms the girl to be '*subhaga*' (fortunate) and '*patibrata*' (devoted to husband) then on the seventh day she is allowed to break her fast. But if the girl turns to be '*durbhaga*' (unlucky) or '*patihina*' (husbandless) then the fast may extend from fifteen days upto one and half month.

Another custom associated with the puberty marriage among the Sonowal Kacharis is the '*Kulaburhi Naach*'. This is performed on the day preceding to the ceremonial function of puberty marriage. The women folk particularly the mothers wear white dress and wishing the girls well being grinds '*gathiyan*' (a special herbal medicine to be used for bathing the girl who has attained puberty). One elderly women used to keep certain things in the '*dola*' (tray like round wicker work used for keeping paddy) or '*kula*' (winnowing fan made of bamboo) and keeps in upon her head, holds a '*thareng*' in her hand and dances in the traditional style . She then places the *dola* or *kula* along with the articles on the lap of the girl and teaches her the responsibilities of her future motherhood. She is also advised to keep away all her childish nature and make her ready to handle various family burdens. The entire ritual is performed by way of traditional song and dances.

Customs associated with death rites

The Sonowal Kachari tribe of Assam has some specific customs associated with the death of a person. There is a custom of cremating the dead body and certain folk beliefs are there related to the death of a person. As soon as person dies, the person is immediately taken outside with the belief that the death of a person inside the house would make the house an impure place to live in. Besides this, if a person happens to die all of a sudden within the house then there is the custom of taking the body immediately out of the house not through the main door but by the backdoor. And if there is no provision of a backdoor in the house then the members of the family will have to cut a door and take the dead body outside. The dead body is kept in the courtyard and then covered with a white cloth and then wrapped in a '*dhari*' (traditional mat used in the Assamese society made of bamboo). When the village folks and the family members gather, the dead body is anointed with '*maah-halodhi*' (paste of pulse and turmeric) and the body is dressed with new clothes. There is also the custom of bringing three 'thuk' (bunches) of paddy from the granary and that bunches are made to cross the hands of the dead person. In the process of doing so the little bit of paddy left is kept back in the granary and the door of the granary is covered by a '*parda*' (curtain). This is done with a belief that '*Lakhimi*' (Goddess of wealth) cannot go away with the dead person. A '*changi*' (bamboo frame used as carriage) is made of a single piece of bamboo from the garden of the dead person. That bamboo is not used for any other purpose for a year. The *changi* is three '*haat*' (cubit of length/ length of the forearm) and one '*muthan*' (length from the elbow to the fist) in length and one 'hat' one muthan in width. '*Tongal*' (bamboo rope) is made from one piece of bamboo measuring the width of the change to tie the dead body. Then a new '*dhari*' is placed on the *changi* and the dead body is put on it and carried to the cremation ground.

In the past the dead body was put in a wooden coffin and buried, but due to the influence of neovaishnavism culture among the Sonowal Kacharis the custom of burying the dead has come to an end. But if a person dies due to drowning or snake bite or commits suicide and minors such persons are buried even today. The dead person is cremated in a common crematory or own land of the dead. The near relative's son, brother, nephew or grandson first holds the '*changi*' to the cremation ground. The eldest or the youngest son holds a burning '*jumuthi*' and '*daa*' (machete) and leads the dead body to the cremation ground. In absence of any sons brother or any near relative has to perform the task. On reaching the cremation ground the upper surface of the area is dug out in the shape of 'plus' sign in the east-west direction. Before digging the soil the cremation area is bought by offering a '*tamul-paan*' and some money. Then four main pillars of bamboo or wood are erected on the four sides of the plus sign. Then two heavy pieces of logs are placed upon which a layer of bamboo firewood is kept. Then in every alternate layer logs are placed horizontally and seven to nine piers are made. After the pier is made the person who would light the fire makes seven circles with two bundles of burning firewoord in both his hands around the pier who is followed by people carrying the dead body along with the 'changi'. After that the changi is kept down and undresses the body and in case of male he is kept upside down and in case of female the face towards the upper side facing the head to the north direction. After that one more layer of heavy logs are placed upon the dead body and every one present in the cremation ground offers a piece of log to the dead. The person who leads the dead to the cremation ground turns his back towards the pier and moves the burning flame in the front and back direction and throws it upon the pier. After that the friends and relatives lits up the pier and burns the body. When the body is burnt completely the fire is put off by pouring water from an earthen pot. Lentil and pulse is scattered, breaks the earthen pot and the people present in the crematorium utters '*jayadhwani*' (blessings in loud voice) and goes back to their respective homes. The people attending the funeral have to take bath and face the '*jaag*' (a fire burnt with paddy husk and other herbs) before entering their respective house.

The family of the dead observes fasting for three days and is allowed to eat fruits, gram etc. On the third day of death a ritual called '*tilani*' is observed. On this day the house is purified, all clothes and all household utensils are washed. The paternal family members even if they are staying apart also have to observe this ritual. On this day the neighbour gather at the house of the dead and fast is broken by serving '*pithaguri*' (uncooked rice flour) with milk. On the tenth day a ritual called '*doha*' is observed. The neighbours cook and serve vegetarian boiled food to the family of the deceased on that day. On the tenth day another ritual called '*doha*' is observed. There is a custom of offering sixteen items and these items are believed to the favourite of the deceased. There is another custom of offering '*pinda*' (act of offering oblation to the dead person). This is done either in land or in water. *Doha* is done according to the advice of the '*brahmin*' or '*medhi*'. On the eleventh, thirteenth or completion of a month '*shraddha*' (ceremony performed for eternal peace of the departed soul) is done. On the *shraddha* all the relatives and friends are invited and the ritual is done by the 'brahmin'. A '*robha*' (temporary shed/pendal) is erected in the courtyard of the house. In the eastern side of the *robha* an alter or '*thapana*' is placed which is known as '*Tiphai*'. Around the '*tipahi*' four tender banana plant, sugar cane plant, twigs of bamboo are placed in some places of Assam. In each banana plant some bamboo cans are tied. There is the custom of keeping betel nuts, three mango leaves and coins. Now-a-days earthen pots are used in place of bamboo cans. In the bamboo cans or earthen pots there is the custom of keeping '*bhujoni*' (eatables for a person) for four persons of the community. There is also the custom of donating certain items which was used by the deceased or '*hullo borno*' (sixteen items which was favourite to the dead). The above custom is followed by the '*Henduria*' cult of the Sonowal Kacharis. There is another cult known as '*Behari*' among the Sonowal Kacharis. There is the custom of observing '*tilani*' on the third day, '*doha*' on the tenth and and '*shraddha*' on the twentieth day. The followers of the '*behari*' cult do not take the assistance of '*brahmin*' in conducting the death rituals. The family is purified by an elderly person of the area on the day of *tilani*. The family members bow down before the village folk and take blessings. An '*outenga*' (elephant apple) is cut into four pieces and are tied by '*tora*' plant. In some areas the items used for '*pinda*' is tied by three '*tora*' plants and other items are tied like garland. The custom of offering '*jal pinda'* (in water) is practised. A temporary shade is made on the river bank and three pools are dug to perform the *pinda*. In this shed an alter is made. The alter is purified by spreading rice flour and puffed rice. Eleven parts are made of the previously prepared items which are carried to the *pinda* spot and nine parts are offered to the ancestors. One of the remaining parts is offered to mother earth and one part is offered to the '*ghatoi*' (holder of the ferry ghat). In each of the offerings a garland is placed and the person who gives the '*pinda*' bows before the alter and the aged persons give blessings. There is also a custom of offering sixteen items in the 'doha'.

The Sonowal Kacharis practise several customs at the death of a person. In both the system there is similarity in customs. In the '*Henduriya*' system after the '*kaaj*' (rituals of death) the families invites some aged persons and have '*naam kirtan'* (singing religious prayers) and the next day a feast is given to the village folk. The death ritual ends with the completion of '*kaaj*'.

Thus the folk custom of the Sonowal Kacharis prove that they have distinct cultural traits. Of course in the present day society there are changes to be seen with regard to the customs and traditions. Despite of changes and conversion into the Neo-Vaishavism, a sizeable section of the Sonowal Kachari community are still retaining their culture and tradition.

References

Bordoloi, B.N., Sharma Thakur G.C., Saikia, M.C. : Tribes of Assam (Part – I) 1st Edition, Tribal Research Institute, Guwahati, 1987.

Borkakoti, S. : Tribes of Assam, Director of National Book Trust. A.S. Green Park, Jagwal Printing Press, New Delhi, 1984.

Boruah, Binita: The Sonowal Kacharis of Assam, published by Assam Institute of Research for Tribal and Scheduled Campus, Guwahati – 22, 1998.

Dorson, R.M. (ed.): Folklore and Folk life: An Introduction, Chicago, University of Caivo Press, 1972.

Kachari, N.: Sonowal Kachari Hamaj-Hanskriti aru Bhakhar Parichoy, Moranhaat, 2007.

Chapter - 17

Transformation in Nyishi Festival, *Nyokum*: An Overview

— *Yora Bathey*

A festival is an event ordinarily celebrated by a community and centering on some characteristic aspect of that community and its religion or cultures. It is often marked as a local or national holiday, Mela, or Eid. Next to religion and folklore, a significant origin is agricultural. Food is such a vital resource that many festivals are associated with harvest time. Religious commemoration and thanksgiving for good harvests are blended in events that take place in autumn, such as Halloween in the northern hemisphere and Easter in the southern (Brandt, 2012: 3-7). In Indian scenario, Diwali, Holi, Durga Puja, Eid, Tribal festivals like Sarhul in Jharkhand (similar to Holi), *Nyokum*, Mopin and many others.

Festivals often serve to fulfill specific communal purposes, especially in regard to commemoration or thanksgiving. The celebrations offer a sense of belonging for religious, social, or geographical groups, contributing to group cohesiveness. They may also provide entertainment, which was particularly important to local communities before the advent of mass-produced entertainment. Festivals that focus on cultural or ethnic topics also seek to inform community members of their traditions; the involvement of elders sharing stories and experience provides a means for unity among families (Pickard, 2012: 1-3).

In Ancient Greece and Rome, festivals such as the Saturnalia were closely associated with social organization and political processes as well as religion (Robertson, 1992: 11-15). Saturnalia festival was to appease the God Saturn, and such reference of appeasing the Hindu God Shani has also been found in India. Such issues show the similar origin of customs in ancient times. In modern times, festivals may be attended by strangers such as tourists, who are attracted to something different from their own culture or historical ones. The Philippines has traditionally been the capital of the world's festivities, as each day of the year has at least one specific Filipino festival. There are more than 42,000 known major and minor festivals in the Philippines, the majority of which are in the village level (Pickard, 2012: 1-3).

There have been many definition of festival, Asian Culture Centre (1975) defined the festivals as an occasion to wear new clothes, decorate the house, sing new hymns, let of fireworks, prepare special meals and exchange good wishes. A.M. Kurup in his article The Festivals of central India stated that, "Festivals derive, for the most part, from collective ritual."(1990:119). Ajit K. Singh in his book the tribal Festivals of Bihar stated that, "the festivals are not mere occasion but deep-rooted tradition and custom woven into the fabric of Indian Life". "Festival is an occasion that reinforces the presence of god in the life of the individuals and family and binds them to community. They are also moments for the young people to absorb and be part of old age, yet still vibrant and living tradition" (Tribhuwan, 6:2003).

Hence we can say is that the Festivals one of the most important part of any culture. It is a collective performance of rituals. The festival of one community has a huge role to play in his community. But with the progressing and very quickly changing world the festival and their mode celebration are also changing to quite an extend.

"The *Nyokum* festival is being celebrated by the Nyishi tribe of Arunachal Pradesh. It is an Agro base festival that is being celebrated in the 26th of the February. The main theme of the festival is to worship the almighty Donyi-Polo to bring peace, prosperity and happiness to all the living creatures of the earth. Moreover, they sacrifice number of animals to appease different malevolent and benevolent spirits and deities, who are the cause for their sicknesses" (Bagang 2006). "Mnyokun (*Nyokum*) is the most important rites and assures prosperity and good harvest" (for the Nyishi). (Pandey, 12:1981). "It is the only festival which is celebrated annually in every village on a community basis in the Bangni (Nyishi) month of Leekar and Lehar corresponding to the English month of March and April, amidst great joy and devotion and unbound enthusiasm (Deuri 26:1983). "Nyishi celebrate different types of festivals based on rituals. Some of the major festivals are *Nyokum*Yullow, Bori Yullow, Longte Yullow and Yullow Uyus Panam. Festivals have a close link with agricultural production, animal husbandry and well beings of human beings. These festivals are perform to ward off natural calamities like flood drought famine, etc. by the intervention of gods and goddesses. The priest plays a dominant role in these festivals and *Nyokum* festival is amalgamation or extension of Yullows" (Nakha, 18:2012). "In the fast changing scenario where the good old practices are generally dying the innovation of *Nyokum* Festival is one of the most remarkable culture heritages in the anal of Nyishi. '*Nyokum*Yullow' festival is an occasion to display the sole features of the Nyishis life style and its socio-cultural and socio-economic pattern besides the religious fervor that are believed to have been inherited from Abotani, since the birth of mankind on the lap of mother earth" (Rikam: 2004).

"The changing atmosphere around the tribe Nyishi is leading them adapt and accept this changes" (Rikam 2004). "The people who are in the traditional faith perform rituals and old people of the interior villages are still believed in their traditional custom and practices. But the education is bringing drastic changes in the Nyishi society" (Bagang 2006). "The people's spiritual and mental outlook are being hijacked by the outside culture, now days some of the natives have started disgusting their own popular faith and belief for the enjoyment of material comfort provided by the alien culture" (Nabam Rikam, 2004). So, the present study is carried out to look closely in the celebration of *Nyokum* festival of Nyishi tribe of Arunachal Pradesh.

The Nyishi tribe

Arunachal has total of 101 recognised tribes/community living in it, 37 of which are animist majority (Nyishi, Apatani, Adi Galo, Tagin, etc.), 23 are a Christian majority tribes (Mossang, Bori, Wancho, Yobin, Tangsa etc.), 15 are a Hindu dominated tribes (Deaori, Mishing/Miri, Aka, Mishmi, Longchang Tangsa.etc.) and 17 are Buddhist (Monpa, Khampti, Momba, Singpho, Sherdukpen.etc.). The remaining eight tribes are multi-faith, which means there is no any dominant religion in these tribes (Nocte, Tangsa, and Naga.etc).

The Nyishis is one of the largest populated tribe of the state. The total population of the Nyishis are over 2,76.622 out of the total 1,42,049 of them is male and 1,34,573 of them are female, the number is though increasing very rapidly annually. The Nyishi inhabit in as many as seven districts viz- Lower Subansiri, Kurung Kumey, Papum Pare, East Kameng, Kra Daadi, Kamle Pakke-kesang and there are some number of Nyishi also found in the parts of west Kameng in Arunachal and in Sonitpur and North Lakhimpur districts of Assam.

"The Nyishi believes that they are the descendents of Abo Tani. The People call themselves Nyesang, Nishi or more appropriately as Nyishi since the time Immemorial. As per their Mythology, the term 'Nyishis' or 'Nyeshang' is derived from two words i.e, Nyi or Nyia- means man or human race that descended from Atu Nyia (first real man on earth) and Eshang or Ishi- means high hills or highlands. Therefore, a compound word 'Nyishi' denotes the descendednt of Atu Nyia who dwells in the highlands." (2005:5, Rikam).

Nyishi, are believed to be the descendants of Abo Tani. Similar to Nyishis the tribes like Apatani, Adi, Tagin, Gallo and Mishings tribe of Assam also considers themselves as the descendants of Abo Tani. These tribes together are also called the Tani Group, since they all decent from Tani. These tribes, because of the different topographical and climatic conditions, may vary from one another in terms of Language, dress, physical, etc. Though they might seem different from one another in many aspects but what categorized them in one Tani umbrella is the tracing of their genealogy from Abo Tani.

"The Nyishi believes that in the beginning, out of nothingness the universe was created by Jingbu Pabu Abu (Almighty). It is believed that, Jingbu-Pabu Abu invoked the power through different supernatural means to create and evolve the present-day universe. All living creatures including man were created and the Abo Tani was the progeny of the first human being on the earth. After the completion of the process of creation of universe and its different components, Jingbu-Pabu Abu the creator disappeared from the scene." (Showren, 2016).

The division of the Nyishis into Anthropolgical division of one community on the criteria of family, Lineage, clan, phratry, moiety and tribe, is bit complicated. The Nyishis belief themselves to be the children of the mythical ancestor who was Semi-god, called Abu Tani. The Abu Tani had different incarnation and there were numerous Tanis like Nyiku Tani, Nyema Tani, Nyiyang tani,Nyidar Tani, Nyekam Tani, etc. When finally Tani took the Homo sapiens form was called by the name Niyah Tani, meaning 'Human Tani'. The Niyah Tani had eight sons and out of it only the four son's genealogy could be traced, who are Haring, Hagung, Habing and Anya Hari. Haring had a son called Tado, who had four sons namely Dopum, Dodum, Dolu and Nyiv. The entire Nyishi population is considered to be the sons of these five fathers, namely Anya Hari, Dodum, Dopum, Dolu and Nyiv.

Festivals

The major festivals of the Nyisis are *Nyokum* Yullo, Boori Boot Yullo and Longte Yullo. These festivals are celebrated to please the god and the goddesses, both malevolent and benevolent. The Longte Yullo are promply being celebratied in the Kurung Kumey District of Arunachal Pradesh, but with the diminishing gap between the Nyishis it also being celebrated in the other Nyishi dominated areas too. The Boori Boot Yullo had its initiation in the Kamle Districts of Arunachal Pradesh, the Nyishis of the region celebrate it with much zeal. The *Nyokum* had its early generalized form of the festival from the Subansiri region, but compared to the other two festival of the Nyishi, the *Nyokum* is the most widely celebrated festival. The *Nyokum* is almost celebrated in all the Nyishi dominated region of the state.

The festivals of the Nyishi are deeply attached to the ritual part. The festivals are being celebrated to seek prosperity and protection from god and the goddesses. Since the Nyishis are animist in religion, traditionally, they worship the nature, the spirits dwelling in them and the ancestral spirits. There festival format and pattern are all governed by the spirits. Festival gives them an occasion to please these Uyus, spirits, and seek their blessing. In fact the festival of the Nyishis is an arranged occasion, with the permission for the spirits themselves, to offer sacrifice to the spirits and in return be blessed by the spirits.

Most of the festivals of the world are the extended or the modified form of the ritual they practiced in the past. The festivals of the Nyishi were also being inspired from the rituals in their past which slowly developed from the individual observed ritual to a family and finally as a village or community observed festival. The festival like *Nyokum* is amalgamation of the rituals, being observed as a festival today. The amalgamation of Nyishi rituals in *Nyokum* is one of the reason it is being widely celebrated festival among the Nyishis of the entire region as compared to the other two important festival of the Nyishi, the Longte yullo and the Boori Boot Yullo.

The *Nyokum* Yullo festival

According to Prof. Tana Showren, "the sole objective of *Nyokum* is to entreat all the God and Goddesses to a specific venue on a particular day and a time. The worship is by all section of people, regardless of age, caste and religion for bumper harvest, rich animal husbandry, peace and prosperity of all Mankind."

"*Nyokum* (*Nyokum*) is the most important rites and assures prosperity and good harvest. Agriculture being their mainstay, they attach great importance to such celebrations. The *Nyokum* is believed to be a harvesting festival so it is being celebrated in the months of February when the Harvesting season begins for the Nyishi tribe, in contrasting to it the *Nyokum*, in actual; it is a Prosperity festival for the welfare of the Nyishi and the whole human being as a whole."(B.B Pandey).

The celebration of *Nyokum*, as a generalized form festival, was started in August 1967 at Joram village, 7 KMS away from Ziro, under the Leadership of famous Nyishi Personalities like lt. Tadar Tang, Dr. Joram Begi, Nabam Tata, Chuku Talar, etc. But before retaining to the present state of *Nyokum*, *Nyokum* itself had to pass through many refineries and generalized process to gain the present pattern of *Nyokum* celebration. As almost most of festival of the globe has evolved from a simple form of ritual, so has the *Nyokum* too.

Literally the term *Nyokum* is derived from two words 'Nyok' and 'um' – means 'earth' (home of living creature) and 'gathering' respectively. The yullo can be understood as festivals. Therefore, the compound word '*Nyokum* Yullow' is a conglomeration of all the things on earth, to be precise the gathering of human beings in order to propitiate the innumerable Weyis(spirits) for the safety and security of mankind with all things needed for its well-being, peace, progress and prosperity. (2005:65, Rikam).

The *Nyokum* originally was in initial period a ritual which the Nyishis performed to please the Uyus (the spirits/gods), both the malevolent and benevolent, either to seek their blessing or to keep away their wrath. And in due course of time with its generalization took the shape of a festival. "In the Past, this ceremony was performed by individual village to protect the paddy crops, from insects and other natural calamities. Now with the advent of development activities and the spread of education the new generation is searching for an important festival which could be observed as a community festival" (Pandey, 1981).

Before one tries to find out the Tangible and Non Tangible cultural changes occurring in *Nyokum* from time to time, one must also know how *Nyokum* have originated. One has to know the Folktales, Folklores and Theories describing or explaining the origination of *Nyokum*. The *Nyokum*, to my observation, has passed through three grand stages before coming to the present form of *Nyokum* celebration.

In the First stage, *Nyokum* was merely a ritual performed by the Nyishis in different occasions, like Nyoying Hingnam, Yullo Panam and Uyu Panam, which were performed to please the Both Malevolent and Benevolent Spirits, in order to achieve prosper and protection from the spirits. It should also be mentioned here that in the first stage the *Nyokum* was not an annual celebrated festival but instead a timely performed ritual, performed only when needed or required. Till today the Nyishi whenever they seek blessing or sense a threat they still conduct these old aged rituals, beside *Nyokum*, to please the Uyus (spirits), both benevolent and malevolent. "Indeed, it can be said with some justification that until recent years tribes such as Nyishi did not have a celebration which could be described as "Festivals" involving all members of a whole community in common activity. The Performance of rites in the service of gods and spirits was generally a domestic affair concerning only the members of a single long house and such ritual experts as had been called in mediators between the donor of a sacrificial feast and the supernatural powers whose help and protection was solicited" (1981:1, Haimendorf)

In the Second Stage, the *Nyokum* became a Village celebrated annual ritual. The Nyishis at that time began settling in particular villages and when ever there was any threat to the village or villagers they performed ritual for the whole village and villagers. Since the ritual performance was for the mass it came to be known as the *Nyokum*, here the 'Nyok' means Earth or piece of land and 'Kum' means together like in 'hakum' meaning coming together, combinely *Nyokum* means practicing ritual together in a common piece of land or earth. In Joram people celebrated *Nyokum* for the agricultural purpose and for the abundant harvest. It was only celebrated among the four villages of Joram annually. Prior to the people of the Joram, the Nyishis did not use the term *Nyokum*. The ritual performed was termed differently at different occasion of the performance. The *Nyokum* celebrated in Joram was purely an Agricultural ritual; later on only *Nyokum* was generalized to a festival for the prosperity of the entire Nyishi community and the world as a whole.

The Third stage was the one which made the present form of the *Nyokum*. In mid 1960s the govt. of India, in order to protect the tribal culture of the North Eastern India, asked the tribal to adopt a festival of its own, which could give identity to that particular tribe. Almost every tribe in Arunachal Predesh, the then NEFA, adopted a festival of their own, like Dree by Apatani, Solung by Adi, Mopin by Galo, etc. The first educating generation of the Nyishi, who were studying in Ziro, came to know about the *Nyokum* being celebrated by the Nyishis of Joram village and they saw it as cnly event which the Nyishi's could consider as a Festival. So they adopted the annually observed community ritual as the festival by generalizing it and making it a festival for the entire Nyishi tribe.

The present form of *Nyokum* seems to be having evolved from the three important rituals being practiced and performed by the Nyishi tribe since the time immemorial, called the Nyoying Hingnam, the Yullo Panam and the Uyu Panam. The practices of these rituals can be found in the folktales, folklores and folksongs of the Nyishis. According to Nyishi tales, these rituals were also responsible for the creation of universe and all the living and non living object of the world. The three ceremonies are being performed at different occasion for the safety and prosperity of the family or clan. The *Nyokum* is the combination and up gradation of these rituals which slowly took the shape of the festival with rightful guide and help of the first educated generation of the Nyishi Community.

The Yullo

Changma Dima Namchang lo, Soma Subu ngam paling nw,
Ho Tama Pate nge, Bwgma Tabeg nge, Nima Tani nge ho sangling nw,
Changtug Namchang lo, Sokku Subu ngam paling nw,
Changjig Namchang lo, Sogig Subu Ngam Paling nw,
Changdar Namchang lo, Sodar Subu ngam paling nw
Changha Changyi Namchang lo, Soha Sohing Subu ngam paling nw,
Donyi pabug nwnem nge, Talu Nyoying Tapung bunyi
Tani pabug nwnem nge, Atang yoyung Pungte bu,
Ho ngulu si palo pabug malo pabug,
Ho sebe pachang be, patung be
Ho si sulu Sokum sobu paling renw, so Nyokum so

These were the Words of Mr. Hillang Palang, a very prominent and popular priest of Sangram. It means that in the Changma Dima Namchang (ground/village/household) Soma Subu (mithun, bos frontalis), was sacrificed, because of which the Pate (Tiger), Tabeg (Snake) and Nima Tani (first Tani) had its birth as the blessing of the sacrifice and so on in Changtug, Sokku Subu was sacrificed; in Changjig, Sogig subu was sacrificed; in Changdar, Sodar subu was sacrificed; in Changha Changyi,

Soha Sohing subu was sacrificed and so on. Each time a mithun was sacrificed it brought great blessing to the Human race and increased their heriditation. The nyub contibues his saying that, so in the same spirits we are sacrificing the mithun in the *Nyokum* as a Sokum Subu (gathering mithun) for the welfare of the entire Humanity. The sacrifice of mithun meant the Yullo itself. The sacrifice of mithuns denotes that the *Nyokum* at a point was inspired from the Yullo.

Nyokum today

As to my observance, the pachung kugnaam ritual started at different timing in different *Nyokum* centres. The ritual was preformed to determine the spirit's will, by viewing the chicken liver after the chicken is being chanted, regarding their view for the coming *Nyokum*, the animals to be sacrificed and the choosing of the *Nyokum* Priest. In case of Nyapin *Nyokum* in Kurung Kumey District, it started almost two months before the *Nyokum* celebration date. In Doimukh *Nyokum*, there were more than four renown Nyibu, who canducted pachung kugnaam ritual and it took them 3 alternative day and more than 30 Chicken livers to finally decide that which spirit would summon this *Nyokum* and on Which Nyok (the place in spirit world where the god and goddesses will accept the sacrifice being made in *Nyokum*) they will accept the Sacrifice. Through the Pachung Kugnam devination they also determined the animals to be sacrificed and the chicken liver devitnation also determined the Nyoukm priests. The priest of Doimukh *Nyokum* said that this time the 'Yullo Uyu' would summon the Doimukh *Nyokum* Yullo, hence a Mithun is to be Sacrificed with other animals. The priests of the Doimukh *Nyokum*, chosen through devination, were Tana Tatang as *Nyokum* Yullo Nyub, Nangbia Taj as Galang Nyub, Techi Ringtu as Peming Topu Nyub and Teshi Tar as Nyoyin Nyub. It is considered to be a very prestigious to be chosen as a *Nyokum* Nyibu by Anne Donyi.

On 16th of January the food stall were being inaugurated in Doimukh *Nyokum*. The Celebration Copmmittee has fixed price of all the commodities that are to be sold in the stalls. Sports activity has also been kicked off. The Sport tournament for Football and volleyball takes bit a long time. The Volleyball seems to be a very prominent sport tournament in the *Nyokum*. There is an entry fee and the winner gets a cash prize, which various from year to year and from centre to centre, with a trophy. The cash prizes for winner in some of the *Nyokum* centres like Itanagar, nirjuli and Doimukh were Rs. 1,50,000, Rs. 1,00,000 and Rs. 50,000 respectively. In some centre only Nyishi players are permitted to participate like that of in Doimukh, believing that our own people should be encouraged in *Nyokum*. Whereas in other centres, they are open towards any team or individual to participate in the Sport in *Nyokum* with a mindset that we should welcome every individual to share a part blessing from Anne *Nyokum*. The other sports included Erri apka, dapo, etc.

The chanting of rituals begins from the 24th of January. In the evening of 23th the *Nyokum* Organising committee reaches the Nyub's house with meat and local bear as gift for the Nyub, that evening whole the committee stays at the Nyub's house, specially the elder member of the *Nyokum* committee. On the Next day i,e. on 24th morning the *Nyokum* committee with due honor escort the Nyub from his house to the *Nyokum* Lapang's Nyub house. The ritual and chanting are being performed in the *Nyokum* Nyub Naamlo, which is being constructed for that purpose. As soon as the nyub reaches the nyub Naamlo he starts his chantings for inviting the god and goddesses to that *Nyokum*. There are special committee engaged for the nyubs, whose main duty is to serve the nyubs and provide them the all the necessary commodities for the ritual, they are called the Nyub In-charge. There are also the volunteer arranged for serving and looking after the needs of the nyubs, most of the time these are elderly women of the community. The volunteers in the Nyub Naamlo, most of the time, were seen working there willingly, even though they were not engaged there, in order to seek some blessing from Anne *Nyokum*.

When the priest are chanting the rituals inside the house the common villager will go to the jungle and collect all the materials for the construction of the Yugang (altar), where the sacrifice is to be made, though some of the materials are being collected before the time, specially to the plants that are not available in the surrounding and which are to be exported from the distant places. There are only certain types of plants that are being used in the construction of Yugang. Some of the important and compulsory plants for the construction of Yugang are Taboo (a type of bamboo), Kura (type of leaves which is used in every kind of altar making by the Nyishis), Hatte (another family of Bamboo with broader leaves), depeg (decorative flower made out of Bamboo), etc. each of these plant used in the altar making has their own importance and story behind their usages. These plants are not replaceable in the altar making process and even if one of them is missing the altar would be considered incomplete, so there collection in advance is very much important.

The construction of the Yugang starts from the 25th morning and most of the time the whole day is enough for the construction, and the Yugang is complete by the evening. There is also a pattern for the constructing of Yugang, and it is a very systematic process, which only the experience elderly people of the community has the detail. Moreover the construction of Yugang will be with the full direction from the *Nyokum* Nyub, the Head priest of the *Nyokum*, who will give the detail and number of gods and goddesses to be represented in the Yugang. There are more than two or three Yugang constructed, representing different god and goddesses.

Previously the Yugang (altar) were constructed in the middle of the *Nyokum* Lapang (ground) but in the present there is definite place made especially for the construction of the Yugang. In Doimukh the place where the Yugang was to be established was well fenced so that the cattle cannot destroy the Yugang, when the *Nyokum* celebration is over

In Yugang is very well decorated and the entire god and the goddesses that are going to be present in that *Nyokum* is symbolized in that Yugang. The Annne Donyi (Sun Godesses) is the most powerful deity in the Nyishi deities, which is why she is represented at the highest. All the god and goddesses who are to be represented in the Yugang is being instructed to the in-charge for the Yugang construction by the head priest who in advance, who with the divination, has already fixed an appointment with the god and goddesses. The representation of only those the god and goddesses are represented in the Yugang who have accepted the proposal of the invitation of the nyub to grace that *Nyokum*. There are also landing grounds made for the spirit through which the spirits can identify the Yugang and land in that Yugang and stay there. The number of deities is not fixed for every *Nyokum* that is why the design of the Yugang of the *Nyokum* may differ from centre to centre and from time to time. There is also space, specially made for the selected women, to offer Attang and Oppo to the god and goddesses. This practice has been taken from ritual performed during Yullo and Nyoying. In *Nyokum* there are huge numbers of applicants who want to offer the Attang and Oppo to the Yugang, out of which the committee selects only few; otherwise the Yugang design may be hampered.

At the time when the priest is chanting the rituals in the Nyub Namlo (the priest house), the other non ritual part of the *Nyokum* members carries on with the other activity like the games and sport competition, the culture competition etc. The culture activities were mostly performed in the night time. There were numerous items for the competition like single, duet and group dance and song on both traditional and Modern. The exiting and interesting traditional completions were the folklore and folk song competitions like Edd binam, Nyimey kabnam, buya kinam, etc. but the sad view of it was that during these competitions the number was almost nil, the people, the self claimed modern people, were all only interested in witnessing the modern form of cultural activity and not the traditional form of cultural activities. The participants, in the traditional folk lore and folk song, were also very less in number with only the elderly people participating, who can be considered as the only few survivor with these ethnic knowledge and interest.

In the evening of the 25th, when the making alter is completed, the Nyub offers a sacrifice to the malevolent spirits in the backyard of the house, the offering usually is of a pig and a chicken. The offering is made so that the malevolent spirit may not disrupt the *Nyokum* celebration and specially the ritual ceremony of 26th day.

On 26th morning the all people who want to participate in the ritual procession gathers in the Ground in early in the morning. The male members bring Tori, a long bamboo stick with a chicken attached to it for offering to the Yugang. All female members get ready with their Oppo to be offered to the Yugang. In the mornig at around 8.00 AM the priest steps out from the Nyub Naamlo and proceeds toward the Yugang with the male members following him with the Tori in their hand. The priest makes some rounds of the Yugang, ringing a bell in his hand, and then finally goes nearby the Yugang and chants the ritual and invites all the god and goddesses to come in the Yugang and accept the offering made to them. With the signal from the priest the animal sacrifice is made to all the altars prepared, one after another. The offerings are made in the decreasing order; the first sacrifice is to the Yullo uyu which is Mithun, followed by the offering pig, goat and chickens in order. Once the sacrifice is made the selected women offers their Oppo to the altars and the left over are being served to the people around, which is considered to be devine one as it was being offered to the god goddesses and people drink it with great zeal. After all the offering is made the women stands in queue and one by one the head priest blesses them and their family, and as a symbol of blessing he plucks a small part of the alter and puts it in their Agey, grain basket. The male members after offering their chicken in the Tori also take back the body of the death chicken, which they offered as a sacrifice to the Yugang, back to their home as a symbol of blessing and even eat it, with their family members, taking it as a blessing from the god and goddesses. After the sacrifice the death animal can be eaten by the *Nyokum* ritual observer as the Uyus accepts only the spirits of the animals and has to observe the taboos related to it.

When all these ceremonies are in process the male member of the *Nyokum* leads a procession called Buya, where they stand in queue and rounds the alter, shouting for the blessing from the god and goddesses, it was confined for the male member of the society but today the female member also joins the Buya, the impact of modernization seeking equality for all genders. The female section performs Rikam Pada, a tradirional dance of the Nyishis for the female section. In Doimukh *Nyokum* celebration the Naarnam Dance was also demonstrated, which is one of the oldest dance form and not practiced anymore by the Nyishis, luckily a member of this dance from the first generation was there to lead.

When all the sacrifice and chanting is done the priest marches toward the Nyub Naamlo. After reaching inside the Naamlo the Nyub place some of the object used during the ritual in horn cone, mithun horn, with which the spirits are have come to the Naamlo for the stay for the night. In the mean time all the male participants divides the pieces of Mithun Meat, which was slaughtered in the ritual, to all the pure observer of the ritual and which is a very holy meat with the blessing. The meat sacrificed in the ritual can only be consumed by the pure ritual observers and one who agrees to observe the taboos related to it. The impure person, that have by any chance practiced unholy practice like adultery, thief, broken a taboo, etc., if consume the sacrificed meat may have to face the wrath of the spirits like illness and sometime death of himself or in the family. For the pure observer of the taboo in the *Nyokum*, the sacrificial meat will act as a medicine and blessing to the individual or in the family.

The ritual parts end in the morning followed by the official program. For the day there is one Chief Guest and Guest of honor invited. There is cultural display for them, the Mega dance as the centre of the attraction. The selected individual reads out the Philosophy of *Nyokum* to the audience, this year Prof. Tana Showren read the philosophy of *Nyokum* Yullo in Doimukh *Nyokum* Yullo celebration. Prof. Saket Khuswaha, the VC of RGU, graced the Doimukh Nokum Yullo as the Chief Guest. The Guests has a say, most of the time on Unity, integrity and the upliftment and preservation of the culture. Most of the time, when the Guest is some Legislator or someone with Executive authority, they announce some development package for the *Nyokum* committee. The Program ends with a Community feast for everyone. In the evening there is cultural programme with the distributions of prizes for every event.

On the 26th a very important ritual is being observed. In the morning the family, who were selected for the offering to the altar with Oppo, goes to Jungle and collects the the Kokam leaves and Bwbrey plants. The Bwbrey plants are designed as Tasang (beads). Then before the sun raises the women offers the Kokam and the Bwbrey plants as the ornaments to the Spirits dwelling in the altar. The spirits that dwelled in the Yugang for the night accepts the ornaments and leaves for their respective place, which is also why the ornaments are being offered early in the morning before the Sun rise as to bid them good bye for the long journey.

On the day, Nyub then selects a place where they lay the *Nyokum* Dapo, a log of Tree, as a symbol to keep away the evil from the particular village or villages. In past the *Nyokum* Dapo were place at the entrance of the Villgae and no outsider were allowed to cross that village for the selected day. The village where the *Nyokum* was organized also followed the strict taboo of prohibition of to-and-pro from the village. If someone broke the taboo, by either entering the village or leaving, was imposed with a heavy fine. But in the present the prohibition of people from one place to another is not possible and moreover there no any definite jurisdiction of any particular village. Therefore the Nyub select a place where usually the people don't go much and lay the *Nyokum* Dapo there. This is the last ritual of the *Nyokum*.

Conclusion

The festivals are usually an upgradation of rituals of the past. The festivals have their central focus, the reasons usually because of which the particular festival is being observed or celebrated, like agriculture for example. The *Nyokum* was also a ritual in its origin and slowly in the course of time it has taken the shape of a festival. It can be very truly said that the *Nyokum* festival is amalagation of the rituals for the prosperity of human civilization. The three major rituals from which the *Nyokum* had evoleved are Nyoying, Yullo and Uyu Panam. There was concept of Sokum Sodar Subu Panam, meaning sacrificing of Mithun, and Sotu Nyotu ritual from the time immemorial in the Nyishi tradition which possibly were also the origins of the *Nyokum*.

The origin of the *Nyokum* can be assumed to have passed through three separate steges of evolution; in the first stage the Nyishi simply practiced many rituals and sacrifice, to both benevolent and malevolent spirits, for the welfare and protection of their existence, the rituals like, Yullo, Sotu Nyotu, Nyoying, etc. are the most ethnical form of rituals. The Nyishi at time were mostly semi-nomadic in their residential nature. The rituals were practiced at the individual level only. The rituals were only performed when there was the need for the ritual and sacrifice to be performed, that too could be known only through the devinition and there was no fixed time for the ritual performance.

In the second phase when the Nyishi started settling in one particular place and built villages they started practicing the rituals in the village level, the perfect exemple can be cited to the *Nyokum* practiced in the Joram village on the basis of yearly basis. The celebration of *Nyokum* in Joram was purely a post harvesting agricultural festival. The rituals were celebrated for the whole village and in a community level. But the fixation of particular time for the celebration was not there.

In the third phase the *Nyokum* took its modern form. It was in the mid 1960s that the government of India, in order to preserve the dying tribal culture and tradition, started encouraging the tribals to popularize their culture in the form of festivals. With the direction from government on India, almost every tribe in Arunachal Pradesh adopted a festival of their own. The first generation educated Nyishi saw it as opportunity to bring Nyishis under one umbrella, those that were living in different topography and zones. The leaders like Lt. Tadar Tang, Dr. Joram Begi, Bengia Tollum, Chuku Tallar, etc. who at that time were studying in the Govt. Higher Secondary school Ziro, took the initiation and convinced the people of Joram village to make their village celebrated Ritual, *Nyokum*, to be celebrated in generalized form for the whole Nyishi community. As a result, in the year 1967 the first generalized form of *Nyokum* was celebrated in the Joram, which was participated from the young Nyishi student brigades studying in Ziro, who later became the champions and pioneers in popularizing the *Nyokum* festival. The *Nyokum* today is the compilation of the many rituals, there is worship of not only one god or goddess but the numerous numbers of deities are invited in the *Nyokum*, where they are worshipped and being offered sacrifices.

One of the reasons, as quoted by one of the informant, Mr. Techi Taura (Priest incharge of Doimukh *Nyokum* Yullo) was that, "in Nyishi community there were lots of necessary rituals needed to be performed in their daily life. The performance like Yullo, Nyoying and Uyu panam ritual had to be performed in the demands of the Uyus (spirits) and the performances of these rituals were quite an expensive and time taking process. That is also an obvious reason why the *Nyokum* was amalgated, so that all those family and individuals who did not have enough financial capacity to perform the individual rituals can participate in the *Nyokum* and get the blessing from god and goddesses. In the present day also most of the people are busy in their day today life and unless they are tempted by any kind problem in their daily life, they forget to please and remember their god and goddesses. Therefore this festival form of amalgamation of the rituals gives the individuals to come closer to their god and goddesses and seek their blessing."

When observed the changes that are occuring in the *Nyokum*, it was found that the modernization and the alien cultures have highly infected the tribal world in its appearance and in beneath. Every aspect and parts of the *Nyokum* can be seen effected by the agents like globalization, assimilation, acculturation, etc. The Nyishis are not the exceptional of the cultural change taking place in its surrounding.

The changes in the *Nyokum* are because of the numerous agents that are responsible for shaking the ethnical existence of the Nyishi. The alien religions are one of the most determining factors for the dilutions made in the ritual part of the *Nyokum*. In some of the *Nyokum* centers, where there is high concentration of the Christian population, the ancestral ritual are very highly discouraged and very strikingly sometime the ritual part is skipped. The reason is obvious that the Christians condiders the sacrifice made to other god and goddesses as sin. The main reason behind the *Nyokum* loosing its ethnicity is the ignorance of the new young generations. The young Nyishis are so busy in modern enlightenment that they are in no interest knowing and learning their traditional culture and ethnical knowledge.

The agents like modernization, urbanization, industrialization, etc. are also playing equal role in bringing this sea of changes in *Nyokum*. The changes in the means of material used, foods, dress, etc. has also changed the outer appearance of the *Nyokum* as well as the soul of the *Nyokum*. Though it has been found that the modernization has brought negative, but it must also be admitted that without the modern tools and technology the celebration of the *Nyokum* in such a large scale will not also be very possible. It can be assuredly said that without modernization aspects the *Nyokum* celebration today will be a very difficult task and with modernization the *Nyokum* faces the threat of its existence.

References

Aier, Anungla, (2004) "The cultural change among the Nagas- festivals and the ornaments." InVenuh,V. (ed), "Naga Society- Continuity and change" published by Shipra Publication, New Delhi, p. 49-60.

Brandt, edited by J. Rasmus; Iddeng, Jon W. (2012). Greek and Roman festivals : content, meaning, and practice (1st ed.). Oxford: Oxford University Press. pp. 3-7.

Chaudhuri,Buddhadeb (1992)Changing religion and festivals cycle of the Mundas. In Chaudhuri, Buddhadeb (ed) "Tribal Transformation in India", published by Inter-India Publications, New Delhi 110015, p. 219-233.

Deogaonkar,Shailaja S. (1992) "Tribal religion and festivals." InChaudhuri, Buddhadeb, (ed) "Tribal Transformation in India", published by Inter-India Publications, New Delhi. p. 131-138.

Deuri, R. K. (1983) "Festivals of kameng- A few selected". Published by Director of Research, Govt. of Arunachal Pradesh, p. 26-29.

Gohain, BirindraKumer, (1993) "The Hill Lalungs", published by AnundoramBorooah Institute of Language, Art and Culture, Assam.

Haldar, A.K and Arora, Sushil,(1992) "The Religious observances and the Festivals of the Artisan Tribal of Chotanagpur." In Bhuddhadeb Chaudhuri, (ed) "Tribal Transformation in India", published by Inter-India Publications, New Delhi.

Hina, Nabam Nakha (2016), "The Nyishi Social and Political Movement in Search of Identity", published by AuthorsPress, New Delhi.

Hina, N. Nakha,(2012), "The Customary laws of Nyishi Tribe of Arunachal Pradesh", published by Authorspress, editorial Q-2A HauzKhas Enclave, New Delhi-110016.

Horam, M, (1988), "Nagas the old ways and new trends", published by Cosmo Publications, New Delhi.

Karmakar, Kavita (2016) "Mopin festival among the Galos of Likabali, Arunachal Pradesh" (unpublished work)

Joshi, H.G (2010), "Arunachal Pradesh: Past and Present", Published by Mittal Publications, New Delhi.

Khoda Bagang, (2006) "The Nyishi Belief and Ritual practices related to the Economy" (unpublished work).

Kurup,A. M. (1992) "Tribal festivals of central India. In Chaudhuri, Buddhadeb (ed) "Tribal Transformation in India", published by Inter-India Publications, New Delhi. p. 119-126.

Makwana, M.H. (1992), "Religion and the Festivals of the tribal of Sagbara". In Chaudhuri, Buddhadeb, (ed) "Tribal Transformation in India", published by Inter-India Publications, New Delhi 110015. p. 127-130.

Nani Bath, (2004), "Religious Belief and practices of the Apatani in transition". In TamoMibang, and Choudhary, S.K, Understanding the Tribal Religion.

Pandey, B.B. (1981), "The festivals of the Subansiri". published by- Director of Research, Arunachal Pradesh. p. 12- 21.

Ray, A.K. (2004), "Change- the Law of Life". InVenuh, V. (ed) "Naga Society-Continuity and change". Published by Shipra Publications, New Delhi. p. 13-36.

Rikam, Nabam Tadar (2005), "Emerging Riligious Identity of Arunachal Pradesh-A study of Nyishi Tribe", Published by Mittal Publication, New Delhi.

Robertson, Noel (1992). "Festivals and legends: the formation of Greek cities in the light of public ritual" (Repr. ed.). Toronto: University of Toronto Press. pp. 11-15.

Tribhuwan, Robin D, "Fair and Festivals of Indian Tribe In Tribhuwan", Robin D and Tribhuwan, Preeti R, "An Introduction to Tribal Fair and Festival: Theoretical Consideration".

Public Health

Chapter - 18

Prevalence of Hypertension and Its Associated Risk Factors among the *Tengaponia Deoris* of Dibrugarh District, Assam

— Anand Sharma, Nitul Kumar Gogoi & Prasanta Kumar Borah

Cardiovascular disease (CVD) is the leading cause of death worldwide. The incidence of CVD is increasing in both developed and developing countries with high morbidity and mortality. The majority of these CVD deaths were attributable to either ischemic heart disease (IHD) or cerebrovascular disease (GBD, 2013). It is a silent killer as very rarely any symptom can be seen in its early stages until a severe medical crisis takes place like heart attack, stroke, or chronic kidney disease (A. V. Chobanian et al, 2003, Wikipedia, Hypertension, J. Prabakaran, et al, 2013). Since people are unaware of excessive blood pressure, it is only through measurements that detection can be done. Although the majority of patients with hypertension remain asymptomatic, some people with HTN report headaches, lightheadedness, vertigo, altered vision, or fainting episode (N. D. Fisher, 2005). As reported by World Health Organization, hypertension (HTN) is the third 'killer' disease, accounting for one in every eight deaths worldwide (WHO,2002) It has been expected that the number of hypertensives may rise from 118 million in 2000 to 214 million in 2025(Kearney et al, 2005). Hypertension is well recognized as a public health problem among urban and as well as among rural adults in India and is directly responsible for 16% for ischemic heart disease, 21% for peripheral vascular disease, 24% for acute myocardial infarction and 29% for stroke in India (Gupta et al, 1996). Premature mortality from CVD could be prevented, to a considerable extent, by the effective control of hypertension (ICMR Report, 2004). There is a paucity of data on the prevalence of hypertension and its risk factor in tribal population and this study was carried out to determine the same in a tribal population from rural Assam.

Materials and method

In the present study, an attempt had been made to estimate the prevalence of hypertension and its associated risk factors of hypertension among the Tengaponia Deoris of Dibrugarh district, Assam. A community-based cross-sectional study was conducted among 100 individuals in the age group of 18 years and above. After taking written informed consent form each informant, data on their socio-demographic aspects, substance use, dietary habits, and physical activity were collected from the informant. In the present study respondents with any gross abnormalities, bedridden subjects, pregnant/lactating women and subjects not providing informed consent were excluded. Systematic random sampling was used to enlist the study of individuals. Joint National Committee VII classification was used to define hypertension and Body mass index was classified as per World Health Organization criteria.

Inclusion criteria

The following inclusion criteria were adopted for recruitment of the study subjects:

1. *Tengaponia Deoris*of either gender and aged > = 18 years
2. Subjects proving informed consent.

Exclusion criteria

1. Subjects unable to provide informed consent.
2. Subjects <18 years
3. Pregnant women
4. Subjects with past history of stroke, transient ischemic attack, congestive cardiac failure, myocardial infarction and angina.
5. Patient with known diseases of kidney, liver and malignancy.

Results

Table 18.1 show that the prevalence of hypertension was higher in females (62.5%) than in males (37.5%). The overall prevalence of hypertension

Table 18.1: Socio-demographic characteristics of *Tengaponia Deoris* of Dibrugarh district, Assam (N=100) according to blood pressure status.

Variable	*Subgroups*	*Group*		*p value*
		Hypertensive N (%)	*Non-hypertensive N (%)*	
Sex	**Male**	9(37.5)	26(34.2)	0.768
	Female	15(62.5)	50(65.8)	
	Total	24(24)	76(76)	
Age group, yrs	**18-30**	0(0)	20(26.3)	0.016
	31-40	3(12.5)	14(18.4)	
	41-50	6(25.0)	16(21.0)	
	51 and above	15(62.5)	26(34.2)	
	Total	24(24)	76(76)	
Educational status	**Illiterate**	9(37.5)	11(14.5)	0.05
	I-V	3(12.5)	9(11.8)	
	VI-X	7(29.2)	22(28.9)	
	HSLC	0(0)	19(25.0)	
	Higher Secondary	5(20.8)	11(14.5)	
	Graduate	0(0)	3(3.9)	
	Post Graduate	0(0)	1(1.3)	
Income	**<5000**	1(4.2)	6(7.9)	0.648
	5001-10000	18(75.0)	44(57.9)	
	10001-15000	3(12.5)	15(19.7)	
	15001-20000	1(4.2)	5(6.6)	
	20001-25000	1(4.2)	2(2.6)	
	>=25001	0(0)	4(5.3)	
Occupation	**Cultivation**	6(25.0)	21(27.5)	0.874
	Service	3(12.5)	6(7.9)	
	Housewife	9(37.5)	35(46.1)	
	Others	6(25.0)	13(17.4)	
Marital status	**Married**	19(79.2)	66(86.8)	0.004
	Unmarried	0(0)	8(10.5)	
	Widow	**5(20.8)**	**2(2.6)**	

was 24% and the prevalence of hypertension was found to be highest in the age group of 51 years and above (<0.001). Educational status states that 37.5% of hypertensive is illiterates followed by VI-X standard (29.2%), Higher Secondary (20.8%) (< 0.05). Out of the total, 75% of hypertensive has an income from 5000 to 10000 and 57.9% was non - hypertensive. The majority of the prevalence of hypertension was found in housewives (37.5%) followed by cultivation (25.0%), others (25.0%), service holders (12.5%).

Table 18.2 states that the distribution of Tengaponia Deoris of Dibrugarh district, Assam according to blood pressure status and found according to Body Mass Index shows that 54.1% of hypertensive were found to be normal followed by overweight (29.1%), obese (12.5%). and underweight (4.1). The habits of tobacco chewing were associated with

Table 18.2: Distribution of clinical characteristics of *Tengaponia Deoris* of Dibrugarh district, Assam according to blood pressure status

Variables		*Hypertensive (%)*	*Non-hypertensive (%)*	*Total (%)*	*p value*
Body mass index	**< 18.5**	1(4.1)	6(7.9)	7(7)	0.451
	18.5-24.9	13(54.1)	50(65.7)	63(63)	
	25-29.9	7(29.1)	16(21.0)	23(23)	
	≥ 30	3(12.5)	4(5.3)	7(7)	
Tobacco consumption	**Yes**	9(37.5)	17(22.4)	26(26)	0.14
	No	15(62.5)	59(77.6)	74(74)	
Alcohol consumption	**Yes**	18(75.0)	32(42.1)	50(50)	0.05
	No	6(25.0)	44(57.9)	50(50)	
Smoking consumption	**Yes**	5(20.8)	4(5.3)	9(9)	0.02
	No	19(79.2)	72(94.7)	91(91)	
Extra salt	**Yes**	10(41.7)	22(28.9)	32(32)	0.24
	No	14(58.3)	54(71.1)	68(68)	
Physical activity	**Light**	12(50)	52(68.4)	64(64)	0.19
	Moderate	12(50)	23(30.3)	35(35)	
	Heavy	0(0)	1(1.3)	1(1)	
Familial History	**Yes**	5(20.8)	10(13.2)	15(15)	0.35
	No	**19(79.2)**	**66(86.8)**	**85(85)**	

Table 18.3: Distribution of anthropometric indicators in *Tengaponia Deoris* of Dibrugarh district, Assam according to blood pressure status

Variables	*Normotensive (N=76) (Mean ± S.D)*	*Hypertensive (N=24) (Mean ± S.D)*	*P value*
SBP (mm/Hg)	119.4±**10.9**	150.3±**13.2**	0.663
DBP (mm/Hg)	74.6±**7.5**	90.7±**6.0**	0.192
Age (years)	43.21±2	55.1±**11.8**	0.001
Height (cm)	155.7±**7.6**	155.7±**8.0**	0.368
Weight (kg)	56.2±**9.5**	59.9±**11.8**	0.252
BMI	**23.2±3.7**	**24.6±3.7**	**0.110**

hypertension 37.5% while 22.4% of tobacco chewing was non - hypertensive. Among 50 alcoholic users, 75.0% were hypertensive and 42.1% were non - hypertensive (<0.005). The prevalence of hypertension among smokers was 20.8% while 79.2% were non-smokers (<0.005). A total of 41.7% of hypertensive was taking extra salt intake. A higher prevalence of hypertension was found with light activity and moderate activity (50%). Familial history possesses 20.8% of hypertensive and 13.2% was non-hypertensive.

Table 18.3 depicts the distribution of anthropometric indicators in Tengaponia Deoris of Dibrugarh district, Assam according to blood pressure status. Age revealed a significant difference and has high value in hypertensive than normotensive.

Discussion

The present study focused on the prevalence of hypertension and its associated risk factors among the Tengaponia Deoris of Dibrugarh district, Assam. The prevalence of hypertension was 24% and was higher among females (62.5%) as compared to males (37.5%). The Prevalence of hypertension was found to be highest in the age group of 51 years and above (41%). Educational status states that 29% of hypertensive are VI-X category (<0.005), 62% of hypertensive have an income of up to 5000 to 10000. The majority of the prevalence of hypertension was found in housewives (52.8%). Similar studies like Hazarika N.C et al (2003) reported that the overall prevalence of hypertension in their study was 63.63%, 64.2% in men and 62.89% in women. An increasing trend of prevalence was observed in the higher age group of 60 years and above in the study population. A higher prevalence of hypertension was also observed in females in the age group 70-79 years in comparison to males. Again, Mishra et al 2014, found that overall, tobacco use was 84 % (men 94%; women 73%, $p<0.001$) and alcohol use was 67 % (men 82%; women 50%, $p<0.05$); 86 % reported vigorous physical activity, (men 91%, women 82%; $p < 0.05$). 68% reported to consume an unhealthy diet (less than five servings of fruits and vegetables/day), 11 % had abdominal obesity, 16 % were overweight and 26 % had hypertension. Non-users of tobacco and those who consumed more fruits and vegetables had a higher prevalence of overweight ($p<0.05$). Mahanta T.G et al (2008) found that the overall prevalence of hypertension was 33.3% with no significant sex difference. A positive trend with increasing age was observed. Singh M. et al (2016) reported that the overall prevalence of hypertension in both sexes is around 36.5% with 29.76% among males and 47% in females. The peak age of hypertension in the study was 60-69 years and a proportionate increase with age was observed in both sexes. The prevalence of hypertension in their study was 52.05% in low socio-economic index families and 30.17% and 30.52% in medium and high socio-economic index families. High prevalence in low socio-economic index families is an inconsistent finding in the study.

In the current study, the distribution of Tengaponia Deoris according to Body Mass Index shows that 54.1% of hypertensive were found to be normal followed by overweight (29.1%), obese (12.5%) and underweight (4.1%) The habits of tobacco chewing were having hypertension 37.5% while 62.5 % not having habit of tobacco chewing were having hypertension. Out of the total number of alcoholic users, 75.0% were hypertensive and 25.0% were non - hypertensive (<0.005). The prevalence of hypertension among smokers was 20.8% while 79.2% were non - smokers (<0.005). A total of 41.7% of hypertensive was taking extra salt intake while 58.3% of hypertensive was not taking extra salt. A higher prevalence of hypertension was found with light activity and moderate activity (50%). A familial history depicts 20.8% of hypertensive and 79.2% are not having a familial history. Similar studies like tobacco use of 94 % reported by men in the present study were higher than the 72 % prevalence among the general men population of Assam. The prevalence of Smoking was 63.6 % among men in the study and Alcohol use in 67 % population (Mishra et al, 2014). Studies like Hazarika N.C et al (2003) reported that extra salt consumption was recorded in 50.90% of the elderly participants, 36.94% of the participants were alcoholics and only 16.78% were current smokers. Apart from smoking, 44.93% of the study participants were habituated to chewing. Mahanta T.G et al (2013) found that tea-garden workers also consumed more salt. Mean daily per-capita salt intake was 29.60 grams, tobacco consumption 85.2% ($p < 0.0001$). Tea-garden workers had higher levels of physical activity and had lower BMI (mean BMI 21.34 kg/m2 vs. 23.59 kg/m2, $p<0.0001$).

Conclusion

From the present study, it is seen that burden of hypertension was quiet high in females in comparison to males among the *Tengaponia Deoris* of Dibrugarh district, Assam. Prevalence of risk factor like alcohol is very common among *Tengaponia Deoris*. Implementation of health promotional measures aiming to reduce alcohol & tobacco consumption, detection and treatment of hypertension, dietary modification will help in decreasing the future risk of hypertension and its complications.

Acknowledgment

The authors would like to acknowledge the people of *Tengaponia Deoris* of Dibrugarh district, Assam.

References

Assessment of burden of non-communicable diseases in India, Final report of Project WR/SE IND RPC 001 RB 02, SE/02/419575, New Delhi: Indian Council of Medical Research, 2004, http://www.whoindia.org/LinkFiles/Assessment_of_Burden_of_NCD_Hypertension_Assessment_of_Burden_of_NCDs.pdf.

Chobanian AV, Bakris GL, Black HR, Cushman WC, Green LA, Izzo JL Jr, Jones DW, Materson BJ, Oparil S, Wright JT Jr, Roccella EJ, 2003, Joint National

Committee on Prevention, Detection, Evaluation, and Treatment of High Blood Pressure. National Heart, Lung, and Blood Institute; National High Blood Pressure Education Program Coordinating Committee., Seventh report of the Joint National Committee on prevention, detection, evaluation, and treatment of high blood pressure, Hypertension, Vol. 42(6), pp. 1206–1252.

GBD, 2015, Mortality and Causes of Death Collaborators. Global, regional, and national age–sex specific all-cause and cause-specific mortality for 240 causes of death, 1990–2013: a systematic analysis for the Global Burden of Disease Study, Lancet; 385: 117–71.

Gupta R, al-Odat NA, Gupta VP, 1996, Hypertension epidemiology in India: meta-analysis of 50 year prevalence rates and blood pressure trends. J Hum Hypertens; 10: 465-72.

Hazarika NC, D Biswas, K Narain, HC Kalita, J Mahanta, 2002, Hypertension and its risk factors in tea garden workers of Assam. Natl Med J India; 15: 63-8.

J. Prabakaran, N. Vijayalakshmi, and E. VenkataRao, 2013, Prevalence of hypertension among urban adult population (25–64 years) of Nellore, International Journal of Research & Development of Health, Vol. 1(2), pp. 42-49.

Kearney PM, Whelton M, Reynolds K, Muntner P, Whelton PK, He J., 2005, Global burden of hypertension: analysis of worldwide data, Lancet; 365: 217-223.

Mahanta T.G., F.U. Ahmed, B. N. Mahanta, A. Barua, 2008, Prevalence of Hypertension and its Risk Factors in a Tea Garden Community of Dibrugarh District, Assam,Indian Journal of Public Health; Vol. 52(1).

Misra, Palash Jyoti, G.K. Mini & K.R. Thankappan, 2014, Risk factor profile for non-communicable diseases among Mishing tribes in Assam, India: Results from a WHO STEPs survey, Indian J Med Res, 140: 370-378.

N. D. Fisher and G. H. Williams,2005, Hypertensive vascular disease, in Harrison's Principles of Internal Medicine, D. L. Kasper, E. Braunwald, A. S. Fauci et al., McGraw-Hill, New York, NY, USA, 16th editionpp. 1463–1481.

Victor RG, Leonard D, Hess P, Bhat DG, Jones J, Vaeth PA, Ravenell J, Freeman A, Wilson RP, Haley RW, 2008, Factors associated with hypertension awareness, treatment, and control in Dallas County, Texas, Arch Intern Med;168(12): 1285-93.

Wikipedia, Hypertension, https://en.wikipedia.org/wiki/Hypertension.

World Health Organization, The world health report 2002: Reducing risks, promoting life. Geneva: WHO.

Chapter - 19

Psychology in the Shade of Global Pandemics: A Brief Note

— *Barnali Sarma*

With the spread of COVID-19 virus, it is understood by everyone what a pandemic is and how susceptible we are to it. A pandemic has overriding influence over people which is associated with concerns over its geographic spread. According to WHO (World Health organization), a pandemic is a new disease, spread over several countries and continents, affecting a large number of people, for which people do not have immunity. However a widespread endemic disease with astable number of infected people is not pandemic. An outbreak of global pandemic causes fear and concern among the general population and it has overwhelming influence on the cognitive and emotional well-being of every individual.Despite hectic planning, quarantine schedules, social distancing, administrative actions, a large majority of people continue to confront with pandemics time to time.

A short history

Disease and illness have plagued humanity since time immemorial. The history of disease is as old as the history of human civilization. Though quite often endemics, epidemics and pandemics are used interchangeably, but there are some distinct differences among them. As modern humans spread across the nook and corner of the world, so are the infectious diseases. Throughout history, nothing has killed more people worldwide and afflicted human civilization than contagious diseases. Recently, COVID-19 which has been declared a pandemic by WHO (World Health Organization) in March 11, 2020 proved how vulnerable are the people to any kind of pandemics. In the course of time such pandemics alter the course of human history. Fig 19.1 depicts few of the most momentous pandemics that have occurred over time.

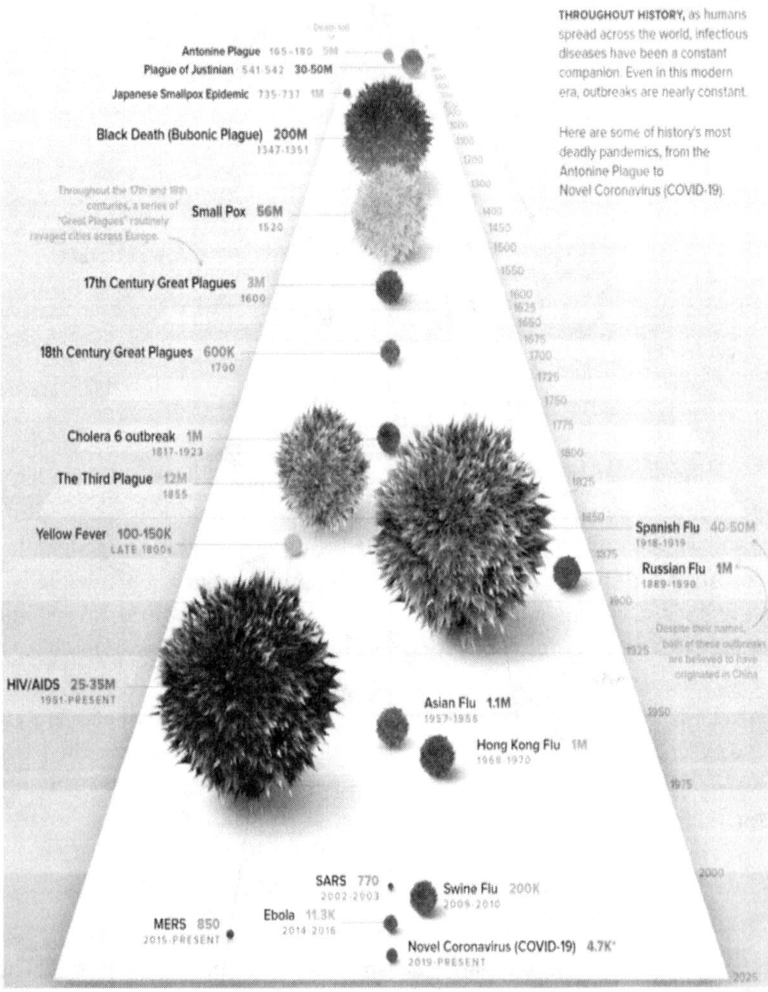

Source: World Economic Forum.

Fig 19.1 Types of Pandemics throughout history.

Psychosocial impacts of Pandemics on patient and the general population

Pandemics that occur over time bring stealthy and growing public health crisis and equally match emergency situation as well as response. A pandemic puts enormous stress on everyone, from health care professionals to other specific groups.

These emergency situations create immense psychosocial disturbances, involving unfamiliar threats which are difficult to detect, combat and challenging to differentiate from other benign illnesses. Such protracted and dynamic pandemic conditions evoke hope and despairsimultaneously and dramatically upset everyday habits, interactions and economic exchanges. Experiencing a potential cascade of tough situations is a challenge. The lives of infected as well as vulnerable population and the whole society are at stake due to the perpetuated potential impacts of any global pandemic. There is always a neuropsychiatric relation between the outbreak of acute respiratory infections and mental disorders as influenza and SARS (Severe Acute Respiratory Syndrome) reported this years ago (Shah, K et al. 2020).

Psychological impact on health care professionals

It is worthwhile to presume that during a pandemic situation, many medical practitioners as well as paramedics face PTSD (Post Traumatic Stress Disorder), depression, anxiety, burnout and other stress related disorder like hypertension during and after the cessation of the incidence of such infections. In addition, during such tough times, medical practitioners have to work extra-hours keeping the fear of own lives, which may lead to generalized anxiety disorder and other mood disorders. A previous study shows that compared to the other health care professionals, clinicians are more prone to distress. A study on SARS outbreak reveals that medical providers experience distress at the onset, during and cessation of the outbreak (Phua, DH et al, 2004).

A step toward nurturing mental health

All the mental health professionals like psychiatrists, clinical psychologists, counselors, psychiatric social workers and other paramedics should build a team to offer mental health support not only to the affected persons or general population but to the medics also. Since a global pandemic engulf the entire population and pose serious challenges for health and economic security of millions of people worldwide.Clear and consistent information should be provided to the medical teams as well as mental health professional on the prevalence of such outbreaks. It is the responsibility of government and other health organizations to ensure secure and legitimate electronic information sharing platforms in order to promote and provide telepsychiatry and telemedicine psychological counseling. CBT (Cognitive Behavioral Therapy), REBT (Rational Emotive Behavior Therapy), Acceptance and Commitment Therapy for anxietydisorders, stress management techniques should be provided to the victims to reduce the cognitive effects of pandemic.

Psychological first aid (PFA) is an important early intervention to provide psychosocial support during any kind of pandemic outbreak like SARS, Ebola and COVID-19 etc. These PSA tools are designed to assess the mental health care needs for the survivors, to minimize and mitigate overwhelming grief and distress by offering practical help, providing safety and comfort (Birkhead, GS and Vermeulen, K, 2018). PFA can be provided by professionals and non-professionals alike in order to build disaster preparedness and response (WHO).

Psychological impact of quarantine

The outbreak of any global pandemic coerces the general population and the people who potentially come into contact with infected people to keep themselves isolated or quarantined for a certain period of time to get rid of these kinds of contagious diseases. Keeping it in mind that prevention is better than cure; people together have to fight against such virus to win over it where the entire humanity is under the unrelenting threat of death.In order to weather the crisis of present hubbub of corona virus, quarantine has become only possible means to prevent it. During the quarantine period, people reports negative psychological effects including PTSD, confusion, anger and hopelessness, helplessness, mood disorders and some other anxiety disorders. The stressors are mainly longer quarantine duration, fears to get infected, frustration, boredom due to isolation, inadequate supplies of necessary amenities, inadequate information and virtual rumors, fear of financial loss and stigma. Of late, COVID-19 outbreak forces the whole world to stay in confinement in order to fight this virus. During the 2003 outbreak of SARS (Severe acute Respiratory Syndrome), citywide quarantine was imposed in different areas of china and Canada and in the year 2014, entire villages in many West African countries were quarantined due to Ebola virus outbreak. Past researches have shown that during SARS in 2014, people reported various negative responses during the quarantine period like fear, nervousness, sadness, guilt (Reynolds DL et al, 2008). It is also witnessed that social isolation during COVID-19 has taken a toll on human psyche all across the globe.

Coping with stress and staying psychologically resilient

It is not unnatural to be scared, unsettled and uncertain about upending of life during the frightening situation of a global pandemic. Quite often the death toll and rise in the spread of such diseases bring negative psychological consequences in human being. When a pandemic becomes more reluctant and government has to issue work-from-home directives as well as social distancing, people start experiencing various negative emotions. Our lives dramatically change overnight and we try to find ways to deal with such deadly reality.Therefore people have to respond effectively to cope up with such pervasive uncertainty about near future and preserve psychological wellbeing.

Accepting the present can be one of the ways to stay resilient. A lot of anxious thoughts and emotions can peep up during such tough times, but accepting such situations rather than escaping or indulging in more negative thoughts will be of more demand. To allow negative emotions to come and let go is the most crucial task in such period, involving oneself in more joyful and productive activities and giving ourselves best possible lives of that period.

Creating new routines for the quarantine period and pampering oneself, leverage hobbies and other skills can be more enriching for the psychological heath. Audio and video technologies can be a source of connection to stay in touch with others during social distancing.

Studies also show that a little stress and negative emotions have positive consequences which is called eustress. Experiencing difficult situations bring stronger sense of psychological resilience, rekindled relationship and teach one to appreciate life (Kecmanovic, J, 2020). So having plethora of varied options can help people become better equipped to tackle the stress.

Another important strategy to stay resilient is to quit overconsumption of news. Checking news and other kind of information from any legitimate and reputed source is momentous.

Conclusion

There have been many significant pandemic worldwide recorded in human history and the catastrophe related to the pandemics cause enormous stress and turmoil in human psyche all across the globe. The spread of such contagious diseases pose serious challenges for the physical health, economic ramification and other psychological and social problems among the millions of people worldwide. Therefore, from the psychological perspective our duty is to strengthen people's resistance to the emotional impacts of such alarming situations and stop the psychological reverberation from meetingits peak.

References

Birkhead, GS.,Vermeulen, K. (2018) Sustainability of Psychological First Aid Training for the Disaster Response Workforce.Am J Public Health.Vol. 108, No. S5 page no 381-382. 10.2105/AJPH.2018.304643

Brooks, SJ., Webster, RK., Smith, LE., Woodland, L., Wessely, S., Greenberg, N., Rubin, GJ. (2020). The psychological impact of quarantine and how to reduce it: rapid review of the evidence. Lancet.Vol. 395, page no 912-920.

Kecmnovic, J. (2020). A Psychologist's science based tips for emotional resilience during the coronavirus crisis. The Washington Post.

LePan, N. (2020).Visualizing the History of Pandemics.

Phua, DH., Tang, HK., Tham, Ky. (2004) Coping responses of emergency physicians and nurses to the 2003 severe acute respiratory syndrome outbreak. AcadEmerg Med. 2005, Vol. 12. Page no. 322-328. Doi10.1197/j.am.2004.11.015

Reynolds, DL., Garay, JR., Deamond, SL., Moran, MK., Gold, W., Styra, R. (2008) Understanding, Compliance and Psychological impact of the SARS quarantine experience. Epidemiol Infect 2008; 136: 997-1007.

Shah K, Kamrai D, Mekala H, et al. (2020) Focus on Mental health During the Coronavirus (COVID-19) Pandemic: Applying Learnings from the Past Outbreaks. Cureus 12(3): e7405. DOI 10.7759/cureus.7405

Chapter - 20

Antenatal Care Practices among the Mog Women of Upper Assam

— *Falguni Roy Barua & Deepanjana Dutta Das*

Antenatal care is a term which denotes and describes the medical procedures and care that are carried out during pregnancy. Antenatal care refers to care given to pregnant women so that they have safe pregnancy and healthy baby. One of the major challenges of reproductive health of women is pregnancy management and the care taken during pregnancy period as well as postpartum period. Since it is sole responsibility of the woman to give birth her baby, is likely that she should attain some special care during her pregnancy, child-birth and just after child-birth. Health Care Practice is more than medical care. It embraces a magnitude of services provided to an individual or community by health professionals aiming at promotion, protection health and restoration of health services through Primary Health Care network. The National Health Policy of India aims to attain the goal of Health for all (HFA) through universal provision of comprehensive primary health care services. Pregnancy is a normal physiological process associated with certain risks to health of the women and the infant bears. The risks can be overcome through proper antenatal care. It is an important factor to dropping down the maternal and prenatal mortality rates. It is to be emphasized that a single antenatal care is better than having none. Out of five optimum antenatal visits one should be in first trimester and at least one in the last trimester. By doing this many a problems can be identified and proper corrective measures can be taken for safe confinement at an appropriate place. During these antenatal visits pregnant women are given TTS vaccine which protects them from toxemia and also iron and vitamin supplements are given for oral consumptions. Low hemoglobin and deficiency in vitamins can cause different morbidities to pregnant women. However the main cause of maternal mortality found to be unhygienic and primitive practices for parturition (Saklani, 2008). Unhygienic practices lead to serious medical complications. Basu (1992) has recommended that tribal women should be convinced to use only modern medicine during pregnancy and conducting deliveries.

The Mogs are a lesser known ethnic group in Assam. They are Arakan tribes who came to this land through Chittagong Hill Tract. The Mogs of Upper Assam migrated from Burma (Das 1994). They speak the Chittagong dialect of Bangladesh. The term Mog is derived from Magadha (present Bihar) the kingdom from where their forefather came to conquer Burma. They strictly follow Theravada Buddhism. They do not use Mog as their surname but commonly use the surname Barua. During British Colonial period from East Pakistan some Barua Mogs i.e. Bengali Buddhists migrated from Bangladesh to different parts of India and abroad. . In India the Barua Mog people are inhabiting mainly in Kamrup, Bongaigaon, Sibsagar, Dibrugarh and Tinsukia districts of Assam, Shillong in Meghalaya, Kolkata and its surroundings, Jalpaiguri districts, Silliguri, Coach Bihar, Durgapur in West Bengal, Jamshedpur, Ranchi in Jharkhand, Lucknow in UP, Sadar subdivision of West Tripura District and Udaipur subdivision of South Tripura District in Tripua and in some parts of Delhi. In India the approximate population of this Barua Mog community is about 200000.

In early writings these people are designated in different names, Magh, Magha, Meng, Mang, and Mugg etc. by different authors but after Independence the Government of India has given them the name Mog. Many ethnographers of British colonial period mentioned about the origin of this Mog community in their writings. Credit goes to Risley (1891) who for the first time gave elaborate details of this Buddhist community of Bengal. According to him there are several sections of people who are known by the name Maghs and basically it was a popular designation given to the Indo- Chinese group of tribes who describe themselves by various names as Marmagri, Bhuiya, Magh, Barua Magh, Rajbansi Magh, Marma or Mayan-ma, Roang Magh, Thogntha or Jumia Maghs. Risley divided all these groups into three major branches. These are:

1. The Thongtha, The Thongcha or Jumia Maghs;
2. The Marma, Mayan-ma, Roang or Rakhaing Maghs ; and
3. The Marmagri, otherwise known as Rajbansi, Barua or Bhuiya Moghs.

O'Malley (1908) furnished the graphical details on the Magh Barua community. He observed the origin and other cultural aspects of this community which suggest that the community came into existence in Bengal in the seventeenth century, and made Chittagong its permanent home. A fraction of the community migrated to other parts of Bengal and nearby districts of Chittagong.

Some people from this community suggest that the surname Barua is derived from Virji, a community of modern Bihar or "Baro-ariyo", meaning the great ones. The surname Barua was thought of and adopted in early nineteenth century as a substitute for Magh or Meng because of the political pressure arose that time in Bengal which compelled them to abandon their Arakan connection. This Marmagri Maghs (Mogs) of Chittagong region branched off in several groups at the end of seventeenth century. Some shifted to Arakan and some are found in Mizoram of North East India. They called themselves Marmagri and still retain their Arakan language and culture. While the Marmagri branch remained in Bengal got a different characteristics that look more close to Bengali culture.

The Mog people are Buddhist by religion. They follow Theravada Buddhism and the religion has become their identity. In every household there is a worship place where the whole family worships Lord Buddha. They call Buddhist temple in their language a *Khyen* which is an Arakan word. The monk or Bhante of Buddha Vihara performs all the vital rituals related to birth, marriage and death. Though they are followers of Buddha some of them also worship Hindu Gods and Goddesses like 'Durga', 'Kali', 'Shiva' etc. The most common religious festivals are: Buddha Purnima, Nababarsha, Chibar Daan and Madhu Purnima.

Their family type is patrilineal. Father is the head of the family. Family property goes from father to son's line. In a Mog family, males take part in the decision making processes. They prefer joint family. In Mog population it is observed that they prefer to marry within their own group i.e. they practice endogamy. In some cases marriage outside the community are not accepted by the members and the couple is restricted to take part in social activities as a member of the community. Marrying a maternal uncle's daughter is permissible because they believe it is auspicious as Lord Buddha had married to his maternal uncle's daughter. But now a day they avoid this type of cross-cousin marriage due to the influence of neighbouring Hindu societies. They have very good knowledge about ethno-medicine. They use different parts of plants available in the locality to treat the common diseases at home. In the earlier times some of them used to earn their livelihood by giving herbal medicine to the people

Material and methods

The present study is carried out to understand about antenatal care practice among the selected Mog women of Upper Assam. For the purpose Bisfutia-Konwari Pathar and Golai of Tinsukia District, Grahambazar-Jyotinagar and Duliajan of Dibrugarh district and Naphuk (Boripara) of Sivsagar district are selected on the basis of random sampling procedure for the study.

The data has been collected through pre designed and pre structured survey schedules in the year 2014-2015. For the purpose 406 ever married women of age group 15 years to 60 years have been selected and information about the topic is collected through personal interview.

Results and discussion

Table 20.1 shows the distribution of ever married women in different age groups according to their present age. In the present study the data have been collected from those ever married women whose age ranges from 15-60 years. The total numbers of 406 ever married women are taken into consideration. From the table it is clear that the number of women under study is highest in the age group 35-39 years (17.75%), followed by the age groups 30-34 years (16.50%) and that of 40-44 years (16.00%) respectively. There is very few number of ever married women present in the age group 15-19 years (0.25%) which indicates that the number of married women below 18 year is very less in the studied population.

Table 20.1: Distribution of Ever Married women according to Age.

Age of Women	*Number of Women*	*Percentage (%)*
15 – 19	1	0.25
20 – 24	13	3.25
25 – 29	49	11.50
30 – 34	66	16.50
35 – 39	70	17.75
40 -44	65	16.00
45 – 49	48	12.50
50 – 54	50	12.75
55 -59	23	5.50
60 -64	**15**	**2.75**

Table 20.2 shows the number of children born to the ever married women of all ages under study including stillbirth and abortions. It reveals that out of 406 women total number of live birth is 930. Total number of uterine wastage (abortion/miscarriage + stillbirth) is 118. Actual number of conception is 1084. Total number of infant death up to the age of 1 years is 18. According to the table average number of live birth per mother is 2.29; average number of uterine wastage is 0.29 per mother. Average number of abortion/miscarriage per mother is 0.25 and average number of stillbirth is 0.04 per mother.

Table 20.2: Average number of children born to the women of all ages including still births and abortions.

Total number of women	*406*
Total number of live birth	930
Total number of conception	1046
Total number of infant death up to the age 1 year	18
Total number of uterine wastage	118
Average number of stillbirth per mother	0.04
Average number of abortion/miscarriage per mother	0.25
Average number of uterine wastage per mother	0.29
Average number of live births per mother	**2.29**

Table 20.3: Utilization of Antenatal Care during Pregnancy and Child Birth.

Utilization of Antenatal care parameters	*Number of women (N)*	*Percentage (%)*
Antenatal Check Ups :		
Not done	48	11.9
At least 1 time	13	3.7
At least 2 times	11	3.2
3 times and above	344	82.2
Immunization Done :		
No	67	16.5
Yes	339	83.5
Iron /Folic Acid Supplement .		
Not consumed	71	17.5
Consumed partially	44	10.8
Consumed full course	291	71.7
Place of Delivery:		
Home	260	28.33
Hospital/PHC	670	71.67
Attendant at Birth:		
Untrained personnel	**249**	**26.77**
Doctor ?trained personnel	**681**	**73.23**

Table 20.3 shows the utilization of antenatal care during pregnancy and child birth. It is observed in the table that maximum number of ever married women under study had three or more antenatal checkups and their percentage is 82.2 and minimum number of the women had at least 2 antenatal check ups during pregnancy (3.2%). 11.9% of the studied Mog women did not have any health checkups during pregnancy. 3.7% of the women had at least one health checkups during pregnancy. 83.5% of the ever married women had TTS vaccine during pregnancy and 16.5% of them did not have the vaccine during pregnancy. 71.7% of the studied women consumed the full course of iron/folic acid supplements, 17.5% of them did not have any iron/folic acid supplement and 10.8% of the women partially consumed the iron/folic acid supplement course. Maximum number of deliveries conducted in hospital or PHC and their percentage is 71.67. 28.33% deliveries conducted at home. 73.23% deliveries have been conducted under the supervision of trained personnel and 26.77% deliveries have been conducted under the supervision of untrained personnel.

Table 20.4 shows the impact of antenatal care on infant mortality. It is observed in the table that infant mortality is highest among the mothers who had three or more numbers of antenatal health check ups during their pregnancy (44.45%) and among the mothers who did not have any antenatal check ups during pregnancy the percentage of infant mortality is 38.89. Therefore, it can be concluded that the number of antennal checkups during pregnancy do not have much impact on infant mortality particularly in this studied population. It is clear from the table that infant

Table 20.4: Utilization of Antenatal Care and its Impact on Infant Mortality.

Utilization of Antenatal Care	*Number of women N (%)*	*Infant Mortality N (%)*
Antenatal Check Ups :		
Not Done	48 (11.9%)	7 (38.89%)
At least 1 time	13 (3.7%)	1 (5.56%)
At least 2 times	11 (3.2%)	2 (11.12%)
3 times or more	344 (82.2%)	8 (44.45%)
Immunization :		
Yes	339 (83.30%)	9 (50.00%)
No	67 (16.70%)	9 (50.00%)
Iron /Folic Acid Supplements:		
Not Consumed	71 (17.5%)	9 (50.00%)
Partially Consumed	44 (10.8%)	7 (38.89%)
Consumed full course	291 (71.7%)	2 (11.12%)
Place of Delivery :		
Home	**104 (28.33%)**	**11 (61.12%)**
Hospital/PHC	**345 (71.87%)**	**7 (38.89%)**

mortality is same among the mothers who had TTS vaccine during pregnancy and the women who did not have the same. Hence we can say that immunization of the pregnant women does not have any impact on infant mortality in the population. Infant mortality is highest (50.00%) among the ever married women who did not consumed iron/folic acid supplements during pregnancy. Among the women who consumed iron/ folic acid supplements partially have been recorded 38.89% of infant mortality and it is lowest (11.12%) among the women who consumed the full course of iron/folic acid supplement during pregnancy. Therefore, it is clear from the table that consumption of iron /folic acid supplement has a negative impact on infant mortality. Place of delivery also is an important factor for influencing the health of new born baby. In the study it has been confirmed that infant mortality is higher among the deliveries conducted at home (61.12%) than among the deliveries conducted in hospital or PHC (38.89%).

Conclusion

It has been observed in the present study that most of the Mog women has availed antenatal care services. All the areas where the study has been conducted have modern health institution within the vicinity. The Mog women are aware of the importance of antenatal health care. In some of the localities under study ASHA worker are also working with great efficiency. Due to which maternal and infant mortality has been controlled to a great extent in the area studied. It is found in the study that infant mortality (0-1 year of age) is influenced by the intake of iron/folic acid food supplement by the pregnant women and the place where delivery has been conducted. Intake of iron /folic acid and delivery conducted in modern health institutions has a negative impact on infant mortality (0-1 year of age).

References

Das, B. M., 1994, Ethnic Elements in North East India, Bulletin of the Department of Anthropology, Dibrugarh University, Vol. 22 : 1-12.

O Malley, L., S., S., 1908, Eastern Bengal District Gazetteer, Chittagong.

Risley, H., H., 1891, Tribes and Castes of Bengal, Calcutta.

Saklani, B., 2008, Culture of silence and reproductive health of tribal women in India, The oriental Anthropologist, Vol. 8(12) : 59-80.

Sha, P.K., 2003, The status of family welfare services in tribal areas: highlights of the evolution process, Indian Journal Of Community Medicine, Vol. 1; 282.

Singer, N.F., 2008, Vaishali and the Indianization of Arakan, A. P. G. Publishing Corporation, New Delhi.

Srinivasan, S., 1987, Health care in rural India: problems and challenges, Kalita, A.K. and K.S. Singh, Anthropology Development and Nation Building (Ed.), Concept publication, New Delhi, 211-220.

Chapter - 21

Relationship between BMI and Percent Body Fat among the Adult Mishings of Dhemaji District

— ***Mayurtrishna Hazarika &***
Sarthak Sengupta

Body composition is used to portray the level of fat, bone, water and muscle bodies and because muscular tissue occupies less space in our body than fat tissue, our body composition, as well as our weight, determines leanness (Jeukendrup and Cronin, 2011). Body composition plays a significant role in qualifying health and nutritional status. It can be influenced by numerous variables including age, gender, genetics, the environment and lifestyle habits related to physical activity and nutrition.

Anthropometric characteristics explain a better way to deal with the knowledge of the growth process and the conspicuous changes in the body composition with increasing age. Nutritional studies can be elevated using globally acknowledged BMI rules. BMI is commonly viewed as a good indicator of nutritional status. Adult nutritional status is assessed with different techniques, the BMI is one of the broadly used inexpensive, non-invasive parameter for large-scale surveys (Bose *et al.* 2006), for explaining growth and development, particularly in the developing nations (Prista *et al.* 2003). The most commonly used measure for the expectation of body fat percentage (BF %) is Body Mass Index (BMI). However, some studies have been seen that BMI and BF% have an imperfect association and some, in contrast, justify a strong association.

WHO, (1998) has characterized obesity as a condition with excessive fat accumulation in the body to the extent that health and well being are antagonistically influenced World Health Organization recommends that

BMI as the most valuable population-level proportion of overweight and obesity. It is utilized as the equivalent for both genders and in all ages of adults (WHO, 2012). Bioelectrical Impedance Analysis (BIA) method to estimate the body fat percent. BIA is known to give a rapid, non-invasive and relatively accurate measurement of body composition. A better measure of obesity should be based on an individual's percent body fat (PBF), which would now be able to be measured by bioelectrical impedance analysis.

The present study aims to assess the age-related changes in anthropometric characteristics and indices thereof among the adult Mishing based on body mass index and percent body fat.

Materials and method

The proposed study was conducted among various Mishing dominated villages of Dhemaji District, Assam which is located in plain areas. The District occupies an area of 3237 km2 and has a population of 6, 86,183 (as of 2011). The total population of the scheduled tribe is 3, 25,560. The area is inhabited largely by Mishings. They are the second-largest group of the plains scheduled tribe of Assam. They came down to the plain areas before the reign of the Ahom Kings. Since then they began to settle in the riverine areas of Brahmaputra Valley of Assam. They belong to the Tibeto-Burman family of the Mongoloid group of languages.

The present study was carried out among 181 female and 120 male Mishings of latak village. Their age group ranged from 20-60 years for males and 18-60 years for females. The subjects of each gender were grouped into ten distinctive age groups with five years interval each, to contemplate the pattern of Height, Weight, BMI, and Body Fat percent (BF%). A relationship between BMI and BF% at five years of age interval is also being studied. The instrument like Anthropometer, Portable Weighing Machine, and Bioelectrical Impedance Analyser was carried out for the study. Anthropometric measurements like height and weight were taken by using standardized equipment. Heights of all participants were measured using Martin's Anthropometer in standing position without footwear to the nearest 0.1cm. Bodyweight was measured with minimum clothes using a weighing machine. BMI was calculated by weight (kg) divided by height (m) squared (kg/m2) Total body fat percentage (BF %) was evaluated by using a commercially available Omron Fat Analyzer system, which works on the principles of Bioelectrical Impedance to quantify an individual's real muscle to fat ratio content. The percentage of body fat was assessed by using BIA and compared with that measure of Body Mass Index.

The data collected for the present study was quantified and analyzed by using standard and proper statistical methods using IBM SPSS Software. Statistical analysis, for example, t-test was done.

Results

Table 21.1 shows the basic data of height, weight, BMI and Body Fat percent (BF %) among the adult Mishing males of Dhemaji District. The mean body height could be seen as a maximum in the age category 25 to 29 years (168.72cm). Then afterward decline. Height shows a decreasing trend after 30 to 34 years. In the age group 45 to 49 years it is again increasing. The lowest mean was found to be 60 years of age category.

Table 21.1: Age-wise distribution of basic data and BMI among the adult Mishing male of Dhemaji District.

Age group (Years)	*N*	*Height(cm)*		*Weight(kg)*		*BMI(kg/m²)*		*BF%*	
		X±SD	*SE*	*X±SD*	*SE*	*X±SD*	*SE*	*X±SD*	*SE*
<20									
20-24	19	168.67±4.560	1.046	55.91±6.052	1.388	19.66±2.130	0.488	15.54±8.114	1.861
25-29	19	168.72±6.143	1.409	64.02±10.03	2.301	22.43±2.834	0.650	19.37±8.068	1.849
30-34	18	166.86±5.243	1.235	60.67±9.985	2.353	21.65±2.704	0.637	20.64±7.897	1.861
35-39	17	166.28±3.747	0.908	57.38±7.346	1.781	20.75±2.542	0.616	13.21±6.787	1.646
40-44	13	166.56±9.044	2.508	61.30±11.91	3.304	21.97±3.317	0.919	20.24±8.005	2.220
45-49	13	167.23±5.631	1.561	62.90±10.74	2.981	22.42±3.100	0.859	19.42±8.148	2.260
50-54	6	163.13±5.064	2.067	57.63±5.659	2.310	21.64±1.631	0.665	18.88±7.802	3.189
55-59	11	163.65±3.382	1.019	54.50±9.751	2.940	20.35±3.523	1.062	17.22±7.244	2.184
60+	4	**161±1.870**	**0.935**	**56.4±10.129**	**5.064**	**21.75±3.879**	**1.937**	**18.57±9.331**	**4.665**

As shown in the above table the mean body weight is seen maximum in the age category 25 to 29 years (64.02). Bodyweight shows a decreasing trend after 40 to 44 years. Mean BMI was found to be lowest among the 20 to 24 years age category (19.66 $kg/^{m2)}$. It was a slight increase in the age category of 25 to 29 years. Then again there is a decline. The highest body fat percent is seen in the age category 30 to 34 years (20.64%) and the lowest mean BF% is 35 to 39 years of age category i.e. (13.21%). The mean value has declined in the age category from 40 to 44 years. It is evident from the table that the mean height, weight, and BMI are showing a maximum in the age category 25 to 29 years.

Table 21.2 indicates the age-wise distribution of basic data and BMI among the adult Mishing females. Maximum height has seen among the age category below 20 years. There is a slight decline between the ages of 20 to 24 years. The mean height is almost similar till 45 to 49 years i.e., (157 cm).

Table 21.2: Age-wise distribution of basic data and BMI among the adult Mishing Female of Dhemaji District.

Age group (Years)	*N*	*Height(cm)*		*Weight(kg)*		*BMI(kg/m²)*		*BF%*	
		X±SD	*SE*	*X±SD*	*SE*	*X±SD*	*SE*	*X±SD*	*SE*
<20	10	158.05±3.869	1.223	48.69±5.614	1.775	19.49±2.068	0.653	23.36±10.051	3.178
20-24	28	156.90±5.426	1.025	51.16±9.906	1.872	20.65±2.894	0.546	24.43±9.369	1.775
25-29	29	157.61±4.413	0.819	48.76±8.325	1.545	19.57±2.868	0.532	24.25±8.852	1.643
30-34	22	157.18±4.545	0.968	52.74±10.008	2.133	21.28±3.374	0.719	26.82±7.553	1.610
35-39	35	157.47±4.666	0.788	52.70±10.642	1.798	21.22±3.972	0.671	26.84±9.270	1.566
40-44	29	157.53±4.285	0.795	53.35±10.833	2.011	21.42±3.965	0.736	27.10±9.589	1.780
45-49	15	157±5.409	1.396	54.25±7.792	2.011	21.98±2.664	0.687	30.53±6.884	1.777
50-54	6	154.41±5.255	2.145	47.83±6.165	2.516	20.02±2.072	0.845	21.75±3.438	1.403
55-59	7	154.6±3.158	1.193	56.6±14.167	5.349	23.57±5.252	1.985	30.48±13.09	4.947
60+									

The maximum number of body weight was found to be 55 to 59 years (56.6%). The highest mean for BMI has seen among the category 55 to 59 years and the lowest mean of BMI is seen below 20 years. The mean BMI is almost similar till 45 to 49 years i.e., (21 kg/m²).

The highest mean value of BF% was (30.53%) found among the 45 to 49 years of age categories followed by the age group 55 to 59 years i.e., 30.48%. the lowest mean value was found among the age of 50 to 54 years.

Table 21.3 depicts the Nutritional status as per BMI among adult Mishing males. The highest percentage of normal BMI is found in the age group of 20 to 24 years. A comparative percentage is found in the age group of 25 to 29 years (8.33%) and followed by a similar age group between 34 to 39 and 35 to 39 years (7.50%). The lowest percentage of BMI among the normal category is found in the age group of 60 and above (2.50%).

The highest percentage of the underweight category has been found in the age of 25 to 29 years and followed by a similar percentage of age categories till 34 years (3.33%). Then afterward there is a decline.

The percentage of the overweight category is found highest in the age group of 30 to 34 years. In the age category from 35 to 39 and 45 to

Table 21.3: Nutritional status as per BMI among adult Mishing males of Dhemaji District.

Age group (years)	*N*	*Underweight (<18.5)*	*Normal (18.5-22.9)*	*Overweight (23.0-24.9)*	*Obese I (25-29.9)*
20-24	19	6 (5.00)	10 (8.33)	3 (2.50)	
25-29	19	2 (1.66)	10 (8.33)	4 (3.33)	3 (2.50)
30-34	18	2 (1.66)	9 (7.50)	5 (4.16)	2 (1.66)
35-39	17	4 (3.33)	9 (7.50)	3 (2.50)	1 (0.83)
40-44	13	2 (1.66)	8 (6.66)		3 (2.50)
45-49	13	1 (0.83)	7 (5.38)	3 (2.50)	2 (1.66)
50-54	6		4 (3.33)	2 (1.66)	
55-59	11	3 (2.50)	6 (5.00)	1 (0.83)	1 (0.83)
60+	4		3 (2.50)		1 (0.83)
Total	**120**	**20 (16.66)**	**66 (55.00)**	**21 (17.5)**	**13 (10.83)**

(Asia Pacific cut off, 2000)

49 years, the percentage is the same (2.50%). In the males obese I category the percentage is less than the other category of BMI. The highest percentage of obese I was to be found similar in the age category of 25 to 29 years and 40 to 44 years (2.50%). There is a diminishing pattern in the age group following 44 years. From the above table, it has been seen that all the category of BMI is observed to be expanded in lower age group and in then marginally change and the later age category there is a decrease.

Table 21.4 shows the Nutritional status as per BMI among adult Mishing females of Dhemaji District. It is clear from the table that the percentage of normal BMI among the female was found in most elevated number in the age group of 20 to 24 years (9.94%) and lower in the age group of 55 to 59 years (1.65%). However minor fluctuation in the percentage of normal BMI has been noticed among the females. It is also apparent from the table that the percentage of the underweight female is highest in the category of 25 to 29 years (6.62%). Both the age group between 35 to 39 years and 40 to 44 years is similar i.e., (1.97%).

The maximum number of overweight females has been observed in the age category from 30 to 34 years and 35 to 39 years (2.76%). A similar percentage was found to be highest in the obese I category in the age group of 40 to 44 years. In the obese II category, the percentage is the

Table 21.4: Nutritional status as per BMI among adult Mishing females of Dhemaji District.

Age group (years)	*N*	*Underweight (<18.5)*	*Normal (18.5-22.9)*	*Overweight (23.0-24.9)*	*Obese I (25-29.9)*	*Obese II (30-40)*
<20	10	3 (1.65)	7 (3.86)			
20-24	28	5 (2.76)	18 (9.94)	3 (1.65)	2 (1.10)	
25-29	29	12 (6.62)	13 (7.18)	3 (1.65)	1 (0.55)	
30-34	22	3 (1.65)	12 (6.62)	5 (2.76)	1 (0.55)	1 (0.55)
35-39	35	9 (1.97)	17 (9.39)	5 (2.76)	3 (1.65)	1 (0.55)
40-44	29	9 (1.97)	13 (7.18)	1 (0.55)	5 (2.76)	1 (0.55)
45-49	15	1 (0.55)	9 (1.97)	4 (2.20)	1 (0.55)	
50-54	6	1 (0.55)	4 (2.20)	1 (0.55)		
55-59	7	1 (0.55)	3 (1.65)		2 (1.10)	1 (0.55)
60+						
Total	**181**	**44 (24.30)**	**96 (53.03)**	**22 (12.15)**	**15 (8.28)**	**4 (2.20)**

same between the four age groups at (0.55%). It is clear from the above table that with the increasing age group of BMI was found to be increased and then afterward declining in the older age category.

Table 21.5 depicts the calculation of the t-test of selected anthropometric variables by sex. Height, weight and body fat percent is statistically significant on the other hand in BMI shows no significant differences between both the sexes.

Table 20.5: Calculation of t-test of selected anthropometric variables by sex

Sex	*Variables*							
	Height		*Weight*		*BMI*		*Body Fat%*	
	Mean ± SD	*"t" value*	*Mean ± SD*	*"t" value*	*Mean ± SD*	*"t" value*	*Mean ± SD*	*"t" value*
Male	166.68±5.832	14.939*	59.42±9.819	6.527*	21.33±2.99	1.059	17.93±8.24	8.137*
Female	157.16±4.746		51.83±9.979		20.93±3.53		26.18±9.26	

Discussion

The relationship between height, weight, body mass index and body fat percent changes with age have been widely studied in this paper. The present paper reveals that with the increasing age in both the sexes the values of height, body weight, BMI and BF% rise but with the subsequent fall. Das *et al.,* (2012) have reported that with the increasing age, the values of height, body weight, BMI and BF% rise significantly but with a subsequent fall, among older rural Bauri women of West Bengal. Begum (1998) studied that decreasing change has also been found among the adult Muslims of Kamrup district in Assam. Mott *et al.,* (1999) studies among the adult of both males and females in various population groups demonstrate that fat mass increases slowly with age and that the rate of increase varies by sex.

In the present study, the percentage of body fat in females is higher as compared to males in all the age categories. Flegal *et. al.*, (2009) reported that females have higher percentages of body fat compared to males of all ages and ethnic groups. Comparative studies on the indigenous Surui Indians of SouthWest Brazil revealed that body fat was higher in women (38.8%) than in men (13.6%) (Lourenco *et al.,* 2008). Gogoi *et al.,* (2018) among the adult Tai Ahoms of Lakhimpur District, Assam also reported that the mean BF% is higher in females than males in all the age categories.

The present study shows the BMI among both the sexes is found to be increasing with increasing age. It has been observed that males have a higher percentage of normal BMI (55.00%) than the female's normal BMI i.e., (53.03%). The present study reported that the total percentage of the occurrence of overweight and obesity among females is (22.63%) whereas among the males it is (28.33%). The prevalence of obesity is more among males than females. Similar studies have done by Santos *et al.*, (2008) among the adults from Portugal reported that the prevalence of overweight and obesity is (52.3%) in women and (61.8%) in men respectively. The frequency of under nutrition (BMI < 18.5 kg/m2) was significantly higher among females (24.30%) as compared to males (16.66%) in all the age groups.

Conclusion

The results of the study show that with increasing age group the mean estimation of height, body weight, BMI and BF% increase in both the sexes. Also, it has been found that in all the categories of BMI is seen to increase in a lower age group and then insignificantly change and the later age category there is a decline. The percent of body fat in females is much higher than the males in all the age categories. Similarly in the underweight category female number is very high as compared to males. In the present investigation, the number of males was found to exceed with regard to the cut off points of normal BMI than females. Body fat percentage strongly correlates with body mass index. The present study also noticed that there is a statistically significant in both the sexes with regard to height, weight and BF%. Otherwise, BMI shows no significant differences between males and females.

References

Begum, G, 1998. Nutrition and Economic Status in Relation to Changes in Adult Growth Among the Assamese Muslim of Kamrup District, Assam. Journal of Human Ecology, 9 (6): 585-591.

Bose, K, Bisai, S, and Chakraborty, F, 2006. Age variation in anthropometric and body composition characteristics and underweight among male Bathudis: A tribal population of Keonjhar District, Orissa, India. Collegium Anthropolozicum, 30(4): 771-775.

Das, S, Chowdhury, T, and Bose, K, 2012. Age variation in anthropometric and body composition characteristics among the adult Bauri females of Paschim Medinipur, West Bengal, India. Scholarly Journal of Scientific Research and Essay Writing, 1(2): 16-24.

Flegal, KM, Shepherd JA, Looker, AC, 2009. Comparisons of percentage body fat, body mass index, waist circumference, and waist-stature ratio in adults. American Journal of Clinical Nutrition, 89: 500-508.

Gogoi, M, and Begum, G, 2018. Relationship between BMI and Percent Body Fat among the adult Tai Ahoms of Lakhimpur district, Assam. Journal of Human Biology, 8(1): 52-56.

Jeukendrup, A, and L Cronin, 2011. Nutrition and elite young athletes. Medicine and Sports Science 56: 47-58.

Lourenco, AEP, Santos, RV, Orellana, JDY, and Coimbra Jr, CEA, 2008. Nutrition transition in Amazonia: obesity and socioeconomic changes in the Surui Indians from Brazil. American Journal of Biology, 20: 564-571.

Mott, JW, J Wang, JC Thurston, DB Allison, SB Heymsfield, and NP Pierson Jr., 1999. Therelation between body fat and age in four ethnic groups. American Journal of Clinical Nutrition, 69: 1007-1013.

Santos, R, Aires, L, Santos, P, Ribeiro, JC, and Mota, J, 2008. Prevalence of overweight and obesity in a Portuguese sample of adults: results from the Azorean physical activity and health study. American Journal of Clinical Nutrition, 20: 78-85.

World Health Organization, 1995. The use of interpretation of Anthropometry – Report of WHO Expert committee. WHO Tech Rep Series 854. Geneva: World Health Organization.

World Health Organization, 2000. Obesity: preventing and managing the global epidemics. Report of a WHO consultation, WHO Technical Report Series 894, 1-253. (Geneva 2000).

World Health Organization, (2012) Obesity and Overweight: fact sheet No. 311; 2012. http://www.who.int/mediacentre/factsheets/fs311/en/index.html.

Chapter - 22

Hygiene and Sanitation Practices among the Mising Tribe of Dhemaji District, Assam

— *Milonjyoti Borgohain*

Unsatisfactory sanitation has direct effect on health of human being, communities and nation as a whole. Good sanitation facilities improve our physical condition and also develop economic productivity. Use of personal hygiene, latrine, clean surrounding, proper disposal of waste products and hygiene activities are under sanitation. However, toilet is taken as a fundamental sign of health and sanitation worldwide.

The tribal inhabitants of India are aboriginal people of the land. India has the second largest tribal population in the world. There are around 461 tribal communities found in India. Basically they are living in various environmental circumstances. Assam is the homeland of diverse ethnicgroups. Each tribal community has their own cultural tradition. As per 2011 censes, the total population of Assam was 31,169,272. The Misings are one of the second largest plain tribal groups of Assam. As per the 2011 Census of India, the population of the Misings in the State of Assam is 6, 80,424 (Male-3, 45,786 Female-3, 34,638). Among them in rural- 6, 63,842 and in urban-16,582 which constitute 17.5% of the total population of the total S.T. population of Assam is 3,883,371. District wise population of the community is as follows (ignoring the Districts where their population is shown as below 25): Dhemaji (2,20,024), Lakhimpur (1,97,886), Jorhat (1,02,270), Golaghat (53,028), Sonitpur (49,028), Sibasagar (27,834), Tinskia (18,145), Dibrugarh (9,285), Kamrup Metropolis (2,290), Nagaon (178), Kamrup (125), Udalguri (67), Bongaigaon (52) and Morigaon (31). The Misings are the second largest

Scheduled Tribe in Assam. The Mishings constitute 680,424 (17.52%) total population in Assam (Taid, 2015).

The Misings are popularly known as "Miri" among the common Assamese people. In their language '*Mi*' is man, '*sing*' is good. Thus, it stands for 'good man'. Gait (1926) and Needham (1886) found that the term 'Miri' is an Assamese word which means 'go between'. J.F. Needham (1886), a British administrator, who published a grammar of the *Sa: yang* dialect of Mising – '*Outline Grammar of the Sa: yang Miri Language'*, was probably the first to point out the Miris call themselves 'Mishing', using 'h' in spelling the word. Similarly, J.H. Lorrain, who wrote about the Misings, used by the same spelling in his '*A Dictionary of the Abor-Miri Language*' (1910).

However, the Mising language, has in its phonemic system only one silent sibilant sound that can be written as 's', but none that can be written as 'sh'. However, the '*Mising Agom Kebang'*, the chief body for the development of Mising language and literature has been spelling the name of the community and language as 'Mising' since the early part of the 1970s.

Materials and methods

This paper is based on fieldwork that was carried out among the Misings of Lakhipathar village, Dhemaji district, Assam, Northeast India. It falls under Sissiborgaon Development Block, Dhemaji District, Assam, India. A total of 155 subjects from 155 households of which 97 men and 58 women in the age group of14-65 years was constituted for the present research. A house-to-house survey was conducted during the months of January 2019 to July 2019. The qualitative and quantitative data were collected during the field work through in depth- interviews, case studies and other field techniques form the basis for developing the research paper.

Objectives

The main objectives of the study are:

1. To analyse the demographic and socio-economic profile of the study area.
2. To examine the level of consciousness about the personal hygiene and sanitary practices.

Results and discussion

Demographic characteristics

The demographic characteristics of the Misings of Lakhipathar villages, Dhemaji district is sum upped as under. A total of 155 subjects were interviewed for the preset research. Among them 62 percents were male and 37.42 percents were female.

With regard to types, the families have conveniently been categorized into nuclear and joint family. It can be seen from the above table, the majority of the families are joint type (56.13%).

Education and literacy rate

Education is an important indicator of social development. The education level of the household members is an important characteristic as it directly affects other socio- economic aspects of life.

Table 22.3 shows that, 8.62 percent females were unable to read and write and 7.22 percent males were unable to read and write. Similarly, only 3.45 percent females were post-graduate while only 5.15 percent males had post-graduate degree.

Occupation

Occupation is the major way for human survival and subsistence. Data on occupation were collected from those males and females who were engaged in different types of work other than household works and studies. In the present study the occupation of the different individuals are as follows: In the surveyed areas females were generally engaged in household activities while males were busy with outside activities. This table represents that about 36.21 percent respondents were housewife, 29.31 percent were engaged in agriculture, and only 8.62 percent were government employed, 10.34 percent were related with private sectors, 12.07 percent were engaged in daily wagers and 3.45 percent were dependent. Similarly in case of male person, 36.08 percent were engaged in agriculture, 13.40 percent were government service holder, 17.53 percent men were related with private sectors, only 9.28 percent were petty business, 11.34 percent were engaged in daily wage labours, 7.21 percent were engaged as contractor and 5.15 percent men were dependent.

Hygienic and sanitation practices

From Table 22.5 it is clear that, most of the respondents used soap after toilet and the percentage was 46.45 percent. Similarly 31.61 percent respondents used water alone followed by mud (14.84%) and ashes (7.10%).The table also depicts that 23.87 percent of the households had toilets with flush system and 71.61 percent had toilets without flushing system. Hygiene practices, like hand cleaning after using toilet and before having meal were practiced less in the studied areas of Dhemaji district, Assam as compared to other areas in Bangladesh where 90 percent reported the use of cleaning hands and feet after using toilet. However, it is one of the basic causes for the occurrence of hygiene related diseases (Rana, 2009). In the study area about 66.45 percent of the respondent used kaccha toilet which were made by bamboo, banana and betel nut leaves and 30.97 percent used pucca toilet made with bricks and cement,while 4.52 percent individuals defecate in open field. This table also revealed that 64.52 percent subjects never used shoe while using toilet, while 12.90 percent subjects hardly used shoes during toilet time. And about 22.58 percent subjects used shoes during toilet time. It is also noticed that only 36.13 percent respondents were used toilet cleaner after defecation, while 18.06 percent respondents were used occasionally and 45.81 percent respondents were never used toilet cleaner after defecation.

Drinking water

Water is life and key component for the survival of living organisms. Human beings consume water for their everyday life like, cleaning of the equipments washing clothes bathing and other various domestic functions. In the present research it was noticed that, the sources of water for the study area were, hand pumps, water supply, dug well, sanitary well, river and pond. The villagers were used the various sources of water for drinking purposes, for cleaning of the utensils and bathing and also used for of the washing clothes. The villagers store the drinking water in still or plastic vessels. The table 22.6 reveals that about 61.94 percent respondents were used safe water i.e. tube-well for drinking purpose. Only 18.71percent respondents were used water supply. Observations in this regards revealed that the villagers used ponds (6.45%), sanitary wells (5.80%) and dug wells (3.87%) for drinking and other domestic purposes such as cooking of food, bathing etc.

Conclusion

The present study is mainly carried out to understand the consciousness of tribal with respect to personal hygiene and sanitation practices. The Lakhipathar village under Sissiborgaon development block of Dhemaji district is inhabited with Mising tribe. They are educationally and economically backward. Most of the household's major occupation is agriculture. However, the awareness regarding the hygiene and sanitation are very poor. Like other state or country, the women folk are mainly responsible for collection and storage of water for domestic uses and as well as maintaining their personal hygiene and sanitation practices. The present study reveals that personal hygiene and sanitary knowledge was low in the study area in comparison to other country or states. However, there should be extensive awareness programme for the inhabitants of the Lakhaipathar village concerning the personal hygiene and sanitation practices. Similarly, government and NGOs should be involved regarding health education program.

References

Dalibandhu Pukkalla. 2016. *Hygiene Practices among the Yanadi Tribe of Nellore District, Andhra Pradesh*. South Asian Anthropologist. 16(1): 65-78.

Ghafoor G. et al. 2014. *Health Status and Hygiene Practices in Slums: A Case Study of Lahore, Pakistan. Biologica. 60(2)*: 273-278.

Karan R. R., B. Bhandari, N. Jha. 2012. *A study on Personal Hygiene and Sanitary Practices in a Rural village of Morang District of Nepal.* Journal of Nobel Medical College. Volume 1. No. 2. 39-44.

World Health Organization, Progress on Sanitation and Drinking Water. 2010 update, Geneva, Switzerland.

Table 22.1: Sex wise distribution of Misings.

Gender	*Number*	*%*
Male	97	62.58%
Female	58	37.42%
Total	**155**	**100**

Table 22.2: Distribution of the household characters including family structure.

Family Type	*Misings*	
	Number	*%*
Nuclear family	68	43.87%
Joint family	87	56.13%
Total	**155**	**100**

Table 22.3: Educational status of the population under study area.

Level of education	*No. of women*	*%*	*No. of men*	*%*
Illiterate	5	8.62%	7	7.22%
Primary	8	13.79%	11	11.34%
Middle	9	15.52%	15	15.46%
High School	11	18.97%	22	22.68%
Higher Secondary School	17	29.31%	27	27.84%
Graduation	6	10.34%	10	10.31%
Post-graduation	2	3.45%	5	5.15%
Total	**58**	**100.00**	**97**	**100.00**

Table 22.4: Occupational status of the population under study area.

Occupations		*Mising*		
	Female	*%*	*Male*	*%*
Agriculture	17	29.31%	35	36.08%
Govt. Job	5	8.62%	13	13.40%
Private job	6	10.34%	17	17.53%
House wife	21	36.21%	-	-
Petty Business men	-	-	9	9.28%
Daily wagers	7	12.07%	11	11.34%
Contractor	-	-	7	7.21%
Dependent	2	3.45%	5	5.15%
Total	**58**	**100.00**	**97**	**100.00**

Table 22.5: Status of hygiene practices and sanitation system under study area

Variables	*N (%)*	*Variables*	*N (%)*
Toilet use		**Washing hands after using toilet**	
Flush system	37(23.87%)	**Soap**	72(46.45%)
Without flush system	111(71.61%)	**Ash**	11(7.10%)
Open field	7(4.52%)	**Mud**	23(14.84%)
		Only water	49(31.61%)
Total	155		155

Variables	*N (%)*	*Variables*	*N (%)*
Toilet types		Washing hands before eating meal	
Pucca	48(30.97%)	**Soap**	44(28.39%)
Kaccha	103(66.45%)	**Ash**	9(5.81%)
Others	4(2.58%)	**Mud**	11(7.10%)
		Only water	91(58.70%)
Total	155		155

Variables

Using shoes in the toilet time	*N (%)*	*Using toilet cleaner after using toilet*	*N (%)*
Yes	35(22.58%)	**Yes**	56(36.13%)
No	100(64.52%)	**No**	71(45.81%)
Occasionally	20(12.90%)	**Occasionally**	28(18.06%)
Total	155	**Total**	155

Table 22.6: Different sources of drinking water under study area

Sources	*N*	*%*
Tube-well	96	61.94%
Water supply	29	18.71%
Dug well	6	3.87%
Sanitary well	9	5.80%
River	5	3.23%
Pond	10	6.45%
Total	155	100

Chapter - 23

Childhood Mortality among the Santals and Tantis of Upper Assam

— *Parishmita Gogoi- &*
Deepanjana Dutta Das

Childhood mortality is one of the important indicators of a country's general medical and public health conditions and consequently, the country's level of socio-economic development. Infant Mortality Rate (IMR) which is defined as the deaths of infants of age less than one year per thousand live births and under five mortality rate (U5MR) probability of dying between birth and age 5 expressed per 1000 live births have been used as measures of children's well being for many years.

Infant and child mortality depends upon a large number of factors such as socio-economic, demographic and environmental factors and these vary across population. These aspects of determinants of infant and child mortality are over studied but the fact remains that findings varies across population. The Santal and Tanti, the tea garden labour population Upper Assam though have similar cultural and environmental setting yet the childhood mortality is varied. Therefore, this paper attempts to showcase the levels and trends of infant and child mortality among the Santal and Tantis of Upper Assam and also the impact of demographic and socio-cultural factors to reducing the infant and child mortality among the same.

The tribe

The present study has been carried out in two ethnic groups, namely, the Santals (tribe) and the Tantis (caste). Both the population belongs to the tea garden labour population of Assam. The Santals, one of the populous tribal communities of India are mainly found in the districts of Mayurbhanj, Keonjhar and Balasor in the state of Odisha. Besides, they are also found in the neighbouring Jharkhand, West Bengal, Bihar and Assam. This tribe was brought to Assam to work as tea workers in the tea gardens from Jharkhand, West Bengal and Bihar. Various researches and studies approve that the Santal had existed in Assam since 150 A.D. They are kolarian aborigines of India among the Mundari group of proto Australoid origin. They bear common features of Austric people. They are generally short in stature, but they have sturdy limbs. Among them the flat nose with a sunken, ridge is fairly common. They frequently have wavy hair, with black eye and dark skin colour. The Santali dialect is the only medium of conversation among them. Their religion is Hinduism. A good number of them in Assam, have accepted Christianity.

The Tanti is a Hindu caste found in the state of Bihar and Bengal in India. In July, 2015, the Tanti was granted the status of schedule castes in Bihar. But in Assam, this group was classified as MOBC. The word 'Tanti' is derived from the Hindi word *tant* which means loom. They were traditionally weavers. They are found in South Bihar, Rachi in Jharkhand and also in Orissa. A good number of them are found in Assam. They call themselves by the names of Kalahari, Kondri, Sambalpuria, Pan Tanti, Tantubaui and Saibasia. They speak Panchpargania dialect. Linguistically, they belong to Austro-Asiatic linguistic family. Their own dialect is known as sambalpuria dialect. They now speak Sadni (tea garden dialect) which is a mixture of Assamese, Hindi and their ancestral dialect. They are of Proto-Australoid origin.

Material and methods

For the present analysis, the data is gathered from the structured demographic schedule of 200 evermarried women of the Santal and 200 from the Tanti population of Upper Assam. Since the focus of this study is a childhood mortality, the information on the number of children who were born, survived or died is of particular concern. The surveyed had asked the women aged at 15-60 years who have give birth to atleast one live-birth and the husbands are alive at the time of investigation. A complete history of their births including for each live birth, the sex, month and year of birth, survival status and age at the time of the survey or age at death are recorded. Information on some demographic and socio-cultural variables are used in the analaysis were drawn from the household questionnaires. The collected data are quantified and analysed statistically in numbers and percentage. The chi-square test has been done to show the differences between these two population groups.

Results and discussion

Table 23.1 shows the distribution of postnatal mortality by age at menarche. Among the Santal the highest frequency of infant (5.85%) and child (2.13) mortality are observed in the women who attained their menarche at the late age (≥14 years). The highest postnatal mortality is observed among the women who attained their menarche in the late age (7.98%). It is followed by the women who attained their menarche in the intermediate age (4.49%), where the infant mortality is 2.81% and child mortality is 1.69%. No infant death has been observed among the women who attained their menarche at early age (≤ 11 years). Only 1.75% child mortality has been found in the early menarcheal age.

Table 23.1: Postnatal mortality by age at Menarch.

Age at Menarche (age group in yrs)	*Santal*				*Tanti*			
	No. of live birth	*Post natal mortality*			*No. of live birth*	*Post natal mortality*		
		Infant (0-1 yr)	*Child (1.1-5 yrs)*	*Total (0-5rs)*		*Infant (0-1 yr)*	*Child (1.1-5yrs*	*Total (0-5 yrs)*
Early (≤11)	57	0	1	1	93	1	1	2
%	9.48		1.75	1.75	18.38	1.07	1.07	2.15
Intermediate (12-13)	356	10	6	16	271	9	4	13
%	59.23	2.81	1.69	4.49	53.56	3.32	1.48	4.80
Late (≥14)	**188**	**11**	**4**	**15**	**142**	-	-	-
%	**31.28**	**5.85**	**2.13**	**7.98**	**28.06**			

X^2 = 10.95, df = 2, P< 0.05, significant at 5% level.

Whereas, among the Tantis highest percentage of infant (3.32%) as well as child (1.48%) and total postnatal mortality (4.80%) have been observed among the women who attained their menarche in the intermediate (12-13) age. It is followed by the women who attained their menarche in the early (≤11) age where the infant and child mortality is same (1.07%) and the total postnatal mortality is 2.15%. No infant and child death are observed among the women who attained their menarche in late (≥14) age. The value of chi-square shows a significant difference at 5% level in between the Santals and the Tantis (x^2=10.95, P<0.05).

The infant and child mortality is increased with the increase age at menarche among the Santal but among the Tanti it slowly increases with the increase age at menarche but in the extreme (≥14 years) have no incidence of mortality. The women of higher age group show the higher frequency of mortality than that of the younger ones (Saikia, 2015) which is similar to the present study. But in the study of Sengupta and Sarmah (2007) the infant and child mortality rate is found to be higher in the menarche of younger ones.

Table 23.2 shows the postnatal mortality by age at marriage. Among the Santal the infant mortality is highest (4.70%) among the women who got married at 20-25 years and the frequency of infant mortality (2.24%) is lowest among the women who got married at ≤19 years. The frequency of child mortality (5.71%) as well as postnatal mortality (8.57%) is highest among the women who got married at ≥26 years of age. Only 1.34% child mortality has been observed among the women who got married at 20-25 years of age. The lowest frequency of postnatal mortality (4.1%) has been observed among the women who got married at ≤19 years.

Table 23.2: Postnatal mortality by age at marriage.

Age at marriage (age group in yrs)	*Santal*				*Tanti*			
	No. of live birth	*Post natal mortality*			*No. of live birth*	*Post natal mortality*		
		Infant (0-1 yr)	*Child (1.1-5 yrs)*	*Total (0-5 yrs)*		*Infant (0-1 yr)*	*Child (1.1-5 yrs)*	*Total (0-5 yrs)*
≤19	268	6	5	11	320	5	3	8
%	44.59	2.24	1.87	4.11	63.24	1.56	0.94	2.50
20-25	298	14	4	18	161	3	2	5
%	49.58	4.70	1.34	6.04	31.82	1.86	1.24	3.10
≥26	**35**	**1**	**2**	**3**	**25**	**2**		**2**
%	**5.82**	**2.86**	**5.71**	**8.57**	**4.94**	**8.00**	-	**8.00**

$X^2 = 2.13$, df = 2, 0.30>P> 0.50, non significant.

Among the Tanti the infant mortality is highest (8.00%) who got married at ≥26 years of age and lowest among the women who got married at ≤19 years of age (1.56%). The child mortality is highest (1.24%) among the women who got married at 20-25 years of age. No child death has been observed among the women who got married at ≥26 years of age. The total frequency of postnatal mortality is highest (8.00%) among the women who got married at ≥26 years of age. However, the Chi-square value (X^2=2.13, df = 2, 0.30>P> 0.50) shows no significant difference in the postnatal mortality.

Table 23.3 shows the postnatal mortality by age at menopause. Among the Santal the highest frequency of the total postnatal mortality 5.76% is observed in the women who have attained their menopause at 41-45 years of age, where the highest infant (2.16%) and child mortality (3.60%) have been observed. It is followed by the women who have attained their menopause at ≥46 years of age with a frequency of 5.17% postnatal mortality, where 1.72% infant mortality and 3.45% are child mortality. The lowest frequency of postnatal mortality is 4.16% observed among the women who have attained their menopause at ≤40 years of age where same percentage of infant and child mortality (2.08%) is recorded.

Table 23.3: Postnatal mortality by age at Menopause.

Age at Menopause (age group in yrs)	*Santal*				*Tanti*			
	No. of Live Birth	*Post natal mortality*			*No. of Live Birth*	*Post natal mortality*		
		Infant (0-1yr)	*Child (1.1-5 yrs)*	*Total (0-5 yrs)*		*Infant (0-1 yr)*	*Child (1.1-5yrs)*	*Total (0-5yrs)*
≤40	48	1	1	2	34	-	1	2
%	19.59	2.08	2.08	4.16	19.54		2.94	2.94
41-45	139	3	5	8	53	1	2	3
%	56.73	2.16	3.60	5.76	30.46	1.89	3.77	5.66
≥46	58	1	2	3	87	2	2	4
%	23.67	1.72	3.45	5.17	50.00	2.29	2.29	4.59

$X^2 = 1.65$, df = 2, 0.30>p> 0.50 non significant.

On the other hand, among the Tantis the postnatal mortality is highest (5.66%) in the women who have attained their age at menopause at 41-45 years of age. It is followed by 4.59% and 2.94% postnatal mortality among the women who have attained their age at menopause at ≥46 years and ≤40 years respectively. The infant mortality rate is highest (2.29%) among the women who have attained their menopause at ≥46 years of age and the highest frequency of child mortality (3.77%) have been observed among the women who have attained their menopause at 41-45 years of age and the lowest frequency of child mortality (2.29%) have been observed among the women who have attained their menopause at ≥46 years of age. However, the test of significance shows the no significant difference in the studied population groups (x^2=1.65, df = 2, 0.30>P> 0.50).

Table 23.4 shows the distribution of postnatal mortality of women by birth intervals. Among the Santals the total frequency of postnatal mortality is highest when the birth interval is ≤ 23 months (6.49%); it decreases up to 2.00% when the birth interval is ≥36 months. The highest frequency of infant mortality is seen when the birth interval is ≤23 months (4.16%). It decreases up to 2.00% when the birth interval is ≥36 months. The child mortality is higher when the birth interval is ≤23 months (2.39%). It decreases up to 1.20% in the group where birth interval is 24–35 months.

Table 23.4: Postnatal mortality by birth intervals.

Birth intervals (in months)	*Santal Postnatal mortality*				*Tanti Postnatal mortality*			
	No. of live birth	*Infant (0-1yr)*	*Child (1.1-5 yrs)*	*Total (0-5 yrs)*	*No. of live birth*	*Infant (0-1 yr)*	*Child (1.1-5 yrs)*	*Total (0-5 yrs)*
≤ 23 %	385 64.06	16 4.16	9 2.39	25 6.49	396 78.26	7 1.78	4 1.01	11 2.79
24-35 %	116 27.62	4 2.41	2 1.20	6 3.61	81 16.00	2 2.47	1 1.23	3 3.70
≥ 36 %	50 8.31	1 2.00	-	1 2.00	29 5.73	1 3.45	-	1 3.45

x^2=0.33, df = 2, 0.80>P> 0.90, non signi.

On the other hand, among the Tantis the total frequency of postnatal mortality is highest when the birth interval is within 24-35 months (3.70%); it decreases up to 2.79% when the birth interval is ≤23 months. The highest frequency of infant mortality is seen when the birth interval is ≥36 months (3.45%). It decreases up to 1.78% when the birth interval is ≥23 months. The child mortality is higher when the birth interval is 24-35 months (1.23%). It decreases up to 1.01% in the group where birth interval is ≤23 months.

However, when the chi-square test of significance is applied, it shows no significant difference in postnatal mortality among the studied population groups (x^2 = .33, df = 2, 0.80>P> 0.90).

Table 23.5 shows the postnatal mortality by family type. Among the Santals the postnatal mortality is highest (5.39%) from the joint family where 4.02% infant and 0.77% child mortality are observed. Among the women from nuclear family the child mortality rate is higher (2.12%) than the joint family. The infant mortality rate is 3.18% and the total postnatal mortality rate is 5.30%. Whereas, among the Tanti women the highest percentage of total postnatal mortality (3.08%) is observed from the nuclear family where infant mortality is 1.96% and child mortality is 1.12% respectively. Lowest percentage of total postnatal mortality (2.77%) is recorded among the women from joint family. The chi-square test shows no significant differences in postnatal mortality (x^2=0.13, df = 1, 0.70 >P> 0.80)

Table 23.6 shows the postnatal mortality by religion. Among the Santal the frequency of postnatal mortality is 5.52% in the Hindu women where 3.62% infant and 1.90% child mortality are observed. No postnatal

Table 23.5: Postnatal mortality by Family Type.

Type of family	*Santal*				*Tanti*			
	No. of live birth	*Post natal mortality*			*No. of live birth*	*Post natal mortality*		
		Infant (0-1 yr)	*Child (1.1-5 yrs)*	*Total (0-5 yrs)*		*Infant (0-1 yr)*	*Child (1.1-5 yrs)*	*Total (0-5 yrs)*
Nuclear	471	15	10	25	375	7	4	11
%	78.37	3.18	2.12	5.30	70.55	1.96	1.12	3.08
Joint	130	6	1	7	149	3	1	4
%	21.63	4.02	0.77	5.39	29.45	2.01	0.67	2.77

$X^2 = 0.13$, df = 1, 0.90> p> 0.95, non significant.

Table 23.6: Postnatal mortality by religion.

Type of religion	*Santal*				*Tanti*			
	No. of live birth	*Post natal Mortality*			*No. of live birth*	*Post natal Mortality*		
		Infant (0-1 yr)	*Child (1.1-5 yrs)*	*Total (0-5 yrs)*		*Infant (0-1 yr)*	*Child (1.1-5 yrs)*	*Total (0-5 yrs)*
Christian	22				72	3	3	6
%	3.67	-	-	-	14.23	4.17	4.17	8.33
Hindu	579	21	11	32	434	7	2	9
%	96.34	3.62	1.90	5.52	85.77	2.00	0.46	2.07

X^2=6.33, df = 1, 0.02> p> 0.50, significant.

mortality is recorded among the Christians, whereas among the Tantis the postnatal mortality is high among the Christians (8.33%).

The higher infant (4.17%) and child mortality (4.17%) is recorded in Christians than the Hindus. Among the Hindus the postnatal mortality is 2.07%, where 2.00% infant and 0.46% child mortality are observed. The difference between the two population is statistically significant in regards of postnatal mortality (x^2=6.33, df = 1, 0.01 >P> 0.02).

The postnatal mortality by maternal education has been revealed from the Table 23.7. From this Table, it is observed that among the Santals the total postnatal mortality is highest (7.41%) among the primary literate women (7.41%), where the infant mortality rate is 4.63% and child mortality rate is 2.78%. It is followed by 5.11% postnatal mortality, where 3.3% infant and 1.78% Child mortality have been recorded from the illiterate women. No death has been reported from the women of higher secondary and above.

Among the Tanti the postnatal mortality is highest in the women from illiterate (3.49%) category, where the highest infant (2.22%) and child

Table 23.7: Postnatal Mortality by maternal education.

Maternal Educational level	*Santal*				*Tanti*			
	No. of live birth	*Post natal mortality*			*No. of live birth*	*Post natal mortality*		
		Infant (0-1 yr)	*Child (1.1-5 yrs)*	*Total (0-5 yrs)*		*Infant (0-1 yr)*	*Child (1.1-5 yrs)*	*Total (0-5 yrs)*
Illiterate %	450 74.88	15 3.33	8 1.78	23 5.11	121 60.50	7 2.22	4 1.27	11 3.49
Primary %	108 17.97	5 4.63	3 2.78	8 7.41	49 24.50	2 1.90	1 0.95	3 2.86
Secondary %	37 6.16	1 2.70	-	1 2.70	27 13.50	1 1.25	-	1 1.25
Higher Secondary and above %	6 0.10	-	-	-	3 1.50	-	-	-

X^2= 1.08, df = 3, 0.30>P> 0.50, non significant.

(1.27%) mortality have been recorded. The lowest postnatal mortality is recorded in the women from secondary literate group (1.25%) where no child mortality has been observed. No infant and child death are recorded from the women of higher secondary and above literate group. The chi-square test shows no significant difference in the studied population groups (x^2= 1.08, df = 3, 0.30 >P > 0.50).

Conclusion

The improvement in childhood mortality is the result of a combination of factor. Amongst these are the expansion of health care facilities and services, disease-specific health inventions, changes in diets and health behaviours and the success of developmental programmes etc. A significant improvement in women's educational attainment must also have played an important roles in reducing mortality. The strong association between mother's education and infant/ child mortality is considered as one of the most consistent and powerful finding in public health (Cladwell, 1979; Bicego and Boerma, 1993, Ozaltin *et al*, 2010). A large body of research suggest that a casual relationship exists between maternal education and childhood health and mortality. In the past 30 years, many hypotheses have been proposed for the mechanisms through which increased education could lead to reductions in child mortality, including individual effects through improved use of health services, economic advantages, empowerment and independence of women and community level effects (Gakidou *et al*, 2010).

The infant morality rate in India is steadily declining. The NFHS-3 estimate of infant mortality is 57 deaths per 1000 live births, compared with the NFHS -2 estimate of 68 deaths per 1000 live births and the NFHS-1 estimate of 79. Still more than one in 18 children died within the first year of life, and more than one in 13 die before reaching age five.

According to bio-social characteristics, mortality variations between these two population viz. the Santal (tribe) and the Tanti (caste) are statistically non significant regarding the variables like – age at marriage, age at menopause, birth interval, family type and maternal education. Only the age at menarche of women and religion show a statistically significant difference between these two groups of population.

References

Bicego, T.G. and J.T. Boerma, 1993, Maternal Education and child survival: A comparative study of survey data from 17 countries, Social science Med. 36: 1207-1227.

Cladwell, J.1979, Education as a factor in Mortality Decline : An Examination of Nigerian Data, Population Studies, 33 (3): 395-413.

Gakidou, E.K. Cowling, R. Lozano and C.J.L. Murray 2010, Increased educational attainment and its effect on child mortality in 175 countries between 1970 and 2009: a systematic analysis, Lancet, 376 (9745) : 959-74.

Saikia, N., 2015, Fertility Performance and Blood group incompatibility among the Sonowal Kacharis of Dibrugarh District, Assam, Unpublished Ph.D. Thesis, Department of Anthropology, Dibrugarh University.

Sengupta, S. and M. P. Sarmah, 2007, Effects of some Bio-cultural Factors on Fertility and Mortality among the Moria Muslims of Assam: A Preliminary Appraisal, Bulletin of the Department of Anthropology, Dibrugarh University, 36: 113-128.

Sharma, 2008, Childhood Mortality and Health in India, Working Paper Series No. E/292/2008, Institute of Economic Growth, University of Delhi Enclave, North Campus, Delhi.

Chapter - 24

Impact of Reproductive Aging on Women's Health

— *Rita Taid*

"A comfortable old age is the reward of a well-spent youth. Instead of it's bringing sad and melancholy prospects of decay, it should give us hopes of eternal youth in a better world" – **Gloria Pitzer**

Reproductive aging as defined by the North American Menopause society (2001) is a natural process that begins at birth and proceeds as a continuum. Clearly it is a process and not an event, and the end (menopause) is much easier to identify than the beginning. Some of the terms used to define various time periods around reproductive aging described as per the World Health Organization technical report series: 866 (1994) are; Menopause: the permanent cessation of menstruation that results from loss of ovarian follicular activity. Perimenopause: includes the period beginning with the first clinical, biological and endocrinological features of the approaching menopause. Pre-menopause: Often used ambiguously to refer to the 1-2 years immediately before the menopause. Post-menopause: should be defined from the final menstrual period regardless of whether the menopause was induced or spontaneous. Menopausal transition: the period of time before the final menstrual period, when variability in the menstrual cycle is usually increased. Flint (1974), was one of the first to carry out a community based investigation on menopause among Indian women, wherein she showed that menopause was experienced differently in India as compared to United States and there is a variation in age at menopause, and associated symptoms (Pathak and Parashar, 2010).

Aging is an inevitable and a universal process, but the female reproductive organ ages first among humans. Today, with better medical facilities and improving life style most women live long enough to become postmenopausal. In the developed world, the percentage of women over 50 years of age has tripled in the last 100 years (US Census Bureau, 2011), as for India we are the second most populated country nearing to become no.1 in no time. So as life goes on, we see a lot of changes occur in women's life cycle. Biologically one of the pivotal reasons for menopause is sharp decline in the hormone estrogen, which eventually leads to loss of fertility and many of the symptoms associated with menopause. Studies have found that menopause is a very important biomarker of not only the loss of fertility but also an increased risk for various mid-life diseases and problems (Ahuja, 2016). Health is the most important aspect for the well being of a person. The attainment of health is also a fundamental right of every human being as enshrined in the constitution. Status of the health awareness and access to hospitals or Services indicate the status of a family, society and nation in regards to development too (Park K 2013)

As for women's health one can surely say that it's the most crucial and of great importance since she is the foundation of a family and the very fact that only she can bore a child validates it all. While prevention and healthy lifestyles are important at all ages, it is increasingly apparent that health in midlife is an important determinant of a healthy and fully functional life in the following decades. Also a woman is provided with requisite care during her reproductive years, and may be during old age too but the time in between which we call the mid-life (induction of menopausal phase) somewhere has always been neglected. Since Menopause has been linked to a number of post reproductive ailments and as women globally are delaying childbearing it is important to make women aware of it so that they make healthy lifestyle choices right from the beginning, as many of these diseases and conditions can be prevented by timely intervention of lifestyle modification, proper dietary habits, menopausal hormone therapy, or other supplements such as calcium, Vitamin D, and micronutrients.

From Anthropological point of view the study on reproductive aging is the perspective used when one questions why women experience universal menopause at the midpoint of the maximal potential life span. A number of ideas have been put forward to explain why menopause and post-reproductive aging evolved in humans. Anthropologists have argued that menopause may have been selected to ensure that old eggs are not fertilized (Hrdy SB 1999). In humans, gametes can wait in the ovary for 15 to 50 years before ovulation. This wait decreases the available reserve of primordial follicles and increases the risk of age-related chromosomal abnormalities and fetal loss (Holman DJ et al., 2000; Pellestor F et al., 2003). Menopause could have been selected to prevent the ovulation and fertilization of abnormal oocytes. Other anthropologists have argued that maternal death threatens the survival of the youngest offspring; therefore, menopause was selected to ensure that mothers are young enough to survive pregnancy, childbirth, and the infancy of their offspring (Hill K et al., 1991; Peccei JS 2001).

The "mother" hypothesis originated from the work of Williams (Evolution, 1957) who pointed out that human infants are extremely altricial and require extended maternal care. Using data from preindustrial Quebec, Pavard et al., 2008 concluded that if maternal mortality, stillbirth, and birth defect probabilities increased markedly with age in the absence of menopause, then menopause could have been selected for in humans' evolutionary past. The evolutionary reasons for why women experience a long post-reproductive life continue to be debated.

Smith (1991) estimated that hominid longevity exceeded age 50 years more than 1 million years ago, meaning that Homo ergaster and early Homo erectus shared the capacity for menopause. Fossil remains from Paleolithic Neanderthals suggested that 10% to 24% of the population survived beyond 40 years (Trinkaus E 1995;2011) Within early Homo sapiens, it seemed that 17% of prehistoric foragers survived beyond age 40 years (Kennedy GE 2003), Estimates vary, but ethnographic and paleo-demographic evidence indicates that more than one third of hunters and foragers—without easy access to modern medicine—lived beyond age 40 years (Hawkes K et al., 2005; Trinkaus E 2011). Strong evidence indicates that some women outlived their capacity to reproduce during much of humans' historical and evolutionary past.

From an evolutionary perspective, the "grandmother hypothesis" is probably the best known contribution of anthropology to the study of menopause. This idea gained visibility from fieldwork among the Hadza of Tanzania (Hawkes K et al., 1997). The argument is that post-reproductive grandmothers provide care and food to their grandchildren and may also have been the first midwives to their own daughters when hominins moved from the primate pattern of solo births to the human pattern of assisted births (Rosenburg K et al., 2002) The central premise is that postmenopausal grandmothers further increased their own inclusive fitness by investing in their daughters' fertility and their grandchildren's survival rather than continuing to produce children of their own.

Even though culturally (as per some research) menopause seems to be adding positively towards the betterment of an aging woman and her family per se but it's possible (negative) biological implications (viz. osteoporosis, hypertension, UTI, etc) on her body and mind can't be neglected.

Reproductive aging, health and its clinical symptoms

In a recent study done by Slopier et.al (2018) on whether menopause increases the risk of type 2 diabetes mellitus (T2DM) independently of aging. The study found that menopausal transition caused metabolic changes including an increase in and the central redistribution of adipose tissue, as well as a decrease in energy expenditure in women. In addition, they also found that there was an impairment of insulin secretion and insulin sensitivity and an increase in the risk of T2DM (type2 diabetes mellitus). Menopausal hormone therapy (MHT) was found to have a favorable effect on glucose metabolism, both in women with and in women without T2DM, where it could possibly delay the onset of T2DM. However the study also suggested that MHT in women with T2DM should be administered according to their risk of cardiovascular disease (CVD). In women with T2DM and low CVD risk, oral estrogens was more preferred, while transdermal 17β-oestradiol was preferred for women with T2DM and coexistent CVD risk factors, such as obesity. According to the study in any case, a progestogen with neutral effects on glucose metabolism should be used, such as progesterone, dydrogesterone or transdermal norethisterone. The study further added that postmenopausal women with T2DM should be managed primarily with lifestyle intervention, including diet and exercise. The study concluded that most of the menopausal women would eventually require pharmacological therapy, for which the selection of anti-diabetic medications should be based on the patient's specific characteristics and comorbidities, as well on the metabolic, cardiovascular and bone effects of the medications.

Nisar and Sohoo (2010) assessed the menopause related symptoms and the impact of these symptoms on the quality of life of menopausal women. It was a cross sectional hospital based survey conducted at the department of Obstetrics and Gynecology Isra University Hyderabad Sindh Pakistan on 220 women of age 40-60 years. Menopause specific quality of life questionnaire (MENQOL) was used to assess the frequency and severity of symptoms. Most prevalent symptom within study subjects was body ache 165 (81.7%). Frequencies of some classical symptoms were

134 (66.3%) reported "hot flushes", 139 (68.8%) and 134 (66.3%) reported "lack of energy" and decrease in "physical strengths" respectively. The less frequently reported symptom was an increase in facial hair 20 (9.9%). Scores of Physical domain were significantly more in postmenopausal group P< 0.002 while the scores of psychological domain were significantly high in menopause transition group P< 0.003.

Lin li et al. 2012 investigated the factors associated with the age of natural menopause and menopausal symptoms in a large population of Chinese middle-aged women. In the cross-sectional study, a total of 20,275 women (40–65 years) attending health screening in Jiangsu Province of China were enrolled. A structured questionnaire was used to collect data of demographics, menopausal status, chronic diseases, reproductive history, etc. Also the severity of menopausal symptoms by Kupperman menopausal index (KMI) was evaluated. They found that the overall median age at natural menopause was 50 years. Lower educational level, poor socio-economic status, lower body mass index (BMI), age at menarche less than 14 years, nulliparity and smoking were associated with earlier onset of natural menopause . The most frequent symptoms in postmenopausal women were sexual problems (57.05%), muscle/joint pain (53.29%) and insomnia (51.02%), while fatigue, insomnia and muscle/joint pain were predominant symptoms in pre- and peri- menopausal women. After adjusting for confounding factors, logistic regression analysis revealed that women with poor educational background, low income, divorce, higher BMI, higher parity, smoking and chronic diseases presented higher KMI scores.

Mishra et al., (2012) conducted a nationally representative cohort study among 695 women aged 47 to 54 years in England, Scotland, and Wales. A small proportion of women (10%, n=63) had a severe psychological symptom profile that peaked at or in the year after menopause. For vasomotor symptoms, 14% of women (n=83) had the early severe profile that also peaked around early post menopause and then declined noticeably; 11% (n=67) had the late severe profile of bothersome symptoms that increased rapidly in peri-menopause and remained high for four years or more after menopause.

Purnungla and Sarthak Sengupta studied Menarche and Menopause Among The Ao Naga Women of Nagaland, India (2002) Data from 150 and 48 women belonging to the Ao Naga tribe were collected for menarcheal and menopausal ages respectively from Chuchuyimlang village, Mokokchung district, Nagaland. Data on menopausal age were collected from those women who had completed their reproductive life without adopting any birth control measure. Necessary information, regarding their date of birth, age at menarche, and age at menopause, were obtained from the subjects by retrospective method depending on recall. Analysis of the data reveals that the maximum number of Ao Naga girls attained menarche at the age of 15 years (36.67%), the range of variation being 12 to 18 years, and the mean onset of menarche is reported to occur at 14.88 ± 0.11 years. Studies on menopausal age of the women of North East India are rather scanty. In the present study, the maximum incidence of menopause among the Ao Naga women is found to occur at the age of 52 years (18.75%), the range of variation being 40 to 55 years with mean menopausal Mongoloid populations of the region so far reported (Sengupta and Rajkhowa, 1996). In the study, it was obvious that there was a considerable variability in the age at menarche and menopause among the populations of Nagaland, thereby indicating the important role played by both genetic and environmental factors.

Bansal and Thaker (2005) conducted a study to determine age and perception of menopause as well as prevalence of various menopausal symptoms amongst underprivileged women of Ahmedabad. A questionnaire was used as a tool for data collection from 100 menopausal underprivileged women in Sheth V.S. General Hospital. The results showed that 29.5% suffered from joint pain, poor memory and fatigue, 25% had irritability, 22.7% had urinary symptoms, 18.18 % had hot flushes, 6.81% dyspareunia, 4.54% leucorrhoea and anxiety and 2.27% had post menopausal bleeding. For the respondents background 62.2% were illiterate and the mean age for menopause was 41-45 years. 93.18% women had not taken any treatment and none knew about pap's test and self-breast examination. The researcher concluded that uneducated and under privileged women are unaware of their right to health care and protection, as some did not realize the need to consult a doctor for their menopausal problems. They also realized the need for educating females for cancer prevention tests.

Zutsi (2005) in Delhi studied the prevalence of urinary symptoms in peri- menopausal age group. 500 women in the age group of 42 to 55 were given questionnaire and results showed – 334 patients were P2 and P3, 4% had urge incontinence, 10.4% complained of stress incontinence, 42 patients had both, 9.4 % complained dysuria, 2.4% hesitancy, 6.4% frequency and 6% nocturia. Prevalence of urinary symptoms was not very high. Amongst those 87 facing symptoms only 30 had taken any treatment – 18 allopathic, 5 homeopathic, 4 ayurvedic and 4 were operated. 13 patients reported recurrence of symptoms after taking any mode of treatment. The prevalence rate has not been found so high. The results do not match with the western figures; probably our women do not give much importance to these symptoms.

As stated by Johnson et al., in 2003, the prevalence of osteoporosis, which is a debilitating bone disease, increases with age. Also, a higher proportion of women are affected by this condition. It is a silent condition and in many cases, the condition is diagnosed only after an individual suffers a fracture. Osteoporosis is preventable. Guidelines in Canada and U.S. suggest that 1200 milligrams of calcium per day is recommended for individuals over 50 years of age. Studies have shown that dietary calcium intake from pre- adolescence through late adolescence is critical for building high bone density. Among those over 50 years of age, adequate levels of calcium intake prevent the rapid age and gender related decline in bone density. Sources high in calcium include certain cereals grains and products (e.g. Ragi), pulses, legumes (e.g. Whole Bengal gram, black gram dhal, rajma and green gram), green leafy vegetables (e.g. Amaranth, agathi, drumstick leaves), milk and milk products and fish with small bones. In terms of exercises, weight bearing exercises such as walking, cycling, running, and stair climbing have been shown to be beneficial in promoting bone health. Also physical activities increase muscle strength and flexibility, increasing independence and decreasing risk of falls and related fractures. An added benefit to the optimal nutrient intake, exercise and not smoking is improved health and decreased incidence of cancer. In addition with the advancement of science, options such as drug therapy (HRT) along with calcium and vitamin D supplementation and exercise are available.

Reproductive aging and depression

Laurie K et.al, (2008) conducted a study to investigate the direct and indirect relationship between psychological distress, psychosocial factors, stress, severity of menopausal symptoms and physical health in women aged 45-55 years. One hundred and sixteen women were selected through community organizations and women's health centers. They answered a short questionnaire asking about psychological distress, menopause symptoms, stress and physical health. This research concluded that high emotional intelligent women have positive attitudes towards menopause and they experience less severe menopause symptoms, psychological distress, stress and better physical health. These results suggested that women, who expect menopause to be a difficult process, are undergoing greater stress than others are, Greene and Cooke in 1980 conducted a survey using a multivariate analysis technique, where life stress in general was shown to have more influence than did the menopause on psychological and somatic symptoms. There was no significant increase in total life stress at the time of the menopause and the highest levels of both psychological and somatic symptoms were found in the 35-44 years old group, after which age there was a steady decline.

Wood (1979) in a comprehensive survey in Australia of women of all ages found no increase with age (including the menopausal transition) of the psychological symptoms investigated and indeed found a decline with age in headaches and irritability. He also found that women with psychological problems frequently seek help at gynecological clinics, at any age. This overlap between gynecological and psychiatric problems partly explains why clinicians often assume a causal relationship between ovarian failure, hot flushes and psychological problems. Wood, the author of an Australian survey, in 1979 suggested ways in which psychological symptoms may become associated with the menopausal phase. Firstly, psychological symptoms may have preceded the climacteric, may be occurring secondarily to hot flushes or may be a result of new stresses, which may occur at any age. Secondly, the propensity to link many psychological symptoms with the menopause may provoke new anxiety; or it may turn the menopause into a scapegoat for patients with chronic anxiety or depressive states. Finally, the author rightly suggests that more information about the general effects of aging, favorable and unfavorable, would put the menopause in a better perspective.

Avis et al. (1994) examined the effect of change in menopause status on depression, while controlling for prior depression. They analyzed longitudinal follow-up of previous cross-sectional analyses reported by McKinlay, McKinlay, and Brambilla who examined the relative contribution of menopause to depression. The data derive from the Massachusetts Women's Health Study, a 5-year longitudinal study of a cohort of 2565 women aged 45 to 55 years at baseline (1981 to 1982). Results showed that prior depression was the variable most predictive of subsequent depression, as measured by the Center for Epidemiologic Studies-Depression (CES-D) scale. Onset of natural menopause was not associated with increased risk of depression. Experiencing a long perimenopausal period (at least 27 months), however, was associated with increased risk of depression. The association between a long perimenopause and depression appeared to be explained by increased menopausal symptoms rather than by the menopause status itself. The observed increase in depression during a lengthy perimenopause appears to be transitory.

Through most of the research work done on reproductive aging in the recent past we can clearly come to at least one conclusion that women all around the globe experience more than one menopausal symptoms in her lifetime, which could be either physical, mental or even emotional and there is a slight variation in the age of attainment of menopause in different populations. One can even see that women's health and menopause is a rapidly expanding field of medical practice and scientific investigation as clinically menopause is not just the end of one's reproductive life but also the outset of many hormonal and age related health issues. Although menopause is a normal event in a woman's life, it has been diagnosed as one of the major reasons for (health) problems (hypo-oestrogenism) seen in elderly women. In general, as women age, lean mass decreases while body fat accumulates, inviting many health related problems. Studies show that women all over experience more somatic and rheumatic symptoms, also depression and the onset of reproductive aging (menopause) share many of the same symptoms, including sleep problems, fatigue, irritability, anxiety and difficulty concentrating. Because of this, depression can go undiagnosed and untreated in women who may think these problems are a natural part of aging. Many of these diseases can be prevented by timely intervention of lifestyle modification, proper dietary habits, menopausal hormone therapy, or other supplements such as calcium, Vitamin D, and micronutrients. Thus it is very important to address this phase of life. It is important that women be aware of the different stages of reproductive aging to understand its impact on body composition and health at each stage, in order to prevent old age malady. Early management and awareness about menopause can help with managing consequences of menopause and menopausal symptoms.

References

Ahuja M., (2016) 'Age of menopause and determinants of menopause age: A PAN India survey by IMS', Journal of Mid-Life Health; 7(3): 126-131.

Avis, E.N., Brambilla, D., Mckinlay, S.M., Vass. K., (1994) 'A longitudinal analysis of the association between menopause and depression Results from the Massachusetts women's health study', Annals of Epidemiology Volume 4, Issue 3, pp. 214-220 Ahuja M., (2016) 'Age of menopause and determinants of menopause age: A PAN India survey by IMS', Journal of Mid-Life Health; 7(3): 126-131.

Bansal, S. and Thaker, R. (2005) Age, symptoms and perception of menopause amongst underprivileged women of Ahmedabad. Cited from Souvenir of IMS Conference '05, Xth Annual Conference of Indian Menopause Society, Ahmedabad, 61.

Burger, H.G, Hale, G.E, Robertson, D.M. (2008) Cycle and hormone changes during peri menopause: the key role of ovarian function, Menopause; 15: 603-12.

Hardy R, Kuh D. Does early growth influence the timing of the menopause? Evidence from a British birth cohort. Human Reproduction 2002; 17: 2474-2479.

Hawkins, M. M, Dale, E. and Vessey, M.P, (2004) Risk of venous thromboembolism in users of hormone replacement therapy. Journal of the British Menopause Society 2004; Vol. 10, No. 4: 166-168.

Hawkes, K. (1997) Human longevity: the grandmother effect. Nature; 428: 128-129.

Hawkes, K, and Burton Jones NG. (2005) Grandmotherhood: The Evolutionary Significance of the Second Half of Female Life. New Brunswick, Canada: Rutgers University Press: 118-140.

Hawkes. K, O'Connell, J. Burton, Jones N. (1997) Hadza women's time allocation, offspring provisioning, and the evolution of post-menopausal lifespans. Current Anthropology; 38: 551-78.

Hill. K, and Hurtado, AM. (1991) The evolution of premature reproductive senescence and menopause in human females: an evaluation of the 'grandmother hypothesis'. Human Nature; 2: 313-350.

Holman, D.J, Wood , J.W, and Campbell, K.L. (2000) Age-dependent decline of female fecundity is caused by early fetal loss. In: Velde ER, Broekmans F, Pearson P, eds. Female Reproductive Ageing, Studies in Profertility Series. Camforth, UK: Parthenon 123-136.

Huerta, R., Mena, A., Malacara, J.M. and Díaz de León, J. (1995) Symptoms at perimenopausal period: its association with attitudes toward sexuality, life-style, family function, and FSH levels. Journal PubMed; Psychoneuroendocrinology. 1995; 20(2): 135-4.

Johnson, S.J., Rajan, I. and Mcleod, W. (2003) Importance of osteoporosis for aging society in India: Status review and recommendations. Indian Journal of Gerontology, Vol. 17, pp. 286-297.

Kennedy, G.E. (2003) Palaeolithic grandmothers. Life history theory and early Homo. J R Anthropol Inst; 9: 549-572.

Laurie, B.K., and Vega Chales (2008) "physical activity improves lipid profile in post menopausal women" Journal Menopause, Vol. 14, pp. 115-122.

Lin, Li. Jie, Wu. Danhua, Pu and Yang, Zhao.(2012) Factors associated with the age of natural menopause and menopausal symptoms in Chinese women. Maturitas 73: 354-360.

Mishra,G.D. and Kuh,D.(2012) Health sympotoms during midlife in relation to menopausal transition: British prospective cohort study. British medical journal, 344 (7846).

Nisar, N. and Sohoo, A. (2010): Severity of Menopausal symptoms and the quality of life at different status of Menopause: a community based survey from rural Sindh,

Pakistan. International Journal of Collaborative Research on Internal Medicine & Public Health, 2 (5):118-130.

Pavard S, Metcalf CJE, Heyer E. (2008) Senescence of reproduction may explain adaptive menopause in humans: a test of the "mother" hypothesis. American Journal of Physical Anthropology; 136: 194-203.

Pathak, R.K. and Parashar, P. (2010), 'Age at menopause and associated Bio- social factors of health in Punjabi women', The Open Anthropology Journal, 3, pp. 172-180.

Purnungla and Sengupta, S.(2002) Menarche and Menopause Among The Ao Naga Women of Nagaland, India. Journal of Human Ecology., 13(4): 323-324.

Rosenberg. K and Trevathan .W, (2002) Birth, obstetrics and human evolution. BJOG; 109: 1199–1206.

Slopien. R, Wender-Ozegowska. E, Rogowicz-Frontczak A, Meczekalski B, Zozulinska-Ziolkiewicz D, Jaremek JD, Cano A, Chedraui P, Goulis DG, Lopes P, Mishra G, Mueck A, Rees M, Senturk LM, Simoncini T, Stevenson JC, Stute P, Tuomikoski P, Paschou SA, Anagnostis P, Lambrinoudaki I. (2018) Menopause and diabetes: EMAS clinical guide. Maturitas.;117:6-10. doi: 10.1016/j.maturitas.2018.08.009.

Sen, B. (2005) Prevalence of menopausal symptoms in upper middle class women in Kolkata. Cited from Souvenir of IMS Conference '05, Xth Annual Conference of Indian Menopause Society, Ahmedabad, 60.

Smith, B.H (1991). Dental development and the evolution of life history in Hominidae. American Journal of Physical Anthropology; 86: 157-74.

Shanley, D.P, Sear, R. Mace, R. Kirkwood, T.B.L.(2007) Testing evolutionary theories of menopause. Proceedings of Royal Society London B: Biological Sciences; 274: 2943-2949.

Trinkaus, E. (1995) Neanderthal mortality patterns. Journal of Archaeological Science; 22: 121-142.

Trinkaus, E.(2011) Late Pleistocene adult mortality patterns and modern human establishment. Proceedings of National Academy of Sciences U S A ; 108: 1267-1271.

US Census Bureau, (2011) Demographic Internet Staff. "United States Census Bureau - International Data Base (IDB)".

Retrieved from: www.census.gov/ipc/www/idb/informationGateway.php.

Zutsi, and Vijay (2005). Prevalence of urinary symptoms in peri-menopausal women. Cited from Souvenir of IMS Conference '05, Xth Annual Conference of Indian Menopause Society, Ahmedabad, 47.

Chapter - 25

Physical Activity Level of Young-Adult Males of Bakarapara Area of Guwahati

— *Sanjeeb Mallick &*
Dr. Chandana Sarmah

Physical activity is defined as any bodily movement produced by skeletal muscles that require energy expenditure (World Health Organization, 2016). Measurements of physical activity include three dimensions, i.e., duration, frequency and intensity of the intentional activities performed at some period in the past (Thomas, Nelson & Silverman, 2005). Duration refers to minutes or hours spent in a specific activity per session. Frequency refers to the number of times, typically weekly, that an individual is physically active. Intensity refers to the level of effort associated with an activity and commonly classified as light, moderate or vigorous (Thomas et.al. 2005).

The maintenance of a certain level of physical activity is important for health, including the prevention of non-communicable diseases (NCDs). WHO has developed the "Global Recommendations on Physical Activity for Health" to provide national and regional level policy makers with guidance on the dose-response relationship between the frequency, duration, intensity, type and total amount of physical activity needed for the prevention of NCDs (WHO, 2012c). These recommendations are set out for 5-17, 18-64, and e"65 year age groups and physical activity categories include leisure-time physical activity, transportation (e.g. walking or cycling), occupational (i.e. work), household chores, play, games, sports, in the context of daily, family and community activities. The recommended physical activity levels for adults (18-64 years) are at least 150 minutes of moderate – intensity activity throughout the week, or an equivalent combination of moderate and vigorous-intensity activity. Aerobic activity should be performed in bouts of at least 10 minutes duration; for additional health benefits, adults should increase their moderate-intensity aerobic physical activity to 300 minutes per week, or engage in 150 minutes of vigorous- intensity aerobic physical activity per week, or an equivalent combination of moderate and vigorous intensity activity; and muscle strengthening activities should be done involving major muscle groups on two or more days a week (WHO, 2010). These recommendation are similar to those of the American College of Sports Medicine (ACSM) and the Centers for Disease Control and Prevention (CDCP) which recommend moderate physical activity for a minimum of 30 minutes on five days each week or vigorous physical activity for a minimum of 20 minutes on three days each week to promote and maintain health for adults aged 18 to 65 years (Haskell et.al. 2005).

Studies indicate that physical activity varies between race/ethnic group, age, gender, environment and socio-economic level. Physical activity is associated with gender and socio-economic position and varies according to the environment of residence. Women in rural areas were found to engage in less frequent physical activity than men, while in cities women were found to be more active. Higher socio-economic position was associated with less physical activity in women but not in men (Ortiz-Hernandez & Ramos-Ibanez, 2010).

Physical activity is positively associated with health-related quality of life (Bize, Johnson & Plotnikoff, 2007). A higher level of physical activity is of benefit for preventing premature death (Heitmann, Hills, Frederiksen& Ward, 2008; Inoue et.al. 2008), and diseases such as breast cancer (Kruk,2007; Kruk &Aboul-Enein, 2003; Slattery et.al., 2007).

Physical activity is also associated with psychological health. Physical activity may improve psychological health as suggested by Akbartabartoori et.al. (2008), including depressive symptoms (Ball, Burton & Brown, 2008; Kamphiuset.al., 2007; Teychenne, Ball & Salmon, 2008).

Physical activity describes the energetic costs with association with voluntary movement and is one of the larger components of the human energy budget. A person's daily energy requirements are determined by numerous factor. The major components of an individual's energy budget are associated with resting or basal metabolism, activity, thermoregulation, dietary thermogenesis, growth, and reproduction (Ulijaszek 1995). Total Energy Expenditure (TEE), sometimes referred to as TDEE, represents the total metabolic costs incurred over a 24-hour period. It includes energy costs associated with processes necessary for survival such as cellular maintenance, thermoregulation, digestion, immune function, and physical activity, as well as, in certain segments of the population, growth and reproduction. Basal Metabolic Rate (BMR) is one of the primary contributors to the human energy budget. BMR is an estimate of the amount of energy used while a person is in an awake, relaxed state. BMR is the single largest component of energy expenditure in most contemporary human populations, occupying approximately 45-70% of TEE (FAO/WHO/UNU 2004). Energy costs of physical activity are typically described over a 24-hour period in energy terms (e.g., kilocalories or kilojoule). The PAL (Physical Activity Level) (estimated as TEE/BMR), is particularly useful in that it minimizes the effects of size and facilitates comparisons between individuals and populations. Physical activity costs vary considerably, but at a population level, the lowest sustained PALs are approximately 1.4, which represents the minimal amount of energy among healthy but essentially sedentary subjects. However, lower PALs (~1.2) are sometimes seen among hospitalized individuals. The upper bound of sustainable population-level energy expenditure is a PAL of approximately 2.4-2.5, which has been documented in several subsistence groups during peak seasonal energy demands (FAO/WHO/UNU 2004; Shetty 2005). Higher PALs are attainable over a more limited period of time (days or weeks), such as seen among certain competitive athletes in training or competition (~3.5; Black et.al. 1996) and in individuals involved in heavy physical labor (>3.0; Diaz et.al. 1991). The 3-week Tour de France bicycle race, with PALs of approximately 4.5-5 among elite male cyclists (Westerterp et.al. 1986), probably represents the energetic ceiling of short-term sustained human performance. However, these levels, and the energy consumption they require, do not appear to be sustainable as a permanent lifestyle over the course of months or years (Shetty, 2005). The most recent FAO/WHO/UNU (2004) assigned PAL ranges to different lifestyle categories: sedentary/light activity (1.4-1.69); active/moderate activity (1.7-1.99); and vigorous/vigorous activity (2.0-2.4).

Review of literature

This chapter contains an exhaustive review of literature on the problem area. A sufficient number of well organized and reputed articles published in the form of research article/books and written by experts in the field of selected problem relating to the Physical Activity Level and its determinants are reviewed which are the following.

AK Vaidya, PK Pokharel, S Nagesh, P Karki, S Kumar, S Majhi examined association of obesity and physical activity in adult males of Dharan, Nepal. They found that the prevalence of overweight and obesity in the population was 32.9% and 7.2% respectively. The study showed that physical inactivity is more importantly associated with obesity in the older population. The trend of young being more obese is reversed after adjusting for physical activity so that those in the older age were more obese than the younger ones. Similarly, those in to the business, vocational and clerical works, those who were more literate and those in the higher socio-economic status were significantly associated with obesity even after correcting for physical activity.

Eva Leslie, Michael J Fotheringham, Neville Owen, Adrian Bauman examined age-related differences in the physical activity behaviors of young adult. The result they found, there was at least a 15% difference in vigorous-intensity leisure-time physical activity from the 18 – 19 years to the 25 – 29 years age groups, and at least a 10% difference in moderate-intensity leisure-time physical activity. For the index of sufficient activity there was a difference between 9 and 21% across age groups. Differences in rates of walking were less than 8%. For all age groups, males had higher rates of participation for vigorous and moderate-intensity activity than did females, but females had much higher rates of participation in walking than males. Age-associated differences in activity levels were more apparent for males. More studies were also done on Physical activity levels in various journals and books with different authors, scholars, etc.

Objectives

1. To assess the level of Physical Activity among the young adult males.
2. To assess the Total Daily Energy Expenditure among the young adult males.

Materials and method

For the purpose of the study Bakarapara area of Guwahati city has been selected. Bakaraparais situated on the south of Guwahati city near Basistha.Bakarapara is the mixture of different populations. The field work for the research work was carried out among the young adult males residing in theBakarapara area of Guwahati City, Kamrup (M), Assam. Total sample size of the research work is 110 young adult males of age ranging from 18-29 years have been considered for the present paper. This age group is further divided into five groups viz., 18 – 20, 21 – 23, 24 -26, 27 – 29. Purposive sampling was done and males in the particular age group consent to be part of the study have been taken into consideration.

Data on Physical Activity levels are collected through the structured questionnaire. The questionnaire includes daily routine, activities, exercise (all forms), modes of commuting work, and types of work. This physical activity questionnaire was downloaded from www.ipaq.ki.se/downloads.html and used it as a tool to find out the physical activities of daily life. A person's physical activity level is a numeric method of expressing one's daily energy expenditure. Which is to say, it's a number given to what is done in a day? The amount of physical exertion in one day determines how many calories must be consumed in the same period to maintain activity and lose or gain weight as desired. Physical Activity Level (PAL) takes into account total daily energy expenditure (TDEE) and Basal Metabolic Rate (BMR). The equation can be written as:

$$PAL = TDEE/BMR$$

To find out the TDEE as a measurement of calories used can be attained through the following equations.

For sedentary people (office workers who rarely or never exercise): TDEE = weight (in pounds) x 14

For moderately active people (construction workers, or those who exercise or play a sport 3 to 5 times a week): TDEE = weight (lbs) x 17

For vigorously active people (agricultural workers, or those who exercise or play a sport daily): TDEE = weight (lbs) x 20

General Physical Activity Levels are expressed as:

Inactive: less than 1.4

Sedentary: 1.4 – 1.69

Moderately active: 1.70 – 1.99

Vigorously active: 2 – 2.4

Extremely active: greater than 2.4

Results and discussion

Physical Activity Level

Regular physical activity helps to improve our overall health and fitness, and reduces our risk for many chronic diseases. There are numerous health benefits related to physical activity. These health benefits include a lower risk of chronic diseases such as diabetes, heart disease and stroke, some cancers and depression.

A person's physical activity level is numeric method of expressing one's daily energy expenditure. The equation for physical activity level (PAL) can be written as:

$$PAL = TDEE/BMR$$

Total daily energy expenditure (TDEE) takes into account the number of calories used in a day both at rest (Basal Metabolic Rate) and during physical activities. General physical activity levels are expressed as follows:

> Inactive: less than 1.4, Sedentary: 1.4 – 1.69, moderately active: 1.70 – 1.99, vigorously active: 2 – 2.4 and extremely active: greater than 2.4

Here the researcher has considered only 110 young adults up to 29 years of age and it was found that all the age group's physical activity level is sedentary i.e., the value between 1.4 – 1.69 (Table 25.1).

Table 25.1: Distribution of Physical Activity Level (PAL) of the young adult males.

Age group (in years)	*No. of individual*	*Range*	*PAL (Mean)*
18 – 20	39	1.18 – 1.89	1.56
21 – 23	31	1.23 – 1.87	1.41
24 – 26	19	1.41 – 1.76	1.58
27 – 29	21	1.23 – 1.59	1.41
Total	**110**		

Total Daily Energy Expenditure (TDEE)

Total daily energy expenditure (TDEE) can be calculated by the following equation:

For sedentary people (office workers who rarely or never exercise): TDEE = weight (in pounds) x 14

For moderately active people (construction workers, or those who exercise or play a sport 3 to 5 times a week): TDEE = weight (lbs) x 17

For vigorously active people (agricultural workers, or those who exercise or play a sport daily): TDEE = weight (lbs) x 20.

In table 25.2, it can be seen that the total daily energy expenditure is the highest among the 24 – 26 age groups which is 2321.33. Age group

18 – 20 has the 2287.49. age group 27 – 29 shows 2265.17 and age group 21 – 23 shows the lowest TDEE which 2109.75.

Table 25.2: Distribution of Total Daily Energy Expenditure of young adult males.

Age group (in years)	*No. of individual*	*Range*	*TDEE (Mean)*
18 – 20	39	1400 – 3100	2287.49
21 – 23	31	1540 – 3100	2109.75
24 – 26	19	1615 – 2898	2321.33
27 – 29	21	1750 – 2686	2265.17
Total	**110**		

Conclusion

From the above tables and discussion we have seen that all the young adult males possess sedentary activity level. But in the same time we have seen that there is difference in total daily energy expenditure. In the age group of 24–26 age the total energy expenditure is the highest. And the lowest total daily energy expenditure (TDEE) is 2109.75 in the age group of 21–23.

References

Akbartabartoori, M., et.al., 2008. *The associations between current recommendation for physical activity and cardiovascular risk associated with obesity*. Nutrition and Biochemistry Department, school of Public Health, Yasuj University of Medical Sciences, Yasuj, Iran. Jan; 62(1): 1-9. Epub 2007.

Ball, K. et.al., 2008. *A Prospective Study of Overweight, Physical Activity and Depressive Symptoms in Young Women*. Vol. 17. *Willey Online Library.*

Bize, R, et.al., 2007. *Physical activity level and health related quality of life in the general adult population: a systematic review.*. Pre Med. 2007 Dec; 45(6) : 401 -15. Epub 2007 Jul. 21.

Briefel, R.R & Johnson, C.L, 2004.*Secular trends in dietary intake in the United States.*Annu Rev Nutr. 2004; 24: 401-31.

Cronk, C.E., Roche, A.F., Kent, R., Berkey, C., Reed, R.B., Valadian, I., Eichorn, D., and McCammon, R. 1982. *Longitudinal trends and continuity in weight/stature from 3 months to 18 years*. Human Biology. 54, 729-750.

Erikson, E.H. 1968. Identity: *Youth and Crisis*. W.W. Norton, 17-May-1994 – Psychology–336 pages.

FAO/WHO/UNU 2004.*Human Energy requirements*. Rome: FAO, Food and nutrition report series 1.

Francis, D. et.al., 2003 – 14. *Assessing the community level impact of a decade of user fee policy shifts on health facility deliveries in Kenya*.International Journal for Equity in Health.

Leslie, E. et.al., 2001. *Age-related differences in physical activity levels of young adults*.Medicine and science in sports and exercise 33(2), 255-258.

Ortiz –Hernandez, L & Ramos – Ibanez, N, 2010. *Socio-demographic factors associated with physical activity in Mexican adults. Public Health Nutr*. 2010 Jul; 13(7) : 1131 -8. Doi : 10. 1017/S1368980010000261.Epub 2010 Mar 3.

McArdle, WD, Katch FI, and Katch VL. 2001. *Exercise Physiology: Energy, Nutrition, and Human Performance,* 5th ed. Philadelphia: Lippencott, Williams and Wilkins.

Schofield, C. 1985a. *An annotated bibliography of source material for basal metabolic rate data*. Hum. Nutr.Clin.Nutr.39c(Suppl. 1): 42-91.

Schofield, WN., 1985b. *Predicting basal metabolic rate: new standards and review of previous work*. Hum. Nutr.Clin.Nutr.39C(Suppl. 1): 5-41.

Teycheme, M., Ball, K., & Salmon, J., 2008. *Physical activity and likelihood of depression in adults:* A review. *Preventive Medicine*, 46(5), 397-411.

Thomson, J, Nelson, J, & Silverman, S., 2005. *Research Methods in Physical Activity* (5th ed.). Lower Mitcham: Human Kinetics.

Vaidya, AK. et.al., 2005. *Association of obesity and physical activity in adult males of Dharan, Nepal*. Kathmandu University Medical Journal (KUMJ) 4(14), 192–197.

https:// en.m.wikipedia.org/wiki/young_adult_(psychology).

https://en.m.wikipedia.org/wiki/youth.

www.census2011.co.in/india.

www.ncbi.nlm.nih.gov/pmc/articles/PMC 4410253.

www.ncbi.nlm.nih.gov/m/rumbed/16146124.

www.youthpolicy.org/factsheets

Index

A

Abdullah Ali Ashraf, 50
Aboriginal people, 259
Abundant water resources, 27
Academicians of Archeology, 51
Additional Director General, 47
Additional health benefits, 291
Adi-Dravida, 64
Adrian Bauman, 292
Agrarian economy of Assam, 38, 39
Agricultural activities, 85, 140
Agricultural modernisation, 79
Agricultural production, 208
Agriculture and communication facilities, 129
Agriculture Development, Bank, 56
Agro-based activities, 79
Agro-climatic condition of Assam, 33
Ahom community, 181
Ahom kingdom, 181, 182
Ahom Kings, 250
Ahom organization, 192
Ahom people of Assam, 184
Ahom territory, 182
Ahom-Mughal conflicts, 182
Ajit K. Singh, 208
Alcoholic users, 230, 231
Alexander Cunningham, 47
Alimayor, 62, 63
Alternate Wetting and Drying, 38
American College of Sports Medicine, 290
Anaikatty, 63
Ancestor worship, 183, 184
Ancestor worship during bihu, 186
Ancestor worship rituals, 188, 192
Ancient Greece and Rome, 207
Ancient mounds, 47
Ancient Sanskrit, 47
Andhra Pradesh, 36
Anglo-Burmese War, 181
Animal breeds, 173
Animal husbandry, 139, 208
Anjaw districts, 89
Annaikatty, 63
Annaipallam, 62, 63
Annne Donyi (Sun Godesses), 217
Antenatal care, 241, 244
Anthropological characteristics, 101
Anthropological research, 56
Anthropology and cultural resource management, 46
Anthropometric characteristics, 249
Anti-social activities sprung, 91
Arakan tribes, 242
Arbi society, 167
Archaeological sites, 47
Archeological Survery of India, 47, 48
Arunachal Pradesh, 26, 49, 50, 79, 81, 87, 124, 125, 161, 209, 211, 213, 221
ASHA worker, 247
Asian Culture Centre, 208
Asiatic Society, 47

Assam, 27, 148, 174, 210, 228, 229, 230, 231, 232, 250, 260, 268
Assamese calendar, 186
Assembly constituencies, 105
Assistant Commissioners, 105
Assistant priests, 156
Associated ritual, 166
Associated taboo, 167
Atchangarai, 62
Attadi, 62, 63
Audio and video technologies, 239
Australia, 284
Austro-Asiatic linguistic family, 268
Autumn rice, 33

B

Bada Marias, 123
Bakarapara area, 292
Balasor, 267
Bamboo bore, 38
Bamchenia Deori gaon, 152
Banana leaves, 187
Bangladesh, 26, 242
Bara and Chota Maria Gonds, 122
Barak River, 28
Barak river basins, 36
Barua Mog community, 242
Barua Mogs, 242
Basal Metabolic Rate, 290, 293
Basavanagiri settlement, 108
Basketry, 133
Below the poverty line, 58
Bengal Presidency, 183
Bengali Buddhists, 242
Bengali culture, 243
Bengia Tollum, 221
Betta Kuruba tribe, 107
Bhagavad Gita, 47
Bhakat Makan hareba, 159
Bhutan, 26
Bibhabasu Das Shastri, 124
Bihar, 268
Bihu festival of Assam, 186
Bihu rituals, 188
Bioelectrical Impedance Analyser, 250
Bioelectrical Impedance Analysis, 250
Biological resources, 173
Birth ceremony, 109
Biswanath Chariali, 161
Black cotton soil, 105
Blood pressure status, 229
Bodo community of Assam, 70
Bodo society of Darrang district, 69
Bodo women, 69, 71, 73
Body composition, 249
Body fat in females, 255
Body Fat percent, 250, 251
Body Mass Index, 228, 229, 231, 249, 251, 256, 281
Bohag Bihu, 186
Bohag Bihu Rituals, 185, 193
Bohagia Bisu puja, 157
Bongaigaon, 242, 259
Bor Khamti, 85
Bordoloni Block, 152
Bosorekiya (Yearly ritual), 193
Brahmaputra and Barak valleys, 27
Brahmaputra River, 28
Brahmaputra Valley, 181, 182, 250
Brambilla, 284
Bramhaputra Valley, 181, 182
Bride-price and dowry, 110
British Colonial period, 242
British India, 183
British Indologist, 47
Buddha Purnima, 243
Burma, 85
Buya kinam, 218
Bwbrey plants, 220

C

Capital of Dimapur, 182
Cardiovascular disease, 227, 280
Case studies, 123
Cash cropping, 79, 94
Celebration Copmmittee, 215
Census reports, 83
Center for Epidemiologic Studies-Depression, 284
Centers for Disease Control and Prevention, 290
Cerebrovascular disease, 227
Chamundi Hills, 104
Chandan Boruah, 49
Chandıgarh, 61
Chandmari, 119
Changing educational preference, 95
Changlang, 89
Chattisgarh, 102
Chhota Maria, 123
Chi Ren Dam, 190
Chibar Daan, 243
Chicken pox, 175
Child mortality, 271
Child-birth, 241
Childhood to adulthood, 161
Chinese middle-aged women., 281
Chinese parents, 184
Chiring chuk village, 175
Chi-square test, 272
Chittagong, 243
Chittagong dialect of Bangladesh, 242
Chittagong Hill Tract, 242
Chittagong region, 243
Chokkanalli, 62, 63
Choronology of the tombs, 50
Chowkham, 83, 84
Chowkham village, 85
Chronic diseases, 281
Chtiya kingdom, 182
Chuku Tallar, 221
Chutiya kingdom, 151
City Corporation, 105
Clinical psychologists, 237
Coach Bihar, 242
Coffee plantations, 61
Cognitive Behavioral Therapy, 237
Colonial era, 90
Commercial extraction of timber, 88
Commitment Therapy, 237
Communal rights, 65
Community based investigation, 277
Community-based programmes, 96
Computer networks, 139
Concept of livelihood security, 25
Conceptual Framework, 57
Congestive cardiac failure, 228
Construction of the Yugang, 217
Controlling floodwater, 39
Coonur Taluk, 63
Cremation ground, 203
Crop production system, 94
Cropping pattern of seasonal rice, 33
Cropping patterns, 106
Cultural and religious functions, 73
Cultural Ecology, 121, 123
Cultural Heritage Management, 44
Cultural Resource Management, 43, 44, 48, 51
Curative measure, 178
Customs and beliefs, 101
Customs associated with birth rites, 199
Customs associated with death rites, 202
Customs associated with puberty rites, 201

D

Daily wage labours, 261
Dangori, 148
David Throsby, 131
Death animal, 219

Death ceremony, 110, 165
Death rituals, 205
Decision-making agency, 93
Defecate in open field, 262
Deori of Dhemaji, 152
Deori societies, 154, 157, 159
Deori society of Assam, 160
Deori villages, 152
Department of Obstetrics and Gynecology, 280
Departmental stores, 115
Dhampus village, 55
Dhebar commission, 102
Dhemaji, 147, 151, 259
Dhemaji district, 250, 251, 152, 253, 260, 261, 262, 263
Dibrugarh, 147, 151, 242, 259
Dibrugarh district, 228, 229, 230, 231, 232
Dibrugarh University, 50
Dietary habits, 228
Dietary modification, 232
Dima Hasao, 161
Dimapur district, 161
Disadvantaged section of society, 129
Discount stores, 115
Dish of bronze, 187, 193
Dissing Passo, 124
Doimukh, 217
Doimukh Nokum Yullo, 219
Domestic uses, 263
Domesticated cattle, 128
Domestication of animals, 72
Dominant crop, 32
Dongri Gerasia tribes, 107
Dravidian origin., 107
Dress pattern, 108
Drinking water, 262
Dug well, 262
Duliajan of Dibrugarh district, 244
Durgapur in West Bengal, 242
Dying tribal culture, 221

E

Ear pain, 178
Early marriage, 71
East Kameng, 209
East Karbi Anglong District, 162
East Khasi hills, 161
East Pakistan, 242
Ecological Anthropology, 121
Economic activities, 109
Economic advantages, 274
Economic and Social development, 57
Economic condition, 98
Economic condition of the society, 74
Economic condition of the village, 70
Economic depression, 89
Economic organisation, 131
Economic productivity, 259
Economic status of women, 70, 72
Economic status of women, 71
Economic Survey of Assam, 28
Economically backward, 263
Edd binam, 218
Educated younger generation, 74
Education and literacy rate, 261
Educational background, 75
Educational environment of the society, 74
Educational status of women, 70
Electronic gadgets, 140
Elephant corridor area, 63
Elephant rearing, 88
Environmental situations, 121
Etymological origin of Mysuru, 104
Eva Leslie, 292
Ever married women, 244
Exclusion criteria, 228
Exogamous clan, 110

Extra salt consumption, 232
Eyes infection, 177

F

Facture, 177
Far Western regions, 53
Farm management methods, 39
Farmer Development Programme, 56
Farmers Training Centre, 94
Fertility status, 73
Fertilizer rate, 94
Festivals, 109
Filipino festival, 208
Fire accident, 201
Fire wood, 63
Firewood collection, 97
First Anglo-Burmese War, 183
First sawmill, 83
Fishery, 133
Flood and erosion, 27
Flood-affected areas, 40
Flood-prone areas, 28, 35, 36, 40
Flood-prone areas of Assam, 39
Folic acid supplement, 247
Folk custom, 205
Folklore and folk song, 218
Food habits, 108
Food Resources, 103
Food. Hunting, 128
Forest based resources, 75
Forest ecology, 122
Forest policy, 65
Forest regions, 108
Forest Right Act, 62, 63, 64, 65
Forest-based industries, 87
Forest-dwelling population, 122
Forest-rich North-Eastern states, 90
Forests and forestry, 106
Fossil remains, 279
Fourth Five Year Plan, 102
France, 49
Funeral ceremony, 110

G

Gajai Puja, 149
Garo Association's census, 134
Garo community, 137, 141
Garo economy, 140, 141
Garo families, 133
Garo females, 134
Garo Hills, 43
Garo life, 131
Garo society, 131
Garo women, 138, 139
Garo young people, 141
Gastric, 176
Gatigiri Puja, 149
Geographical displacement, 122
Ghai Dam, 190
Girl child's education, 74
Glimpse of poverty in Nepal, 54
Global pandemic, 238
God fearing people, 159
Golaghat, 147, 161, 259
Good harvests, 207
Good sanitation facilities, 259
Goods used in rituals, 187
Government school, 75
Governmental annual reports, 83
Govt. Higher Secondary school Ziro, 221
Grahambazar-Jyotinagar, 244
Grandmother hypothesis, 279
Great earthquake, 28
Green leafy vegetables, 283
Green revolution, 32
Gross Cropped Area, 30
Group discussions, 123
Gujrat, 102
Gunanagar, 84
Gunanagar in Namsai district, 92

Guwahati, 43, 116
Guwahati city, 117, 292

H

H.D. Kote, 104
H.D. Kote taluk, 104, 108
Hakki Pikki tribe, 107
Handicrafts, 139
Handmade implements, 87
Hand-woven dress material, 88
Haryana, 28, 36
Health care professionals, 237
Health for all, 241
Health services, 274
Healthcare facilities, 110
Health-related quality, 290
Healthy lifestyle choices, 278
Heggada Deva, 107
Heggadadevanakote, 104
Hemispherical stone slab, 49
Herbal medicine, 177
Herbal medicine, 85
Herbal medicines, 175
High blood pressure, 177
High dependency ratio, 59
High interest rate of loan, 59
High school level education, 74
Highest mean value, 252
Hill Broom Grass, 65
Hill Karbi community, 162
Hindu God Shani, 207
Homo Sapiens, 51, 210
Honey gathering, 107
Horticultural cash crops, 133
Horticulture, 106
Household census, 123
Household level rituals, 189
Howraghat sub-division, 162
Human civilization, 220
Human Ecology, 122
Human Tani, 210
Human-environment relationship, 123
Hunsur, 104
Hunting and food gathering, 132
Hybrid crop varieties, 87
Hybrid seeds, 96
Hypertension, 227

I

Idol making, 166
Impact of economic development, 139
Important source of income, 81
Impure person, 219
Inadequate breast milk, 176
Inclusion criteria, 228
Indian Council of Historical Research, 48
Indian Forest Act, 137
Indian peasantry, 142
Indigenous Bodo people, 70
Indigenous tools, 136
Indo-Mongoloid group, 151
Industrial workers, 140
Inequality income, 59
Infant and child mortality, 269
Infant morality rate, 267, 275
Infant mortality, 247, 271
Influence of evil eyes, 178
Intangible Heritage of Humanity, 44
Integrated Tribal Development Projects, 103
Integrating Historical Property, 48
International border, 26
International markets, 39
Interview method, 162
Iron Age of India, 49
IIrrigation, 106
Irrigation potential, 27, 37
Ischemic heart disease, 227
Isra University Hyderabad, 280

J

Jaintia Hills, 161
Jalpaiguri districts, 242

Jammu and Kashmir, 102
Jamshedpur, 242
Jaundice, 175, 176
Jenu Kuruba, 103
Jenu Kuruba Tribe, 107
Jharkhand, 102, 242, 268
Jiangsu Province of China, 281
Joint family, 272
Joint National Committee, 228
Joint Pain, 177
Jokorua Dam, 190
Jorhat, 147, 151, 259

K

K.R Nagara, 107
K.R. Nagar, 104, 105
K.R. Nagar taluk, 105
Kabini River, 105
Kaccha toilet, 262
Kacharis of Assam, 149
Kadalur, 104
Kalahari, 268
Kal-honghoti, 184, 192
Kal-honghoti Ahom people, 193
Kallampalayam, 62, 63
Kamle Districts, 211
Kamle Pakke-kesang, 209
Kamrup, 161, 242, 259, 292
Karbi Anglong, 43
Karbi Anglong district, 161
Karbi clan system, 167
Karbi religion, 162, 167
Karbi society, 167
Karimganj, 161
Karnataka, 104, 107, 108
Kasaba hobli, 104
Kati Bihu, 186
Kati Bihu Rituals, 185, 193
Kengarai, 63
Kenya, 78
Keonjhar, 267
Khamti society, 97
Khamti village of Namsai, 83
Kharif food grains, 35
Kharif season, 27, 28, 38
Kherem, 84
Kherem village, 93
King Suhungmung, 182
Kingdom of Tai people, 181
Kitchen garden, 63
Kodagu district, 105
Koilpatti, 63
Kokam leaves, 220
Kolkata, 242
Kollikarai, 62
Kondri, 268
Kora tree, 126
Kosu tree, 126
Kothakiri taluk, 63
Kovilpatti, 63
Kra Daadi, 209
Kupperman menopausal index, 281
Kurumbarpallam, 63
Kurung Kumey, 209
Kurung Kumey District, 211, 215

L

Lack of awareness, 71, 95
Lack of irrigation facilities, 58
Lack of market facilities, 59
Lack of transport communication, 126
Lakhaipathar village, 263
Lakhimpur, 147, 151, 161, 259
Lakhimpur district, 174
Lakhipathar village, 260, 263
Land Reforms Co-operative Movements, 56
Language, 108
Large family size, 59
Laterite soil, 105
Leisure-time physical activity, 291
Lever Disorder, 176

Life cycle rituals, 109
Lift irrigation, 38
Light activity, 291
Livelihood patterns, 91
Local Folklore and Traditions, 48
Local plant, 173
Lohit, 89
Lohit district, 81, 87, 88
Long bamboo stick, 218
Lord Shani Puja, 167
Low hemoglobin, 241
Low productivity of land, 59
Lower Subansiri, 209
Lt. Tadar Tang, 221
Lucknow, 242

M

Madhu Purnima, 243
Madhya Pradesh, 28, 102
Magh Bihu, 186
Magh Bihu Ritual, 185, 193
Maghio Bisu Puja, 159
Magical practitioner, 178
Mahapuruxiya Dharma, 182
Maharashrta, 102
Mahisurapura, 104
Major factors of poor education, 74
Majuli, 147
Makan Chiban, 158
Malaria, 175
Management of cultural organization, 46
Mandya taluk, 104
Mangaldai town, 70
Manipur, 26
Marmagri Maghs, 243
Married man and woman, 190
Maternal education, 275
Maternal mortality, 241
Mavanalla, 62, 63
Mayurbhanj, 267
McKinlay, 284
Medicinal use, 91
Megalithic tombs, 49
Meghalaya, 26, 133, 134, 161, 242
Meghalaya Forest (Conservation) Rules, 137
Meghalaya Forest Rules, 137
Melkoopu, 62, 63
Menarche and Menopause, 281
Menopausal hormone therapy, 280
Menopausal status, 281
Menopausal symptoms, 281
Menopause among Indian women, 277
Menstrual disorder, 176
Menstruation troubles, 179
Metropolis, 259
Metuwa and Bor Metua, 158
Michael J Fotheringham, 292
Mid-life diseases, 278
Minimal amount of energy, 291
Minor forest produce, 62, 137
Minor forest produce collection, 63
Minor Forest Products, 65
Mishimi habitats, 89
Mishing dominated villages, 250
Mishing females, 253
Mishing males, 251, 252
Mising language, 260
Misings, 259
Misings of Lakhipathar villages, 261
Mithun Meat, 219
Mizoram, 26, 243
Mobile phone, 140
Moderate activity, 291
Modern Ahom people, 181
Modern health care, 179
Modern health institutions, 247
Modern medical system, 174
Modified Area Development Approach, 103
Mog family, 243

Mog women, 247
Mog women of Upper Assam, 244
Mokokchung district, 281
Momong, 84
Mongoloid group, 161
Mongoloid group of languages, 250
Mooperkadu, 62, 63
Morigaon, 161, 259
Motorcycle, 140
Mudumalai Tiger Reserve, 63, 64, 66
Mughal architecture, 49
Mundari group, 268
Museum of Gauhati University, 50
Music system, 140
Muslims of Kamrup district, 255
Myanmar, 181
Myocardial infarction and angina, 228
Mysore district, 108
Mysore Mallige (Jasmine), 106
Mysuru, 104
Mysuru city, 111
Mysuru District, 104
Mysuru Rural, 105
Mysuru Urban, 105

N

Na Dam, 190
Naarnam Dance, 219
Nababarsha, 243
Nagaland, 26, 161
Nagaon, 161, 259
Namibia, 78
Namsai, 89
Namsai district, 79
Namsai region, 87
Namsai town, 95
Nanjangud, 104, 105
Nanjangud blocks, 105
Na-pam village, 192
Naphuk (Boripara), 244
Napoleon Bonaparte, 69
National Health Policy of India, 241
National holiday, 207
National level trends, 80
National Planning Commission, 55
National Register of Historic Places, 45
National Trust for Historic Preservation, 48
Native American Grave Protection, 43
Natural calamities, 212
Natural deaths, 162
Natural disaster, 27, 89
Natural menopause, 281
Natural resource, 87
Natural resource management, 45
Natural resource use, 83
Natural resources, 98
Natural rubber, 32
Nealo tree, 126
Neolithic period, 49
Neovaishnavism culture, 203
Netherlands, 49
Neville Owen, 292
New born baby, 247
Nilgiri District, 62
Nilgiri forest land, 90
Nilgris, 63
Niyah Tani, 210
Non governmental organization, 59
Non Tangible cultural changes, 212
Non timber forest product, 66
Non-communicable diseases, 290
Non-timber forest produce, 62
Non-vegetarian, 108
North American Menopause society, 277
North Bank, 181
North East India, 47, 50, 243
North East Indian megaliths, 50
North Eastern India, 213
North Lakhimpur districts, 210

North-East India, 132, 260
North-eastern region, 26
North-eastern states, 28
Nuclear and joint family, 261
Nurturing mental health, 237
Nutritional and health security, 26
Nutritional status, 252, 253
Nyimey kabnam, 218
Nyishi, 125
Nyishi community, 221
Nyishi student brigades, 221
Nyishi tribe, 209
Nyokum Yullo festival, 211
Nyoying Hingnam, 213, 214
Nyub Naamlo, 218

O

Observation method, 162
Occupational pattern of people, 29
Omron Fat Analyzer, 250
Opium consumption, 91
Original Tai language, 189
Orissa, 61, 102
Orphaned ghosts, 184
Overseas Development Institute, 78
Overweight, 231
Overweight and obesity, 291

P

Paddy fields, 127
Pakke-Kessang district, 124
Pan Tanti, 268
Panchpargania dialect, 268
Pandemic outbreak, 238
Papum Pare, 209
Papumpare district, 161
Paralysis, 175
Parashuram Kund, 94
Parliamentary Constituency, 105
Passa Valley, 124
Paste of coconut, 177
Pastoral, 132
People in rural hills, 59
Per-capita salt intake, 232
Percent body fat, 250
Periyapatna, 104
Persian texts, 47
Personal hygiene and sanitation, 263
Phi-Sua-Mung Worship, 191
Photographic method, 162
Physical activity, 228
Physical Activity Level, 291, 293
Physical activity level, 293, 294
Physical appearance, 107
Physical strength, 141
Physical strengths, 281
Piggery, 133
Piles, 176
Pillangkatta, 133, 134
Pillangkatta village, 134, 136
Plastic vessels, 262
Pneumonia, 175, 176
Political connections, 85
Popular tourist attractions, 45
Portable Weighing Machine, 250
Portugal, 49
Post harvesting agricultural festival, 221
Post reproductive ailments, 278
Post Traumatic Stress Disorder, 237
Post-graduate degree, 261
Postnatal mortality, 269, 272
Pot lamp, 187
Poultry, 133
Power tillers, 140
Practice of hunting and gathering, 102
Pregnant women, 241
Pre-monsoon months, 28
Primary Health Care network, 241
Primary Rural Health Care Centre, 110
Principality, 183
Principle deities, 156

Process of the ritual, 186
Production-consumption, 141
Prof. Saket Khuswaha, 219
Protection of Monuments Act, 47
Protein requirements, 128
Proto Australoid origin, 268
Psychiatric problems, 284
Psychological first aid, 238
Psychological impact of quarantine, 238
Puberty, 109
Puberty marriage, 202
Punjab, 28, 36

Q

Quarantine duration, 238

R

Rachi, 268
Rajashik Puja, 153
Rajasthan, 102
Ranchi, 242
Rangagarah Village, 148
Rational Emotive Behavior Therapy, 237
Red clay, 105
Religious and educational field, 138
Religious festivals, 149
Religious Head, 149
Reproductive aging, 285
Reproductive aging and depression, 283
Reproductive history, 281
Revengeful ghost, 189
Revenue taluks, 104
Rheumatic symptoms, 285
Ri-Bhoi, 161
RI-Bhoi district, 133, 134, 135
Rice-fish-horticulture model, 38
Rickets, 178
Rikam Pada, 219
Rilloh village, 125, 129
Ritual foods, 155
Ritual performance, 221
Ritual period, 155
Ritual practices, 183
Rituals at community levels, 191
Rituals at family level, 185
River and pond, 262
River bank, 166
River Cauvery, 105
River Dighalpani, 165
Riverine areas, 250
Rivers Brahmaputra, 26
Rural Bauri women, 255
Rural dwellers, 86
Rural livelihood, 122
Rural poverty in Nepal, 53, 58

S

S.T. population of Assam, 259
Sacrificing of Mithun, 220
Sadar subdivision, 242
Saibasia, 268
Sale of cash crops, 140
Sambalpuria, 268
Sambalpuria dialect, 268
Sandy farmlands, 88
Sandy loam, 105
Sangria tree, 126
Sanitary well, 262
Sanitation practices, 263
Santal (tribe), 275
Santals (tribe), 267
Sarthak Sengupta, 281
Sat Labiruba, 158
Sattik Puja, 153
Saturnalia festival, 207
Sauna Puja, 158
Scientific investigation, 285
Semi-nomadic, 221
Semi-urban residents, 86
Semmanathan, 63
Seri tree, 126
Settlement pattern, 108

Severe Acute Respiratory Syndrome, 237
Severe acute Respiratory Syndrome, 238
Sexual problems, 281
Shifting cultivation, 127
Shillong, 242
Shri Keshabdev Mahanta, 148
Shrine and its rituals, 157
Shyamalee Gogoi, 49
Sibasagar, 259
Sibsagar, 151, 242
Sikkim, 26
Siliguri Corridor, 26
Silliguri, 242
Sindh Pakistan, 280
Sissiborgaon Development Block, 260, 263
Sivasagar, 147
Small size of land holding, 59
Snowball sampling method, 84
Social discrimination between, 69
Social Folk Custom, 199
Social status of Bodo women, 69
Social status of women, 70
Socio-cultural practice, 162
Socio-demographic aspects, 228
Socio-economic profile, 260
Socio-religious practices, 178
Soliga tribe, 107
Sonitpur, 151, 161, 259
Sonowal Kachari community, 200
Sonowal Kacharis, 147, 148, 149, 199, 205
Sonowal Kacharis of Assam, 201
South Bihar, 268
South Indian tombs, 50
South Tripura District, 242
SouthWest Brazil, 255
Spinning and weaving, 133
Sriyure, 63
Staple food crops, 39
State of Assam, 259
Status of the health awareness, 278
Stomach disorder, 174
Stomach pain, 177
Storage of water, 263
Subansiri region, 211
Substance use, 228
Sub-tropical monsoon, 28
Suddhi Hobah, 201
Sukaphaa, 181
Super markets, 115
Surui Indians, 255
Sustainability of seasonal crops, 33
Sustainable livelihood approach, 81
Sustainable livelihoods framework, 80
Swarga Narayan, 182
Symbol of blessing, 218

T

T. Narasipura, 104, 105
T. Narasipura taluks, 106, 107
Tai Ahoms of Lakhimpur District, 255
Tai Khamti, 83, 95
Tai Khamti culture, 95
Tai Khamti Development Society, 86
Tai Khamti livelihood, 92
Tai Khamti livelihood scenario, 91
Tai Khamti Singpho Council, 86
Tai Khamti society, 85, 87, 88, 89
Tai language, 193
Tai prince, 181
Tai-Khamti society, 92
Taj Mahal, 49
Taku tree, 126
Talacauvery, 105
Tamil Nadu, 62, 63
Tamilnadu, 61
Tana Showren, 219
Tanti (caste), 275
Tantis (caste), 267
Tantubaui, 268

Tanzania, 279
Taram tree, 126
Tea garden dialect, 268
Tea gardens, 268
Tea worker, 268
Tea-garden workers, 232
Tengaponia Deoris, 228, 229, 230, 231
Thakkal, 63
Theravada Buddhism, 242, 243
Thottulingi, 63
Tibeto-Burman family, 250
Tibeto-Burman group, 161
Tibeto-Burman linguistic group, 147
Timber forest produce, 65
Timber industries, 93
Timber trade, 95
Timber traders, 93
Tinskia, 259
Tinsukia, 147, 151
Tinsukia District, 89, 148, 242, 244
Titan clock shop, 119
Tobacco chewing, 229, 230, 231
Tobacco consumption, 232
Toilet cleaner, 262
Toilets with flush system, 262
Tonsil, 177
Topographical and climatic conditions, 210
Total daily energy expenditure, 292, 293, 294
Total Energy Expenditure, 290
Trade regulations, 92
Traditional agricultural work, 135
Traditional Assamese towel, 200
Traditional belief system, 162
Traditional calendar year, 156
Traditional concept, 115
Traditional crafts, 46
Traditional culture, 222
Traditional festivals, 140
Traditional folk lore, 218
Traditional Forest Dwellers, 62, 137
Traditional forest dwellers act, 65
Traditional health care system, 174
Traditional health practices, 174
Traditional Hindu marriage, 147
Traditional knowledge, 173
Traditional local market, 115
Traditional market system, 119
Traditional Medicare system, 179
Traditional method of agriculture, 38
Traditional practices, 149
Traditional rainwater harvesting, 98
Traditional religious beliefs, 157
Traditional religious rituals, 148
Traditional rituals, 151
Traditional seeds, 136
Traditional song, 191
Traditional system, 179
Traditional tribal religion, 148
Traditional values, 101
Transient ischemic attack, 228
Transport and communication, 111
Treaty of Yandabo, 181
Tree moss, 65
Tribal community, 122
Tribal Festivals of Bihar, 208
Tribal inhabitants, 259
Tribal societies, 75
Tribal Sub-Plan, 103
Tribal Welfare, 64
Tribal women, 72, 73
Tripua, 26, 242
TTS vaccine, 246, 247
Turkey Berry, 65
Turmeric paste, 202
Types of Pujas, 153

U

Udaipur subdivision, 242
Udalguri, 259

Underprivileged women of Ahmedabad, 282
Underweight, 231
Underweight category, 252
Unemployment, 59
Unholy practice, 219
Union Territories, 61
United Kingdom, 45
United Nations, 44
United Progressive Alliance, 61
United States, 44, 277
Unmarried individual, 192
Upper Assam, 151, 268
Upper Assam Division, 181
Urban society, 138
Urinary symptoms, 282
Urine trouble, 176
US Census Bureau, 278
Uttar Pradesh, 28, 36
Uyu Panam, 213, 214
Uyu panam ritual, 221

V

Vaishnavisim, 148
Variation in the topography, 165
Vazaithottam, 62, 63
Vegetables, 187
Vegetarian boiled food, 204
Video camera, 140
Vigorous activity, 291
Vivekananda Memorial Hospital, 110
Voluntary movement, 290
Vomiting, 176
Vulnerability and coping mechanism, 89
Vulnerable Tribal Groups, 102

W

Wakro circle, 94
Weekly markets, 115
West African countries, 238
West Bengal, 26, 28, 36, 102, 255, 268
West Kameng, 50
West Kameng district, 49
West Tripura District, 242
Western Ghats, 105, 107, 108
Wild animals, 128
Wild boar, 64
Wild forest tract, 107
Wild life protection Act, 63
Wild plant leafs, 154
Wildlife conservation, 78
Winter rice, 33, 35
Women education, 76
Wooden coffin, 203
World Bank, 54
World Health Organization, 227, 249, 235, 289

Y

Yearly rituals, 187
Yerava tribe, 107
Young adult males, 292, 295
Young adults, 294
Younger generation, 150
Yugang, 216
Yullo Panam, 213, 214
Yullo uyu, 218
Yunnan Province, 181, 182

Z

Zila Parishad, 106